Moral Idealists, Bureaucracy, and Catherine the Great

Moral Idealists, Bureaucracy, and Catherine the Great

Walter J. Gleason

Rutgers University Press
New Brunswick, New Jersey

Library of Congress Cataloging in Publication Data

Gleason, Walter, 1944–
    Moral idealists, bureaucracy, and Catherine the Great.

    Bibliography: p.
    Includes index.
    1. Russia—History—Catharine II, 1762–1796.
2. Russia—Politics and government—1689–1800.
3. Russia—Intellectual life.   I. Title.
DK171.5.G58   947′.063   80–18658
ISBN 0–8135–0917–3

To Judy

Contents

Acknowledgments

The writing of this book benefited from the advice of many individuals. I am indebted to Richard Wortman for his unflagging interest in this project, his testing scrutiny of its hypotheses, and his constant regard for felicity of expression. David Ransel was generous in his interest in every stage of the preparation of this work and improved its theses immeasurably by his challenges. Like so many other historians of tsarist Russia, I want to record my appreciation to Marc Raeff for his detailed comments on a draft of this volume. I would be quite remiss if I did not thank J. L. Black for his careful examination and reflections on the entire manuscript. I hasten to add in what is by no means a pro forma disclaimer that the refinements to the text are due to the interest of these individuals while the imperfections are the responsibility of the author.

The final draft of this book was purged of a number of extravagances by the careful editing of Barbara Westergaard. The care of this book at the Press was very capably handled by Joseph Esposito. Martha Rosso succeeded where so many others could not, namely in reading my handwriting and typing final copy in splendid and expeditious fashion. I am grateful to Rutgers University for providing released time under the Faculty Academic Study Program. Finally, I want to thank the Research Council of Rutgers University for grants to pay the costs of typing drafts of this book.

All dates are listed according to the Julian calendar which was eleven days behind the Gregorian calendar in the eighteenth century. All titles of eighteenth-century works are printed as they were originally spelled. Familiar names are given in their English equivalents rather than in transliteration, that is, Paul rather than Pavel. All translations, unless otherwise specified, are by the author.

Everyone who criticizes the Sovereign
in the fullness of his autocratic power
is a pilgrim in the land where all
tremble before him.

—Alexander Radishchev
"Spasskaia prolest' "
Journey from Petersburg to Moscow

Introduction

In the early eighteenth century Peter the Great sponsored a series of reforms to westernize Russia. He revamped the bureaucracy, reorganized the army and navy, advocated by policy and personal example the introduction of Western cultural styles of speech, dress, and behavior, and, by a variety of measures, attempted to remake Russia on the model of a European state. To make his many initiatives intelligible to his contemporaries and to give his efforts a sense of order, the tsar felt the need for invoking a set of political ideals. Peter cited the intellectual authority of contemporary German natural law theorists, particularly Gottfried Wilhelm von Leibniz, Samuel Pufendorf, and Christian Wolff. His choice was not haphazard. Out of the rich variety of political ideologies then available in Europe he quite deliberately chose the theoretical system that could best be adapted to the practices of his state—a choice that also happened to set him off from his predecessors.

Peter's predecessors, the grand princes and tsars of Muscovy, had relied on their own version of the Byzantine imperial ideology. The Byzantine emperors were in theory exalted as men-gods serving in harmony with the ecclesiastical representatives of the God-man. The Muscovite rulers revised this mythology to stress the military exploits of the most illustrious members of their dynasty, Ivan III and his grandson Ivan IV. To bolster their claims to legitimacy the Muscovite princes drew up elaborate and fraudulent genealogies proving the kinship between the rulers of Muscovy and those of the Roman Empire.[1] Peter divested himself of the accouterments of this ideology and was willing to forgo the exalted, sacerdotal status ascribed to the office of the monarch in the Byzantine ideology. In its stead he adopted a secular philosophy that assigned him the post of first servant of the state. His obligations were to govern and administer, rather than to conquer and rule. The tsar was to direct an administrative order that regulated all the affairs of his realm, economic, social, and political, and to do so under the banner of legality.

Peter did not always abide in practice with the theoretical demands of legality, but in stressing its importance he created a problem that was to plague his successors, particularly Catherine the Great. By giving state sanction to the politics of German natural law he defined the ideas and myths which the rulers were obliged to reconcile with their activities, selected the language the monarchs used in their official documents, and shaped the notions the tsars and tsarinas had about their responsibilities to "society." As Robert Wolff noted, "the ideology of the autocracy establishes its own tyranny." [2]

The ideas, language, and sense of the rulers' duties were no less binding on the tsars than on those who commented on the monarchs' functions.[3] While Peter and his successors tried to achieve some correspondence between the demands of theoretical legality and the practice of administrative routine, others tried to sort out imperial policies and evaluate them on the grounds of their fidelity to the theoretical prescriptions of the Germans' writings. German natural law provided the legal language in which the monarchs spoke to their own governments and subjects. It also furnished the language that eighteenth-century political commentators used to voice steadily more sophisticated versions of what they expected from a ruler.

Rather than studying what the state was saying, this book is interested in those who were listening and particularly in three men prominent during the reign of Catherine the Great. The journalist Nikolai Novikov, the poet Ippolit Bogdanovich, and the leading playwright of Catherinian Russia, Denis Fonvizin, will be referred to throughout this book as members of the Fonvizin group. The "Fonvizin group," however, is only a construct of the historian; these men did not think of themselves as a group. To the historian their careers, writings, and ideas exhibit a marked similarity, which makes them stand out from their contemporaries. Fonvizin, Novikov, and Bogdanovich were introduced to German natural law at Moscow University in the 1750s. All of them served under Catherine's chief minister, Nikita Panin, or one of his allies, which brought them the protection of one of the most powerful individuals at Catherine's court but also made the progress of their bureaucratic careers dependent on the success of Panin's political schemes. Their writings clearly exhibit partiality for Panin and opposition to his rival at the court, Grigorii Orlov. Their activity was important for the literature of the 1760s, and although they were not an explicit group, they were aware of one another's work. Because of their education they were singled out for important posts. They were for a time the movers and doers in the bureaucracy. Experienced in the most important affairs of government and protected by connections with important figures in the administration, the Fonvizin group rendered judgment on Catherine II from within the offices of her own bureaucracy.

The importance of their service careers and of natural law ideals has been all but neglected in the works published on each member of the Fonvizin group. The three men were considered by eighteenth-century commentators as literary figures whose bureaucratic posts were sinecures giving them the time and means to pursue their vocations. Novikov himself fostered this reputation in his *Historical Dictionary of Russian Writers* (1772), and it was perpetuated by many literati of the early nineteenth century. For example, Karamzin wrote a two-part review of Bogdanovich's life for the *Messenger of Europe* in 1803. Most of the column space was allotted to a single work, Bogdanovich's literary masterpiece *Dushenka*.[4] Similarly, it was common for nineteenth-century literary critics to remember Fonvizin for his classic comedies of morals, the *Minor* and *Brigadier,* and Novikov for his journals of 1769–1774. Novikov's own book, however, was obviously intended to be about writers and would therefore have considered their service careers irrelevant. Furthermore, the *Historical Dictionary* consisted of brief entries and did not pretend to be exhaustive.

Biographers of the nineteenth and early twentieth centuries often allowed their interpretations to fall into what became a pattern of reconsidering and modifying the existent monographic literature without asking any new questions about their subjects' lives. To cite but one example, Novikov won the attention of several important scholars, including Longinov, Shumigorskii, Bogoliubov, and Nezelenov,[5] but these scholars limited their discussions to a few set points. Invariably Novikov's journals of 1769–1774 were studied, not so much to examine what he wrote as to evaluate why he wrote what he did. The publication of the periodicals became a benchmark for the critics' general assessment of Catherine's relationship to writers of her time. If the empress tolerated the journals, it was a calculation designed, as Longinov and Bogoliubov argued, to deflect attention from her policies. Novikov was the victim of Catherine's plans to deceive "public opinion." If she genuinely wanted the social commentary carried in the journals for her own information, as Shumigorskii contended, then her good intentions were thwarted by the zealousness with which Novikov took advantage of her forbearance and launched an attack, albeit a literary one, on her regime. Nezelenov argued both cases for different periods: in 1769 Catherine deceived Novikov, but by 1774 was instead being used by him. There is obviously a point of diminishing returns in these disputes. To hold Novikov and Fonvizin up as examples of serious challengers to the empress puts them in a heroic pose, exalting their stature and assuming that Catherine considered them as serious threats. It lends to men of the eighteenth century a political importance and an adversary disposition toward the autocracy more like that of critics of the regime in the last half of the nineteenth century.

The reputation of the three men in scholarly literature was revised by several prominent Soviet and émigré scholars, particularly in works published in the 1950s and 1960s. Both the general interpretive works of G. Gukovskii, D. Blagoi, and P. Berkov and the monographs of G. Makogonenko, K. Pigarev, and I. Serman consider the political significance of the three men's literary works.[6] In these works the emphasis is on identifying the members of the Fonvizin group as representatives of the Russian Enlightenment. Makogonenko's biography of Fonvizin placed its subject in the ranks of the "enlighteners." Fonvizin's satires were interpreted as evidence of his criticism of serious flaws in Catherine's feudal, despotic government and his hopes that her autocratic prerogatives could be restricted and her government reformed along the lines of a "liberal" "constitutional" regime. Makogonenko cast Fonvizin in the role played by his Western European counterparts, namely as a participant in a European-wide revolt against the *ancien régime.*

This literature on the Russian Enlightenment is valuable because of the attention it draws to the theoretical bases of the Russian enlighteners' political activities and literary interests, but the direction of these revisions must be carefully considered. Makogonenko and his peers advanced their interpretations of Fonvizin, Novikov, and Bogdanovich within the framework provided by Lenin's general description of all enlighteners. In his article "What Is the Heritage We Disavow?" Lenin claimed that Russian enlighteners were direct intellectual forebears of the Decembrists, the gentry revolutionaries of 1825, and, in Western Europe, of critics of the old order.[7] Thus Soviet scholars are drawing on an interpretation that dates from tsarist times. As a result they argue from many of the same premises originally advanced in biographies of Fonvizin and Novikov written in the last half of the nineteenth century. What was for Bogoliubov and Longinov a case of Catherine the deceiver became for Gukovskii and his peers a study of Catherine the defender of the feudal order. An embattled adversary of the empress was transformed into a prescient advocate of a new political and economic order. Though Soviet historians broke new ground by referring to the intellectual background of the individuals under study, their conclusions were, in general terms, similar to those of the typical nineteenth-century biography.

The relationship between literature and politics advanced by Gukovskii in the early 1930s was not revised until the 1970s when two prominent scholars, I. Shchipanov and Z. Kamenskii, refined it in three valuable ways. The distinction was made between an enlightener in the political sense, one who met Lenin's criteria, and a *prosvetitel'* in a broader sense, one who only required the individual's commitment to the general cause of improving his contemporaries' quality of life and furthering the spread of knowledge.[8] Kamenskii and Shchipanov accredited as enlighteners some who were not even political opponents of the imperial state. With this more inclusive definition, Russian enlighteners could be appreciated for the variety of their activities rather than exclusively for their politics. Shchipanov and Kamenskii stated explicitly that the *prosvetiteli* did not merely convey intact European political philosophies but adapted them to circumstances peculiar to Russia in the eighteenth century. These historiographical initiatives hold out the promise that future studies will view Russian enlighteners with greater sophistication and detail than was previously possible.

While these breakthroughs challenged some old premises, they also created new problems. The new approach is, I think, a subtle means of reemphasizing the primacy of politics. Both Kamenskii and Shchipanov were clear in their claim that enlighteners, however diverse their interests and varied their political convictions, were driven by some inner mechanism to achieve system in their ideas and activities. A *prosvetitel'* who was initially committed to cultural improvement but not political reform inevitably sorted out these concerns and arranged them in a systematically "progressive" direction. What was the driving principle unifying the concerns of Russian enlighteners? What prompted their adaptations of contemporary European philosophies to the realities of imperial Russia?

The answers to these questions lie in a number of other questions which serve as the basic referents to the present volume. What was the intellectual relationship of the Fonvizin group to its predecessors and successors? This book puts Fonvizin, Novikov, and Bogdanovich in a line of Russian enlighteners that began with Lomonosov in the second quarter of the eighteenth century, revealing the configurations of relations between the Fonvizin group and writers of early and late eighteenth-century Russia. A survey of prominent literati in the first half of the century outlines in some detail their positions and their links to the Fonvizin group. Since it was ideas that linked these men, it is vital to determine how well versed they were in German natural law. In general terms, theorists of natural law were not familiar to many well-educated Russians before mid-century. The opening of Moscow University in 1755 provided the first forum for training a small number of men in the specifics of natural law. Even then, the impact of the German philosophy on the educated elite was strongest in politics and ethics rather than metaphysics, epistemology, or cosmology.

How did the enlighteners maintain their principles while also advancing their careers? German natural law was not a matter for deliberations conducted *in vacuo.* The *prosvetiteli* were members of what Ransel described as clientele networks; that is, patrons at the court or in the bureaucracy used their power to reward their clients and enhance their own status. The types of services expected by the chief of each network changed over the course of the eighteenth century. The direction of this evolution drew the clients into steadily more complex involvement in the politics of their day. When the demands on them assumed an exclusively political character, the enlighteners' ability to reconcile theoretical conviction and client loyalty was tested. This difficulty was exacerbated by their relations with the throne. As the men under consideration were spurred by service to bureaucratic superiors to refine political ideals, how did these revisions alter their relations with the throne? Writers from Lomonosov to Fonvizin became increasingly idealistic in their political expectations. Quite sporadically in the 1740s and 1750s but very predominantly by the end of the century, there appeared in their works a vision of a utopian ruler, state, and society. This ideal polity came to approximate the theoretical dictums on ruler, state, and society in German natural law. The more elaborate this ideal order, the more the enlighteners drew the fire of several monarchs for describing a utopia that put in unfavorable contrast the realities of imperial state and society. This juncture during the reign of Catherine the Great precipitated the confrontation of the Fonvizin group with the empress.

When the Fonvizin group was eventually driven into opposition to the Russian autocracy, its members had only two courses of action available to them. To the extent that they recognized the limits of their theoretical expectations in the monarch, they learned that, to extend Robert Wolff's comment, the ideology sanctioned by Peter the Great exerted its tyrannical rule over the ruler's subjects no less than over the monarch himself. To the extent that this lesson was not accepted, the Fonvizin group vested their convictions in an ideal polity, apart from the real world of Catherinian Russia. To accept the first alternative was to abide by the intellectual heritage bequeathed by Peter; to embrace the second was to open the way toward the definitions of political ideals and loyalties typical of early nineteenth-century political thought and discourse.

—— I ——

Careers and Convictions: Lomonosov and Sumarokov in Elizabethan Russia

—— 1 ——

Russian literature in the age of Empress Elizabeth (1741–1761) was dominated by the figure of the hero. He was portrayed as a monarch of utopian stature, at once the symbol of timeless political virtues and the embodiment of the political fictions typical of Elizabethan Russia. In the literature of the 1740s and early 1750s, he was described as one whose realm was far removed in time and space from Elizabeth's Russia. In the late 1750s the utopian monarch remained within the bounds of remote kingdoms but was increasingly and explicitly used as a standard to evaluate the policies of the empress. The literati of the late 1750s returned recurringly to a single point: Elizabeth's failure to embody the political ideals they ascribed to the utopian ruler.

The utopian monarch was most elaborately portrayed in the literary imagery of the two leading men of letters in Elizabeth's Russia, Mikhail Vasil'evich Lomonosov (1711–1765) and Alexander Petrovich Sumarokov (1717?–1777). Lomonosov first sketched his image of the ideal ruler in 1739 and revised it over the next two decades. For Lomonosov the monarch was a moral figure of radiant virtue; he expressed almost no concern for the ruler's view of his state or subjects. This model of the utopian monarch was altered by Sumarokov in the 1750s and 1760s. Sumarokov's ideal ruler was a legal figure, the representative of a state that governed according to law. His duties were to see to the welfare of the individual and the commonweal by the proper administration of the law. Neither writer described the monarch in terms taken from the officially sanctioned political philosophy of German natural law. The writings of Lomonosov and Sumarokov were testimony not to the adoption of German natural law but, rather, to a growing appreciation for legality. Sumarokov was only one of several Russian men of letters who

8

believed literature should serve political interests and deliberately attempted to promote the ideal of the hero as legal ruler. These attempts were bound to heighten contemporaries' interest in Elizabeth.

The definition of the utopian monarch was not the work of men writing in monasteries or university libraries. Lomonosov and Sumarokov were very much men of the world: the first a famous scientist and member of the Academy of Sciences in St. Petersburg; the second the preeminent dramatist of his day. Both sought to advance their careers by associating themselves with influential men at the court. As protégés of some of the principal figures around Elizabeth, they could not write in a way that would harm their interests or those of their patrons. Both writers wanted to win the favor of the empress. They could not afford to be idealists, refashioning their image of the ruler without due regard for Elizabeth herself. Since neither Lomonosov nor Sumarokov was prepared to abandon his career or his convictions, they brought on themselves a dilemma: they could continue to write about the utopian monarch, and in Sumarokov's case refine the image to accentuate the features of a legal ruler, only as long as their work did not incur the displeasure of the throne.

—— 2 ——

Lomonosov's first description of the ideal ruler appeared in his verse composed in 1739 on the occasion of the Russian military victory over the Turks at Khotin. He portrayed Empress Anna (1730–1740) as a prudent, restrained monarch, reluctant to engage in hostilities. She committed her troops against the Turks to ward off the unprovoked aggression of a state that had chosen to make itself an enemy of the Russian throne.[1] Furthermore, this war was justifiable because of the character of the Turks.

> O! How well-remembered are those places,
> Where the cruel yoke was cast off,
> And the terrible burden once imposed by
> the Turks is now borne by them,
> And those hands, those barbarous hands,
> Which enslaved so many,
> Are now themselves fettered.[2]

The war was acceptable since it was directed against "barbarous" Turks who were neither as civilized nor as enlightened as their opponents. Lomonosov coupled these justifications for the war with one that was no more than an argument from enthusiasm. Khotin had been a glorious opportunity for Anna's armies to display their martial prowess and chastise the Turks for standing in the way of Russia's march to the south.

> Let the land quake and the sea quiver,
> Let the multitudes everywhere cry out,
> The darkest smoke will envelop all mankind,
> The Moldavian mountains will be crimson from blood;
> But you, O Russians, are not endangered,
> Fate has shown its will
> To protect you to make Anna happy.
> Already your zeal and enthusiasm for her
> Have carried you through the ranks of the Tatars
> And opened before you the way to distant horizons.[3]

The poet described scenes of battle with brash, even arrogant, pride in Russia's military success. The image of the ruler was, at best, ambiguous. Lomonosov managed to praise in one poem a ruler who engaged in none but defensive wars, one who sponsored certain expansionary military ventures, and one who pursued any successful policy of aggression.

The Khotin ode expresses political thoughts in terms typical of mid-eighteenth-century Russia. Lomonosov wished to articulate in poetic language the standard political opinions of his audience. No poet could afford to make comments that seriously deviated from the preferences of his readers or listeners, and Lomonosov wanted to describe in verse a ruler whose characteristics would be understandable and popular with those at the court and the then minuscule reading public. His premises were to serve as the bases for political comment for the next three decades. The thought was not rigorously logical, the terms not juridically precise. Lomonosov was not a political theorist, and the ruler imagery in the Khotin ode was hardly a model of legal clarity. There was no question of who was to possess political sovereignty. Lomonosov was a monarchist. No distinction was made between the ruler and the state. Lomonosov fastened his attention on the person of the sovereign without worrying about the intricacies of governmental operation, decision making, or policy planning. There was extensive comment on the ruler's exercise of sovereignty. Lomonosov expended a great deal of his literary energies defining the proper functions of the ideal ruler. In so doing he posed, but did not solve, the problem of what was to be done in the event a monarch was delinquent in the performance of his official duties. For Lomonosov the primary duties of the ideal ruler were military. Any consideration of the legitimacy of the sovereign's rule or concern for its *modus operandi* was, in 1739, subsumed wholly within the image of the ruler as knight, charged with protecting the cause of civilization.

Anna's war policies against the Turks could quite plausibly be described as at once defensive and aggressive. The Russian advance across the southern steppes was both a defense of the southern borderlands and an expansion into areas claimed by the Porte.[4] Lomonosov could not enjoy the luxury of this ambiguity when he had to comment on the next empress's military venture: Elizabeth's decision in 1748 to send a Russian expeditionary force to the Rhine to defend the interests of her English and Dutch allies against France. In an ode written on the seventh anniversary of Elizabeth's accession,[5] he praised the dispatch of Russian troops. This time, however, the terms of his approval were more consistent than was the case in 1739. Elizabeth's willingness to intervene in Western Europe and arrange a peaceful reconciliation of diplomatic conflicts was witness "to Europe and the whole world, millions of different peoples, how virtue is now resplendent on the Russian throne." [6] Her peaceful intentions were not called into question even by her vigorous prosecution of the hostilities with Sweden (1741–1743).[7] He did not, however, in his ode of 1748 cater to the patriotic euphoria aroused by the victory. Lomonosov stood by his preference for none but defensive wars, but qualified the circumstances under which a ruler should commit Russian troops. Elizabeth's victories over the Swedes were justified, for the latter had been "willful"; her intervention in Western European affairs was an opportunity to exhibit her "virtue"; her goal was to help "Europe," not her diplomatic allies. Lomonosov justified the empress's policies by creating a moral framework for them. By defining an acceptable military engagement according to moral standards, he refashioned the image of the ideal monarch. The ruler as knight was divested of a cultural mission and morally obligated to accept military commitments so that he could give witness to his own righteousness.

In the 1750s Lomonosov's odes seemed to be exercises in repetition. When the Seven Years' War began, he supported Elizabeth's decision to intervene.[8] He described her actions as a protective measure necessary to guard her own interests and those of her "faithful" allies against the encroachment of the "arrogant" enemy.[9] Then, in a surprising message to the empress on her nameday in 1759,[10] he called on her, "the angel of peace,"[11] to withdraw from the war.

> We await the longed for words:
> "Enough of victories—no more,
> No more the ravages of battles."
> O Lord, Lord of peace, arise,
> Let your love for all of us be shown,
>
> . . . .
>
> Let the gate to war be forever closed.
> . . . Have we not endured enough
> Of the woes of this world?
> Behold the tears of the orphaned,
> Behold the blood of thy servants,
> It is to you that Elizabeth calls on this day . . .
> Banish wars from the ends of the earth.[12]

This poem was unique among Lomonosov's writings on the ruler's military duties. Three odes, one to Elizabeth in 1761, one to Peter III in the same year, and one to Catherine II in 1762, contained remarks on war similar to those made in his earlier odes, particularly the one written on the occasion of the victory at Khotin.[13]

The image of the military ruler came to be mingled in Lomonosov's fictional representations with the image of the utilitarian monarch. Lomonosov charged the ideal monarch with responsibility for developing the economic and social resources of the realm on grounds similar to those justifying his military duties. Economic expansion was permissible when directed against peoples less civilized than the Russians—in this case not the Turks but the inhabitants of Siberia. His remarks came at a time when Russian settlements along the Pacific coast and penetration across the Bering Straits into Alaska revived interest in the economic wealth awaiting those who would pursue it. Many of Lomonosov's contemporaries, particularly Sumarokov, extolled in verse the natural resources of Siberia. Lomonosov had sufficient reason to describe Russia's purposes in Siberia as a legitimate economic concern of the ruler.

Lomonosov's poetic image of Siberia was one of a region rich in natural resources. This abundance was, however, not cited as evidence of available economic wealth, but rather as proof of the idyllic character of the territory. The inhabitants were "innocents," uncorrupted by the presence of any government and free of any moral deficiencies.[14] The unsullied, guileless state of these people imposed a special obligation on Elizabeth. This bucolic life was threatened by unspecified persons whose rapacious interest in Siberia could ruin the tranquility and moral purity of the Siberian natives. Those who would rule the area only to exploit its resources were not to be tolerated. Elizabeth should demonstrate her munificence and intervene to protect the local inhabitants and fend off any threat, whatever its source. The empress had a duty to enlighten these peoples and coax them out of their ignorance. Lomonosov thought the ruler's duty to defend Siberia had priority over her obligation to encourage its development. He would not fault a monarch who paid attention to military matters and expansion even if it meant disregarding her utilitarian role.

Implicit in Lomonosov's remarks about Siberia is an argument that could serve to limit the ruler's military function. If expansion into Siberia was acceptable on the grounds that the Russian presence would guard against any threat to the region's social and economic stability, the same considerations would enjoin the ruler from pursuing a war policy that would threaten central Russia's own social and economic equilibrium. Lomonosov contraposed the ideal of domestic security to the potential disarray attendant on foreign military ventures and gave some thought to favoring the former. In an ode celebrating the sixth anniversary of Elizabeth's accession, he described in exuberant and wonderstruck terms an idyllic picture of a Russia rich in natural beauty and resources.[15] Genuinely enthusiastic, he added a plea to the empress not to jeopardize these advantages or be diverted from attending to their development by engaging in military operations abroad. With this priority of the utilitarian over the military in mind, he wrote a number of works extolling the activities of several Russian rulers as appropriate to their utilitarian duties. His praise was meant, in some cases, to do no more than commend a monarch for being a benefactor of the sciences in Russia. In other, more significant instances, he wanted to draw the ruler's attention to a particular project and, once the focus was fixed, extrapolate to general social benefits. For example, in one sequence he urged the sovereign to find a new sea route to "India." As corollaries he recommended the collection of the necessary meteorological and naval information, establishment of the rudiments of seafaring sciences in Russia, and, finally, the founding of a naval academy to teach students the basics of navigation and other marine sciences.[16] The emphasis in all these proposals was on practical skills and knowledge of immediate usefulness to the ruler.

Lomonosov's apparent preference for the utilitarian rather than the military monarch proved to be illusory when he described how the throne was to fulfill its utilitarian function and who would benefit from the ruler's initiatives. In a typical lecture delivered in 1751 at the Academy of Sciences, Lomonosov praised particular scientific uses of chemistry, cited cases in which the application of chemical techniques led to specific results, as in the field of metallurgy, and closed by stressing the benefits of chemical studies to society. The same extrapolation was made time and again in the 1750s and early 1760s in his discourses on the advantages of the salt trade, mercantile ventures, and a rising population rate.[17] Once the line of argument moved from a specific topic into broad issues of social purpose, he was but a short step away from integrating these general opinions into a corporate vision of the state, economy, and society. Potentially each of these interests would be interdependent or, in his words, members of a "pyramid." [18] This step would have entailed defining the bonds among the various constituents as reciprocal and imposing mutual obligations and restrictions. Yet he never took this final step. Lomonosov not only shunned the consequences of consistency, he even came to deny them. He based his arguments for the development of Russia's metallurgical industries on grounds that circumscribed their potential political significance. He clearly implied that the purpose of developing the economy and society was to serve the interests of the ruler.[19] In so designating the beneficiary of the monarch's utilitarian initiative, Lomonosov did not state that the ruler's utilitarian role was ultimately subordinate to the military one but rather allowed the sovereign to govern without any limitation by function.

Lomonosov reasserted the primacy of the monarchy over its constituent parts and did so in a way that invalidated any idea of "society" as a corporate entity with characteristics and purposes distinct and possibly autonomous from those of the state. Lomonosov never reached a sophisticated understanding of "society" because he never altered his belief that political considerations took precedence over all others. His political theories were limited by his fascination with the ruler. In the end his ideal monarch would subordinate his utilitarian functions to his military ones, and the assurance that both sets of duties would be fulfilled came only from the self-imposed moral obligations of the monarch.

—— 3 ——

Lomonosov's image of the ruler did not include the quality that was most important to his most famous contemporary, Sumarokov, and that was to be primary to Fonvizin and his peers in the 1760s: the ruler as legislator. Lomonosov's direct references to the role of laws were cursory and vague.[20] His ideal ruler was fettered not by legal restraints but by the integrity of his own moral personality. He was to be above all else a model of virtue. Lomonosov made his point in the well-known oration to Elizabeth on the occasion of the eighth anniversary of her accession, a work that was republished four times in the poet's lifetime.[21] He lavished praise on the empress by making a comparison between sovereigns who were exemplars of virtue and those who were only executors of the laws. The second type governed by striking fear into their subjects but found that such behavior neither corrected their people nor enhanced their own power. The first type would be assured of the obedience of their subjects by their own example as generous, kind, and humane rulers. They would be able to lift up the moral standards of their people.[22] "However useful the strict enforcement of the laws on one's subjects may be, it fails to reward virtue and serves more to drive the good into a state of despondency than to correct the evil ones. In comparison one can be particularly effective and have singular success in the correction of human mores by rewarding virtue and making allowance for personal merit along with the gentle disciplining of vices." [23]

Lomonosov was plainly enthralled with an iconic image of the ruler. Moral considerations might even make legal ones unnecessary. Witness Lomonosov's image of the ruler in the tragedy *Demofont* (1750–1751).[24] Demofont, the play's hero, had to endure a series of trials as he returned from Troy to assume power in Athens. His voyage was interrupted by a visit to the palace of the alluring Fillida, with whom he soon fell in love. He had to choose between his love for Fillida and his obligations to the citizens of Athens. One of his aides reminded him that his legal obligations were paramount,[25] yet, as one of Fillida's lieutenants pointed out, his departure would undermine the rule of law in her realm.[26] The hero's anguish over whether to follow his passions or honor his legal obligations was typical of classicist literature. In this play, however, the denouement was brought about when Demofont became enamored of a second woman, considered himself disgraced by his inconstancy, and committed suicide. Considerations of legal obligation were not discarded but absent. Demofont lacked the moral requisites of a ruler, and that alone sufficed to explain his failure and his forfeiture of office.[27]

Virtue, not adherence to the law, was the prime attribute of the ideal ruler. The stress on the monarch's moral worth made irrelevant any distinction between the ruler's personal and public selves, yet this separation of the person of the sovereign from his office is the potential basis for judging the legitimacy of his actions as monarch. The image of the ruler as exemplar of virtue reinforces the identity of the monarch, both in person and office, with the state.

This image of the ruler was repeated in Lomonosov's works consistently and therein lies its importance. Whether he was writing of Anna, Elizabeth, Peter III, or Catherine II, he depicted them in similar terms as the embodiment of "goodness," "virtue," and "kindness"; each would save the "people" or the "fatherland" from the abuses of either the ruler's predecessor or unnamed "foreigners"; each was the protector against the "powerful ones"; each ended the disarray of the previous monarch's reign and restored tranquility and security; and, most important, each was the military defender of the "people." This consistency was maintained even when it was awkward. Lomonosov lauded Peter III for eliminating the abuses of Elizabeth's reign only to extol Catherine II a few months later for ridding the people of the abusive practices of Peter III. When Lomonosov described Peter the Great, he disregarded Peter's own measure of himself as the legal ruler and imposed the same, albeit magnified, image on Peter as he had on Peter's successors. The image of the monarch was composed of a set of constants and appeared in varying degrees of clarity in many of Lomonosov's works for over twenty years, transcending inhibitions of logical consistency and historical accuracy. The features of the image were neither so bland as to be pointless nor so unrelated as to be casually chosen.

Lomonosov's image of the ruler was a mythical one whose origins lay not in Petrine and post-Petrine Russia but in Muscovite times. Yet the iconography of the ruler did not correspond to that of the grand princes of Moscow or the initial tsars.[28] Those political ideals confirmed the sovereign power of the ruler by referring to his military exploits and elaborate ideological claims. Lomonosov's mythical ruler carried no hint of historical justification or religious sanction. Rather he was an immutable figure of metahistorical stature, an exalted archetype of moral rectitude, free of spiritual and civic responsibilities. He represented the mythical fiction that characterized the imagery associated with seventeenth-century Russian tsars, particularly those who ruled after the church schism of 1667.[29] Lomonosov resorted to the mythical language of the tsars of the seventeenth century to complement the functional properties attributed to the monarchs of the eighteenth century.

The ideals present in Lomonosov's odes were certainly not compatible with those to be found in the works of German natural law jurists. Since the ideas of Pufendorf and Wolff had been given the status of the official political philosophy by Peter the Great, it would be reasonable to expect some evidence of these ideas in the works of a writer of Elizabethan Russia. This is particularly the case for Lomonosov, who studied for three years at Marburg under the personal supervision of Wolff himself. After his return to St. Petersburg, Lomonosov patterned his lectures at the Academy of Sciences on those Wolff had delivered at Marburg and was ready for the rest of his life to acknowledge his intellectual debt to Wolff. Yet Lomonosov refrained from accepting with rigorous, thoroughgoing consistency Wolff's political principles in their original form or formulating his own adaptation of Wolff's political theories. What is striking is not the presence of German natural law but its absence.

Lomonosov's example is all the more significant because his image of the ruler was similar to that of no less a figure than the famous theoretician of Peter's Russia, Feofan Prokopovich (1681–1736). Prokopovich ought to have been an advocate of German natural law. He was well known for his treatise *The Justice of the Monarch's Will,* at once a theoretical explanation and an apologia of Peter's policies. In this work and its summary in the "Sermon on Royal Authority and Honor," Prokopovich defended the tsar by relying heavily on the political doctrines of Pufendorf, Hobbes, and Grotius. The intellectual origins of much of the essay can be readily traced, as Gurvich has demonstrated, to works of contemporary natural law theory.[30] Prokopovich, the Russian disciple of Pufendorf, Hobbes, and Grotius, was at the same time the popularizer of the figure of Peter the Great as a paternal ruler, concerned not with legalities but with the protection of his subjects and the maintenance of spiritual bonds joining the tsar to his people. In the *Russian Primer,* a catechism written in 1720, Prokopovich posed the question: "What doth God require in the fifth Commandment?" "He commands us to honour and obey our parents, a name which includes our Sovereign, our Spiritual Pastors and Civil Governors, our Teachers, Benefactors, and Elders."[31] The qualities expected of monarch and subject alike were derived from the ten commandments, not from natural law theory. The image of the ruler as paternal guardian was joined in Prokopovich's odes to that of virtuous warrior smiting a morally unworthy foe. Prokopovich delivered a sermon celebrating Peter the Great's victory over the Swedes at Poltava on June 27, 1709.[32] The tsar was described as a pious ruler striking fear into the hearts of his diabolical enemies, Charles XII and the Hetman of the Ukraine, Ivan Mazepa. In the person of Peter the Great Russians had their David to conquer the Philistines. Peter's exploits were to be compared, Prokopovich instructed his audience, with precedents—unnamed ones—in Roman and biblical history.

Prokopovich's ideal ruler was not identical to Lomonosov's. Prokopovich sought to fit the tsar into a chronological schema of religious and classical history and thereby removed from his imagery the particular features that identified Lomonosov's conception of the ruler as peculiar to seventeenth-century Russia. Nonetheless there was a common characteristic in Prokopovich's and Lomonosov's writings. Both men described the monarch in two images that were parallel and not meant to be reconciled. While neither man drew on the thoughts of the other, both wrote with a recognition of the need to comprehend the ideal of the ruler as defined by German natural law without dispensing with pre-eighteenth-century traditions of kingship. As Prokopovich's writings demonstrate, Lomonosov's ruler imagery was not composed of the unusual notions of a single person but was born of an effort he shared with Prokopovich to reach his own understanding of the meaning of German natural law.

Lomonosov was not interested in legality, either as a general value or as it was presented in German natural law. Pufendorf and Wolff provided quite specific definitions of legitimate and illegitimate activities by the monarch, both in his person and office, and subordinated the throne to the state. They shared the assumption of many other theorists of the German Enlightenment that the legal status of the ruler rendered moot considerations of his moral nature. In describing their political ideals Pufendorf and Wolff wrote with the security that came from the theoretical lineage of their ideas about the legal ruler. They and their contemporaries were common participants in the intellectual evolution away from the medieval scholastics' ideas of the monarch as preeminently a moral personality. Political theorists of the German Enlightenment could also benefit from and build on the common heritage of the Renaissance with its stress on the definition of the sovereign's legal obligations to his subjects. These traditions meant nothing when German natural law was taken up by Russians of Lomonosov's time.

The political ideals of the German Enlightenment differed substantially from those of Muscovite Russia. The subtleties of the Germans' definition of the ruler's role were meaningless to Lomonosov. If he was to understand and make understood the policies and activities of the Russian rulers of his time, it was not at all surprising that he clung to the imagery of the political myths associated with the tsars of the seventeenth century. The accuracy of this image is obviously not the point. The myths served as subjective truths to explain what might otherwise be unintelligible, to make legitimate what might be unacceptable. The language of myths was the medium for ordering and reducing the poet's own political experience into terms he could understand. His use of mythical ideals did not affirm or deny the validity of the legal ideals of German natural law. Rather his writings were clear evidence that the theoretical abstractions of the German Enlightenment had to be translated into correspondent mythical symbols, intelligible and acceptable to Russian thinkers of his times. Otherwise, the German political ideals would, however rationally persuasive, fail to be psychologically satisfactory. Until the legal formulas of German natural law could render unnecessary the mythical imagery of seventeenth-century Russian tsars, its maxims would not be fully intelligible to Lomonosov and his contemporaries.

Lomonosov had made paramount the ruler's virtue, yet also emphasized his utilitarian role. The two faces of the monarch were complementary. One image was essentially passive, the other quite dynamic; one was timeless, the other particular in time and space; one was foreign to the ideas of German natural law, the other readily reconcilable with the tenets of many contemporary European thinkers, including Pufendorf and Wolff. To be sure, the features of Lomonosov's utopian monarch were not rigorously interrelated, but the lack of system was a conscious choice. Lomonosov had available a large number of books by contemporary European theorists and must have been familiar with many schools of political thought. As the shelf lists of his personal library attest, he was familiar with Wolff's political works.[33] Drawing on his knowledge of Western and Central European political theory, Lomonosov contributed to his contemporaries' capacity to appraise the policies of the Russian rulers from Anna to Catherine by interpreting the legal language of German natural law in a political vocabulary intelligible to the Russian thinkers of his age.

Because Lomonosov was not interested in legality he provided later political commentators with little in the way of theoretical guidelines for assessing the legitimacy of the monarch's policies. As long as the law was not recognized as the regulator of the ruler's conduct, no meaningful distinctions could be made between the ruler and the state.

In evaluating Lomonosov's political writings, we must remember that his interests were not primarily political. In 1760 he described his studies in chemistry as "my chief profession." [34] He did not know much about political personalities and policies. His poetic descriptions of each monarch were conventional and quite lacking in distinctions that would differentiate one from another. Nor should Lomonosov's lack of interest in the rule of law be held against him. He was writing at a time when any expectation that the imperial government could regulate the Russian polity by laws would have been a call for it to police a political and social order that did not yet exist.[35] Nevertheless, his emphasis on the ruler's utilitarian function to the virtual exclusion of his legal status had the potential to inhibit the eventual acceptance of the concept. Lomonosov's writings allowed for a monarch who would not be the regulator of social order, still less the instrument of that goal, but the despot capable of deciding on goals and *modi operandi* solely on his own.

—— 4 ——

The image of the ideal ruler in Lomonosov's works beguiled his contemporaries and accounts for a misapprehension of his political ideas by his biographers, then and now. In much of the literature on Lomonosov he has been miscast in the role of a sycophant, composing on demand the appropriate verses to the appropriate magnates on the appropriate occasions. If this were accurate, his political ideals would not be worthy of scholarly attention.[36] This interpretation originated during Lomonosov's lifetime when he became known at court for his odes and orations rather than his varied and specialized scientific research. His remarkable studies in the physical and biological sciences were not known to his contemporaries because many of these works were written in Latin and not published during his lifetime. When Lomonosov put out an edition of his *Selected Works* in 1751, he chose to include his odes, *Russian Grammar, Rhetoric,* and other literary works but only a few, brief essays on physics and metallurgy. His reputation as a littérateur rather than scientist was prolonged by the biographical sketch in Novikov's *Historical Dictionary of Russian Writers* (1772). Novikov referred in passing to his subject as a chemist, but allotted most of the entry to Lomonosov the poet, historian, rhetorician, and linguist. "I cannot give adequate praise," Novikov wrote, "to this great writer." [37] Lomonosov's death was, to Novikov, "deeply mourned by every lover of the literary arts." [38]

Lomonosov's reputation as a literary figure remained unaltered until the mid-nineteenth century when it was revised to emphasize his status as a "progressive" intellectual. His most famous tsarist biographer, P. Pekarskii, described his subject's many interests as a clear-cut example of the struggle for progress against the resistant forces of tradition. In the twentieth century many Soviet scholars, notably G. Vasetskii, I. Shchipanov, and Z. Kamenskii, rephrased and refined this "progressive" reputation in political terms.[39] According to this version of Lomonosov's career, he was a forerunner of the Decembrists, a political forebear of nineteenth-century critics of autocracy, and one of the initial advocates in Russia of constitutional limitations on the regime.

The claims of Kamenskii and his colleagues are vulnerable on two counts. Wolff was a theoretician of absolutism, not constitutionalism in any Western European sense. Moreover, these Soviet scholars extend the ties of political kinship to an inordinate range by associating Lomonosov with Belinskii, Chernyshevskii, and Dobroliubov. Kamenskii and his associates are open to the accusation that they suffer from what Marc Bloch has termed the *"maladie des origines."* Kamenskii's case can best be sustained by reference not to Lomonosov's position in the genealogy of Russian political figures, but rather to his intellectual connections with contemporary writers on German natural law. Morozov amended the interpretation of Lomonosov as the political progressive to stress his subject's ability to reinterpret the intent of Wolff's political theories and conceive his own ideals.[40] Morozov is certainly correct in emphasizing Lomonosov's ability to adapt German political ideals to circumstances particular to Russia in the mid-eighteenth century, but the nature of this adaptation remains at issue. Lomonosov revised Wolff's maxims by referring to the political myths of seventeenth-century Russia. His political ideals were quite conservative, even for his own times. Lomonosov's principles have been given glosses by his commentators, both imperial and Soviet, rather than taken directly as evidence of his effort to understand the politics of his day. Novikov's version at least was a sober estimate of Lomonosov's literary interests, though it too readily consigned him to the ranks of a littérateur. To be sure, he was that but not simply that. The question none of his commentators have come to grips with is why the content of what he wrote remained so immutable over the course of his long career. Why was the image of the ideal ruler a static one, imbued with a sense of stillness and serenity, and removed from the vagaries of events and personalities?

— 5 —

The timeless quality of Lomonosov's political ideals was due, in part, to circumstances far removed from the lofty realm of the utopian rulers—the particulars of his career. The principal facts of Lomonosov's life are well known. The son of a peasant, he came to Moscow in 1731 to enroll in the Moscow Slavonic-Greko-Latin Academy. His native talents and his diligence led to his being recruited for advanced studies at the Academy of Sciences in St. Petersburg. After a five-year stint abroad, Lomonosov returned to Russia in 1741 and received the first of a series of appointments at the Academy of Sciences. Over the course of a long scholarly career at the Academy, Lomonosov was not only a poet but also a geographer, playwright, mosaicist, philosopher, journalist, physicist, historian, demographer, and chemist. Pushkin called him Russia's first university. Lomonosov could sustain so many interests only by frequently doing without extensive experimentation and reflection. Many of his works were briefs of projects proposed but never carried to completion. He played the part not of the dilettante but of the eighteenth-century man of letters, unbound by the fetters of any one discipline and confident in his involvement in many. The one constant in his career was his affiliation with the Academy of Sciences. Within this academic haven he pursued his divers interests and encountered the individuals whose influence left a mark on his writings.

At the time of Lomonosov's initial appointment on January 8, 1742, the Academy retained many of the characteristics imparted by its founder, Peter the Great. The tsar had wanted to staff the Academy by recruiting professors from German universities.[41] When Lomonosov joined the Academy its senior officials were German by birth and training. A testy fellow, quick to feel slighted and difficult to satisfy, Lomonosov saw himself as an embattled scholar besieged at the Academy by the attack of the Germans. Three colleagues in particular drew his fire: the secretary of the Academy's chancellory, Johann Daniel Schumacher, and the historians August Ludwig Schlözer and Gerhard Friedrich Müller. To Lomonosov every initiative he undertook seemed to lead to a dismaying sequence of events: a confrontation with one or another German academic, an appeal to the Academy's secretary, and often a ruling against him.

Consider his quarrels with Müller. In 1749 Müller wrote an oration on the occasion of the empress's nameday, entitled "De origine Gentis et nominis Russorum," in which he made the case for the famous Norman theory on the origins of the first Russian state in Kiev. Müller argued that the Kievan state was founded not by the native Slavs in the Dnieper basin but by the "Varangian Russes," warriors from Scandinavia. The Slavs turned to the Varangian Russes to provide the political organization they could not themselves supply. When Müller's speech was submitted to the Academy, Lomonosov was one of six selected to review the work. His recommendation was that the Academy withhold its imprimatur. The essay "cannot be so drastically revised as to make it suitable for publication." [42] He again criticized Müller's hypotheses in his own *Ancient Russian History* and still again in his handbook, the *Short Russian Chronicle*. Lomonosov did not always dispute his colleagues' claims. When he was assigned in 1751 to review Müller's *History of Siberia,* his judgment was initially quite favorable, though later he reversed himself. If Lomonosov had opposed Müller and, on other occasions, Schumacher and Schlözer on purely theoretical grounds, his remarks could be considered as no more than a spirited critique of his colleagues' work. But Lomonosov turned differences of opinion into confrontations with academic rivals and personal enemies. Note this comment on Schlözer's work: "It is clear to anyone that Schlözer is a madman. . . . How can one put any faith in a man who is so utterly lacking in intelligence and honor? Who is he but an emissary from those who wish me only ill?" [43] Frequently at odds with other academicians, Lomonosov found in the writing of history a means of allaying his antipathy to all foreign-born individuals who wrote Russian history.

This particular resort was significant for reasons that transcend the petty rivalries within the Academy. Lomonosov's personal interest in rewriting Russian history came to be linked in his mind with the quest for national pride. History was to be a means of chronicling the heroic feats of past rulers and reviving their memory among Lomonosov's contemporaries. As he noted in the introduction to *Ancient Russian History,* history "provides sovereigns with examples of government, subjects of obedience, warriors of courage, judges of justice, the young of the wisdom of their elders . . . and to each and all unforgettable enjoyment and untold benefits." [44] Lomonosov's use of history to arouse patriotic zeal was a measure of his own and many contemporaries' appreciation of national sentiments. This awareness of the worth of Russia's past was to have momentous consequences. Lomonosov evoked scenes of past glories to exalt the figure of the Russian ruler as the symbol for his sense of national pride. Many later writers of history were not so ready to accept this identity of monarchy and nationality.

Lomonosov's difficulties within the Academy prompted him to seek shelter and support from powerful figures at the court. He won the favor of several magnates. In the late 1740s he ingratiated himself with Count K. G. Razumovskii (1728–1803), the president of the Academy from 1746 to 1765. In the late 1750s and early 1760s he came to the attention of Mikhail Vorontsov (1714–1767), the chancellor from 1758 to 1763 and the leading political personage at the court. During the initial years of Catherine's reign Lomonosov was shielded from his opponents—real and imagined—by Grigorii Orlov (1734–1783), Catherine's lover and political adviser. Most important to Lomonosov was the protection he enjoyed from his association with Ivan Shuvalov (1727–1797), who attracted the affections of Empress Elizabeth in 1749 and enjoyed an unassailable position of influence at the court. Lomonosov's contacts with Shuvalov were definitely made by August 1750 and lasted until 1761. Their dealings provide a classic example of how patron-client relations worked at Elizabeth's court.

The relationship was based, before all else, on services rendered. When Lomonosov encountered personal animosity, he usually turned to Shuvalov and implored him to intercede in his behalf.[45] When he required subsidies from the state treasury to fund his projects, Shuvalov might try to arrange for the necessary money. When Lomonosov needed assistance in advancing a particular proposal through the bureaucratic channels within the Academy, he might turn to Shuvalov to use his influence to expedite the process and then again to carry the project to the Senate. When Lomonosov prepared major plans for the direct consideration of the empress, Shuvalov often acted as their sponsor and thereby improved their chances of success. Shuvalov was instrumental in winning Elizabeth's approval for one of Lomonosov's most famous projects: the founding of Moscow University in 1755. Shuvalov became its first curator, a post he held for forty-two years and relinquished only a few months before his death.[46]

The link between patron and client was not simply one between a benefactor and supplicant. In the privacy of his letters, Lomonosov made remarks to Shuvalov quite unlike those he addressed to Razumovskii, Vorontsov, or Orlov. To these three, he was exultant when the occasion demanded, vapid when he sought support, and profuse in expressions of gratitude, using the formulas required by social and literary convention.[47] With Shuvalov the tone of his letters was quite assertive. In one instance, when he suspected Shuvalov's interest in Moscow University was flagging, he remonstrated with him, referring to the institution as the potential "origin of countless numbers of Lomonosovs." [48] Lomonosov was ready on occasion to use the influence of one patron to reinforce that of a second one and thereby ensure the success of his own venture. In 1751 he wanted to establish factories to produce his mosaics, an enterprise that required a large subsidy and an allowance to employ serfs. Lomonosov appealed to Vorontsov to petition the empress for approval of the project.[49] Then he wrote Shuvalov requesting that he use his good offices to support Vorontsov's petition.[50] Lomonosov's tactics succeeded in this case.

This apparent independence with Shuvalov hides the degree to which Lomonosov was actually dependent on him. Shuvalov provided his protégé not only with funds and protection but also with many of the ideas that aroused Lomonosov's interest in several projects and led to their eventual completion. Shuvalov and Lomonosov collaborated in 1754–1755 in sponsoring a new journal, *Monthly Compositions.* This was the successor to the *Supplements* and the scholarly *Commentaries* of the *St. Petersburg News* (1728–1742) and the predecessor to the literary journals of 1759–1764. Many scholars, including the distinguished Soviet literary historian P. Berkov, have assumed that the prime mover of this initiative was Lomonosov.[51] Berkov cited two points of evidence: a letter Lomonosov wrote to Shuvalov on January 3, 1754, about the need for a periodical, and an essay he composed in the same year on the duties of journalists. The letter, however, did not propose the journal but was a reply to Shuvalov's suggestion to do so.[52] The "Discourse on the Duties of Journalists" was not an appeal to Russian men of letters to solicit aid in starting a journal. Rather, Lomonosov addressed the "Discourse" to Central European critics of his current chemical studies.[53] When *Monthly Compositions* began publication in 1755, it represented a project conceived and subsequently sponsored by Shuvalov. Lomonosov's role was quite secondary. He was not even chosen as editor.

Lomonosov's dependence on Shuvalov has given rise to a claim, common to Berkov and to Vavilov and his associates, the editors of the most recent edition of Lomonosov's *Complete Collected Works,* that the links between patron and client forced Lomonosov to serve the immediate political interests of the Shuvalovs.[54] Here again the evidence compels a reconsideration of this contention. Lomonosov certainly had the occasion and his patron the need to employ his literary talents to promote Shuvalov's political designs. During the late 1750s Ivan Shuvalov and his brothers, Peter and Alexander, were vulnerable because of their pro-French diplomatic views. When Russia became involved in the Seven Years' War in league with France and Austria, the Shuvalovs came to be associated with a foreign policy that had led to protracted military involvements with ruinous economic consequences.[55] Despite the clear threat to the Shuvalovs' position at the court, Lomonosov did not voice any support for his patron's opinions. He did write in praise of the Russian military commitment in 1757, but he also supported imperial military policy in 1762 when Russia's ally was no longer France but Prussia and, with no less readiness, the decision to withdraw from the war in 1762. The absence of literary support for Shuvalov's political interests is striking evidence of Lomonosov's impartiality. His political ideals were free of any taint of partisan favor for his patron. By the same token, when Ivan Shuvalov was exiled in 1763 by Catherine, Lomonosov could seek the protection of Mikhail Vorontsov and then Grigorii Orlov without anticipating that either man would force his political interests on him. Lomonosov's political involvements with magnates at the court did not require him to compromise or to deny his ideals.

Lomonosov's dealings with Shuvalov were typical of the relations between many poets and playwrights of eighteenth-century Russia and their patrons. The literati sought the favor of the rich and powerful to protect themselves and find sponsors for their projects. Their status vis-à-vis their patron was that of a ward, not a retainer or apologist. In turn the patron remained aloof from his client's daily affairs. Lomonosov never served in a bureaucratic office under Shuvalov's control and, in fact, had only occasional meetings with him. Shuvalov's intercession on Lomonosov's behalf was an intermittent, albeit occasionally crucial, element in the academician's career. Like many other men of letters Lomonosov enjoyed a casual affiliation with his patron, one that did not make any demands on his literary skills or political loyalties. Shuvalov did not employ Lomonosov's talents in his own cause; Lomonosov risked no compromise of political principle from his association with Shuvalov. Only when a patron sought to use a client's literary abilities to serve his own political interests could the relationship acquire the dynamic quality that transformed the client into a political retainer, whose services and ideals were available to promote the politics of the patron.

Lomonosov's relations with the throne were troubled. Dependent on their favor and munificence to support and fund his many projects, he was no more partial to one ruler than to any other. Though each had his particular policies and style of governing, these distinctions were of no concern to Lomonosov. He could not let his attitude toward them be anything other than that of a supplicant. The throne, however, did not remain removed from his activities but intervened in his life whenever the occasion suited the needs or pleasures of the monarch.

Lomonosov's lifelong interest in chemistry and metallurgy grew out of a choice made for him by the government. In 1735 a chemist was needed to accompany an expedition to Siberia. When the Academy of Sciences was asked to provide a qualified individual and could not find one available, it recommended that several Russian students be sent abroad to acquire the necessary training in the chemical sciences. Lomonosov was one of those selected, despite the fact that he had been recruited from the Moscow Slavonic-Greko-Latin Academy that very year to come to the Academy of Sciences because of his demonstrated aptitude for philosophy.[56] He went abroad in September 1736 to be schooled for the Siberian excursion and returned to St. Petersburg on June 8, 1741, to discover that the expedition had already set off for Siberia without him. Nevertheless, he maintained his interest in chemistry and eventually came to regard it as his "chief profession."

His research was interrupted by new assignments from the government. In the winter of 1749–1750, Elizabeth, bored by the weather and court routine, ordered Lomonosov to write plays that could be presented at court. He quickly completed two tragedies, *Demofont* and *Tamira and Selim*.[57] Once he satisfied this particular whim of Elizabeth, he never wrote another play.

In the early 1750s the government led Lomonosov into another area of its, not his, choosing. Even though his historical works were a release for his antagonistic feelings toward the German academics, Lomonosov became a historian in spite of himself. In January 1749 he had told the historian Vasilii Tatishchev that he did not himself write any historical works because "I have no time. My principal occupation is metallurgy, and it was to study this particular discipline that I was sent to Saxony. Moreover chemistry and physics together with the dispatch of business and meetings in the Academy demand most of my time."[58] Yet by 1753, Lomonosov was devoting so much of his time to history that, as he wrote Shuvalov, "I hope that I may be allowed some relief from my labors on the collection [of documents] and composition of 'Russian history' . . . so that I may allot a few hours each day to [my] experiments in physics and chemistry." [59]

What had happened between the two letters, apparently, was that the empress had intervened. Soon after he wrote his commentaries on Müller's manuscripts in 1751, Elizabeth encouraged—to the point of ordering—the writing of what became his *Ancient Russian History*. This project came, as Lomonosov's letter to Shuvalov attests, to consume his time and energies. [60] The *History* was but a prelude to four later works, three of which were refutations of individual sections of Voltaire's *Histoire de l'Empire de Russie sous Pierre le Grand*. It is no wonder that Lomonosov described his new duties as a historian in rather plaintive and beleaguered terms: "I have been forced not only to play the role of a poet, orator, chemist, and physicist but also to become a historian and that to the virtual exclusion of everything else." [61]

Lomonosov served the autocracy under conditions he found personally trying. He was buffeted by the varied and onerous assignments he was given. Utterly dependent on the will of the ruler, there was no possibility that he could share with the monarch any values and purposes. It would never have occurred to Lomonosov to have any definite expectations about the proper conduct of a particular ruler; his ideals were equally relevant to all rulers. His ruler imagery could be immutable because he never associated his ideals with any single sovereign nor committed his services exclusively to any one monarch.

Lomonosov had difficulties with the last autocrat he served, Catherine the Great. When the palace coup of June 28, 1762, brought her to power, the new empress was careful to strike a favorable pose before her subjects. She publicized her own version of the coup and the benefits that it could be expected to bring her loyal citizens. As will be described shortly, she closely monitored the comments of her contemporaries to make sure they praised her dutifully and in the same terms she used herself. Because Lomonosov was seriously ill in June 1762, he did not celebrate Catherine's triumph in the manner she had prescribed nor repeat the political formulas he had used to describe the accession to power of her predecessors. Unable to offer Catherine the congratulatory verses as quickly as convention and prudence required, Lomonosov was also handicapped by association with his patrons Shuvalov and Vorontsov. The two had enjoyed substantial influence in the councils of Peter III's government, a past that did not endear them to his successor. When he remained silent for a full week after the coup, his inaction was taken by Catherine's advisers, particularly Grigorii Orlov, as a signal of his lack of enthusiasm for the new regime. By the time he wrote Orlov and praised the empress, his motives were suspect and he was ignored.[62]

Lomonosov ran afoul of the sovereign and suffered the fate of the political outcast. He requested permission to retire. His petition was approved on May 2, 1763, only to be rescinded on May 13. At the time of his death soon thereafter, Lomonosov was mourned by few of his contemporaries. Sumarokov, who never did have a reputation for tact, could not resist the opportunity to comment at the funeral that the deceased "was a noisy fool whose mouth is forever shut." [63] Nevertheless, the fact remains that Lomonosov stayed true to his ideals while forgoing political commitments. His ideals and political commitments remained in the sixties what they had been in the forties and fifties, namely parallel interests.

—— 7 ——

Lomonosov's difficulties with Catherine followed a long record of unstinting service and harmonious relations with her predecessors. Throughout his career he maintained mutually exclusive concerns with serving his sovereigns and describing in verse his image of the ideal ruler. This relationship between career and conviction identifies Lomonosov's contribution to the political ideals and activities of his contemporaries. He succeeded in constructing a model of an ideal ruler, a political fiction whose qualities were not unlike those described by other writers of his time. Through his image of an ideal ruler he made intelligible to the men of his age—or at least to the literate few who thought about such matters—an autocracy whose form had been radically changed by Peter the Great. Lomonosov's response to the potentially quite bewildering actions of Peter and his successors was not to grapple with the complexities of the reforms or the consequences of the monarchy's new guise. Rather he reduced the scope of these events and personalities to the characteristics expected in the person of the ruler. In so doing he achieved comprehension at the price of limitation.

His image of the monarch was static because it was moral. As long as the ideal ruler was one whose position was validated by his own virtue, there was no need to invoke standards that did not rely on his evaluation of his own conduct. The moral integrity of the ruler discredited the worth of any estimate but his own of the legitimacy, even the moral one, of the sovereign's actions. Lomonosov's interest in the nature of the ideal ruler rendered quite moot any consideration of distinguishing between the person of the monarch and his office or between the monarch and the state. Lomonosov's vision of the ideal ruler obscured everything but the personality of the monarch.

The image of the monarch was untroubled by any concern for legality. This single feature would have enabled the ideal ruler to shed his moral quality and define his status as an individual apart from his office and as a political figure apart from his government. It was also the standard against which the conduct and legitimacy of the ruler could have been independently judged. As legal rather than moral considerations came to define the expectations of many political commentators of the 1750s and 1760s, the relationship Lomonosov had made between political ideals and commitments was gradually replaced by one that assumed not mutually exclusive interests but complementary ones. In turn, this change compelled the throne to relinquish its hitherto benign regard for the formation of political ideals. While the crown could quite easily accept Lomonosov's ideal ruler, it could not possibly countenance those of his successors. Russian sovereigns, particularly Catherine the Great, would certainly not be passive witnesses to the growth of a sense of legality with its consequent expectations for the conduct and policies of the throne. The monarchs, Catherine before all others, would try to redraw the features of the ideal ruler to make the image accord with that of the actual rulers, just as some commentators would attempt to impress that image on the policies of the throne.

Lomonosov's version of the ideal ruler was similar to the model rulers in the literature of the 1750s and 1760s. Many writers of the late Elizabethan and Catherinian eras shared his political ideals, as well as his understanding of the relationship between principles and position at the court. Gradually, though, a new element came to prominence in the literature of the fifties and sixties. The ideal monarch changed from being a moral guardian and defender to being the embodiment of legality. The moving force behind this revision was a new perception of the conduct expected of the ruler, one that was brought on by the influence of political ideals quite foreign to Lomonosov's thinking. This revision of political theory was lent a sense of urgency by what many writers of the 1750s considered to be the threats posed by Elizabeth's style of ruling.

Both the new demands of political theory and the appraisal of contemporary political circumstances were evident in the writings of Lomonosov's rival, the leading court poet of the second third of the eighteenth century,

Alexander Petrovich Sumarokov. He was interested in imparting a legal personality to the rulers in his literary works. He defined and publicized his version of the ideal monarch in his writings between 1750 and 1758. These descriptions were increasingly at odds with the policies of Elizabeth's government and led Sumarokov to do what Lomonosov had not: he committed his ideals to the service of the then Grand Duchess Catherine. This involvement of principle with politics had a price; Sumarokov was to learn that he could change the terms of political debate from moral to legal ones but not the fact that the monarch would remain the interpreter and judge of these values. Catherine was to assume that she was herself the custodian of legality and was not prepared to relinquish that post. How was Sumarokov to dispute the claims to legitimacy of the monarch when the standard of legality was defined by the ruler? Sumarokov attributed quite different values to the sovereign than Lomonosov had done, but the change did not diminish the ruler's capacity to transcend theoretical inhibitions on his conduct and still remain in office.

— 8 —

Sumarokov refashioned the image of the ideal ruler by describing in his tragedies and odes a sovereign of staunch military inclinations and contrasting this model with other less military monarchs. In the tragedy *Khorev*, first presented in 1750 in St. Petersburg at Elizabeth's behest, Sumarokov depicted the disarray in Kiev when it was conquered and ruled by one Kii, a ruler who could maintain his authority in the city only by force of arms.[64] His brother Khorev, however, questioned the value of wars and military valor. "Under the guise of courage, we are sanctifying brutality. . . . Murder and plundering are called heroism!"[65] Sumarokov was certainly not denying the need for military action, and Khorev did eventually overcome his qualms. The playwright wanted to use the example of a ruler with a predominantly military orientation to represent a monarch whose actions were unrestricted by limitations of any type.[66] Such a ruler could no longer be expected to exert a morally restraining influence on his own conduct. Divested of this moral element, the military ruler was not the gallant protector of his kingdom but, potentially, "the plunderer" (*khishchnik*), as Kii was labeled, motivated by nothing more noble than his ambition for personal power and glory.

Rulers of this type had to be scorned and the "civil" monarch, that is, one with primarily legislative concerns, encouraged. A civil ruler governed by laws, not force. Sumarokov contrasted the characters embodying and denying the qualities desirable in a sovereign in the tragedy *Artistona* (1750).[67] The plot follows the misfortunes of the heroine, Artistona, who was at the mercy of the Persian King Darius. Her anguished efforts to avoid an unwanted marriage to Darius were symbolic of the fate of a country that was not ruled by a civil ruler. Artistona rebuked Darius for his lack of respect for laws and his reliance on force: "Has God entrusted you with the scepter so that the order of things is burdened by your rule? Although a ruler of peoples is famous, much more famous is a lover of the fatherland. Where a love for society is linked to the crown, oh, then, how blessed is that country!" [68] Artistona and her appeal for laws were supported when an army of dissatisfied subjects attacked Darius's capital city. Only then did he admit that he should heed Artistona's appeals and not rule as a "tyrant."

Implied in the contrast between the characters was the idea that civil rulers, governing with legal and moral standards, sought peace to improve conditions for their peoples, while military rulers, ruling by force and making arbitrary decisions, disregarded their subjects' welfare in their exclusive attention to military matters and territorial expansion. Sumarokov advocated these political principles with no less tenacity than Lomonosov did his. Each man stood by his utopian monarch for roughly twenty years. The reasons for this constancy were in some respects the same for both men and reveal why they wrote what they did. Each had to emphasize features of an ideal ruler that would be popular with his readers or theater audiences. Whenever one wrote about a ruler, even a fictional one from distant times and places, he could be sure that the Russian monarch, be it Anna, Elizabeth, Peter III, or, in particular, Catherine II, would learn of any questionable comments. To curry the favor of the throne as well as to win the attention of those at court or in the minuscule theatergoing and reading public, Lomonosov and Sumarokov had to exercise discretion in their selection of particular political ideals. It was as convenient for Lomonosov to praise the military feats of the ruler in 1739 when the victory at Khotin had aroused the enthusiasm of capital society as it was for Sumarokov to disparage, as will soon be discussed, military ventures during the unpopular Seven Years' War. It was hardly surprising for Lomonosov to omit any comment on laws in his Khotin ode inasmuch as the victor, Anna, governed by relying on favorites. Her court was studded with personal friends—Biron (Bühren), Korff, and the Löwenwolde brothers—and advisers inherited from previous regimes—

Münnich, Iaguzhinskii, Ostermann, and others.[69] When Sumarokov identified the unacceptable figure of the military ruler with a character of foreign birth (for example, Kii had ousted the native prince of Kiev, one Zavloch), he drew on what were by the 1750s unfavorable memories of Biron and the German influence at Anna's court. By the same token, he could associate the civil monarch, abiding by the rule of law, with the renewed appreciation in the 1750s of Peter the Great that grew out of Voltaire's interpretation of Peter as the legislator-tsar, and with Elizabeth's efforts to identify her reign with that of her famous father.

Despite the element of opportunism in their work, neither Sumarokov nor Lomonosov was simply a court poet whose verses were available on demand from the monarch. Lomonosov's odes were primarily exercises in comprehension and explanation and incidentally paeans to a particular ruler. His purposes required an ordering of political ideals that did not need to achieve harmony with the personalities and events of his time. His poem to Anna in 1739 was written in circumstances fortuitously compatible with his ideals. But in the late 1750s he did not cater to his audience's disenchantment with the Seven Years' War. His was a symbolic language of mythical and legal fictions which were divorced from the literal subjects of the verses. Sumarokov did seek a degree of correspondence to the actual persons cited in his verses and thereby a claim to judge them. Forgoing the language of myths, Sumarokov insisted throughout his career on the value of consistency. Like many of his European contemporaries, he accepted the premise that the monarch should avoid inconsistent policies. Restraints regulating the ruler's fulfillment of his proper duties were necessary. His genuine concern for consistency enabled Sumarokov to define adherence to legality as the principal feature of his image of the monarch. He could not possibly have accepted Lomonosov's ruler imagery because military rulers of the type described in the Khotin ode relied on force rather than moral suasion and on arbitrariness rather than law. A ruler whose personal behavior was consistent would, Sumarokov expected, observe legality in his official capacity. His steadfast advocacy of the need for a legal ruler was a matter of conviction, not of opportunism.

Many of Sumarokov's tragedies depicted a ruler's struggle between his duties as a ruler and his personal passions. This literary convention provided Sumarokov with the means to recognize the two legal persons of the monarch. In *Sinav and Truvor* (1750) he described the perplexities of Sinav, "a Russian prince," called to Novgorod by the *boiar* Gostomysl to restore order in the city.[70] The appeal to Sinav was coupled with an offer of the hand in marriage of Gostomysl's daughter, Il'mena. Ordered to marry Sinav, Il'mena was continually admonished to put her political duty ahead of her private sentiments. Sinav, tempted to give in to his passion for Il'mena, did admit that his obligations as a ruler went for naught if he failed to control his passions and forced Il'mena into marriage. "For what do I rule the peoples in this land if I do not have more power over myself!"[71] If the two were to marry, Sinav would have to act "tyranically." If they did not, Il'mena would have allowed her political duty to become secondary to her personal feelings. Il'mena remained true to her duty but committed suicide shortly after the ceremony. The point of the tragedy was summarized by Sinav himself who bemoaned his image as a tyrant. The ruler's public and private selves were set against one another, the latter requiring control if the former was to meet his political obligations without resorting to tyrannical conduct. A monarch who failed to control his personal life was unable to fulfill his civil responsibilities.

Sumarokov was, however, not one to bother with defining these duties. Consistency required the ruler to act in conformity with the laws. Yet this deference to legality was a vague notion, a sense that the political fashion of the time required homage to the ideal of a legal ruler rather than any rigorous, systematic definition of the proper functions and specific *modus operandi* of a legal monarch. Sumarokov mentioned only the ruler's need to recognize quite general duties to his subjects. "Love for the fatherland is the prime virtue and indisputable witness to our honor: not only is it impossible to be a hero without it, it is even impossible to be an honorable man [*chestnyi chelovek*]. . . . All of us should love our fatherland, but the ruling branch should love it more."[72] "We are born for you, but you are born for us: you cannot be happy alone, if you love yourself; you must love us."[73] Rulers who were inconsistent in their official conduct and policies were, Sumarokov was apparently suggesting, violating not only their proper political duties but also a sense of reciprocity between the throne and its subjects. This bond confirmed the monarch's tenure in office. Were a ruler to act inconsistently, he would be liable to the charge that Artistona, the symbolic representative of the people, directed at Darius, the archetype of the military ruler, that he was a tyrant.

Sumarokov had succeeded in linking, in his unquestionably nebulous way, the monarch's conduct in office with his possession of sovereign power. The link was indeed a fragile one. Sumarokov described neither exactly how a monarch was to lay claim to being a civil ruler nor precisely why he should be removed from office. He only hinted at the bases for separating the monarch from the state and alluded to the idea that the monarch's policies could be subject to the law. Nonetheless, Sumarokov had set the terms for considering an ideal ruler and evaluating an actual one, criteria that potentially could serve to spell out with precision the monarch's duties to his state. Sumarokov had removed the ideal ruler from the mythical realm of Lomonosov's works. As legal ruler rather than warrior-king, the monarch was vulnerable to legal restriction.

---— 9 ——

Since, unlike Lomonosov, Sumarokov was not fascinated by the personality of the ruler, he was able to consider what Lomonosov had termed the "pyramid." He could think in terms of "society," which had interests that were not automatically dependent on or identical with those of the state. Sumarokov did not, of course, bring scientific subjects into his discussion of society. Above all a littérateur rather than an academician, Sumarokov's social comments were directed at representatives of personality types and social classes. The primary target of his satirical attack was the noble class. He sought to identify and explain the role of the nobility in a state governed by a civil ruler. The fictional noblemen in his plays were to serve for the Russian nobles in his audiences as worthy examples of ideal noblemen who had adopted the same civil concerns and moral values as the ideal monarch. Though this intention should have required Sumarokov to question the nobility's military functions, he always played down this point lest he test the readiness of his readers and audiences to endure direct criticism. Like his descriptions of the ideal ruler, Sumarokov's writings on the nobility spanned his entire literary career but did not change in approach, topics, or stress.

For Sumarokov the principal problem with the nobility was the superficiality and laxity of its value system. He described these flaws in his picture of the fictional Chuzhekhvat in the *Guardian*.[74] Chuzhekhvat was a seventy-year-old nobleman, ignorant, provincial, and traditional in his tastes. Yet he also pretended to be a devotee of the latest French styles, a pose he used to win the affections of his seventeen-year-old servant, Nisa. Chuzhekhvat's modishness was consistent. He always followed the latest and only the latest vogue, unconcerned with whether it was modern or traditional. His circle of personal friends included some who accepted the new modes and others who remained faithful to the old styles. He did not care which mode each made his own, but required only that each one's modishness be consistent. This silly man was contrasted to Nisa's lover, Valerii, who was not led astray by the beckoning of the newest fad but followed his "candid, healthy reason, the simplicity of nature and decency of taste; this mode never changes and is followed only by those worthy of being called a human being." [75] Valerii recognized the superficial aspects of Chuzhekhvat's Francophile, perhaps even Francomaniacal, sentiments and refused to follow the whims of French fashion himself. Nor did he lapse into mawkish delight over traditional values. His problem was to identify a positive set of values that would stand in contrast to and eventually correct the examples of individuals of the Chuzhekhvat variety. What this alternative should be was only vaguely mentioned by Valerii. He was more direct in warning that, should the nobles be unsuccessful in their search for acceptable moral and civil standards, "there would not be enough security in society for good men. All the less that lawless ones [*bezzakonniki*] are not punished by justice, all the more do innocent ones perish at the hands of lawless people." [76]

The nobles had to accept standards that took as their primary point of reference the moral value of service. Sumarokov began his poem "Concerning the Nobility" (1772) with the coy disclaimer that "nobles know their debt well enough without me," [77] then went on to remind them of their duty to serve the state. His strictures were directed at those who were ready to dismiss their service obligations and seek fulfillment by withdrawing from society. The price of this serenity was self-denial. In the *Hermit* (1758) the hero Evmenii abandoned his family in Kiev and gave up his official position to flee the vices and corruption of society and find contentment in personal communion with God. [78] "I have paid my debt to society and am leaving it; I flee worldly cares in order to be even more pleasing to the Creator." [79] Evmenii was willing to sacrifice even his passionate love for his wife, if that was the price of perfecting a more intimate relationship with God. [80] He was, however, reminded by his parents that filial and marital duties were also God's commands [81] and by his brother Visarion that service was required by God. [82] Sumarokov described the ideal of moral self-perfection as "barbaric," [83] unrealizable, and detrimental to its advocate. Moreover, it was futile to seek personal contentment apart from service. Sumarokov was stating explicitly that a noble had to fulfill equally his inseparable obligations to family, state, and God. Evmenii had erred in assuming that these links could be broken and he could reach God without serving his government and fellow man. Sumarokov called those who chose a life of withdrawal individuals of noble ancestry who were not themselves noble.[84]

A nobleman was obligated to serve not as an impassive and obedient instrument of the monarch but with the same consistency that was binding on the ruler. Consider, Sumarokov asked his public, the plight of Angelika, in the *Malicious One* (1768).[85] Her father was so impoverished that he was forced to give her hand in marriage to the wealthy Gerostrat, and Angelika was as reluctant to disobey her father as she was adamant in her refusal to consent to an unwanted marriage. The character of Gerostrat was contrasted with that of Dromon, a servant, so as to suggest the means by which a noble could lead an honorable life. Gerostrat eagerly curried favor with magnates; his every action was designed to increase his wealth and power. Dromon had little regard for Gerostrat's values. Gerostrat's ambition for financial and political gain, Dromon declaimed at one point, was an abdication of his duty to check his passions and regulate his behavior. Gerostrat's covetousness was due to his inability to curb his own arbitrariness (*svoevolia*).[86] Delinquent in his responsibilities to himself, he was unmindful of others; his self-centered regard for personal advantage was a danger to society.

How was this personal and social malady to be cured? Sumarokov brought his audience to recognize the need for restraints on the nobles' activities but carried his point no further. He avoided mention of what was the crux of the matter—how Dromon's moral dictums were to be enforced. The plot itself was given a trite resolution: Angelika's anguish was ended when she was suddenly left a fortune by a long-lost relative. Clearly Sumarokov believed that consistency should be the nobleman's moral guide in his conduct with others, yet he failed to identify clear-cut ways to achieve this goal. Aside from this call for restraint and his reaffirmation of the value of service, Sumarokov said little else about the nobility.

When Sumarokov's political ideals are given scholarly attention, it is these remarks about the need to reform the nobility's values that are understood to be significant. Gukovskii, Berkov, and, because of their prestige, many recent Soviet scholars have advanced a common opinion about Sumarokov's comments on the nobility. Sumarokov was himself a nobleman whose knowledge of European literature had led him to an exalted sense of self and disdain for those nobles who failed to appreciate an abstract, moral sense of honor.[87] His estimate of his own moral worth led him, Gukovskii argued, to value highly the sanctity of his person and the need for laws and class privileges to guarantee the inviolability of his person. Once a nobleman's rights were secured, he could be expected to take his leave of a government wont to dismiss his personal rights and to depart for the presumed security and tranquility of his estates. Sumarokov's political ideals were those of a *frondeur*. He was ready to participate in a *fronde nobiliaire* which would institute the rule of law so as to return the state to the alleged agrarian orientation of pre-Petrine times.

This interpretation, argued more explicitly by Gukovskii than Berkov, was invaluable in accrediting its subject's political ideals as worthy of scholarly interest and in rescuing Sumarokov from an undeserved relegation to the category of court poet. Gukovskii performed a particularly valuable service in calling attention to the shift in interest away from the ruler, so typical of Lomonosov's works, and toward consideration of all social classes. Sumarokov's call for consistency (*zakonomernost'*) was, however, inseparable from his demand that consistency as a personal value be fulfilled only by service to the state. Was not the *Hermit* a condemnation of those nobles who withdrew from society to perfect themselves in the sanctuary of a rural retreat? Moreover, it is not necessary to extrapolate, as is done in the fronde theory, from Sumarokov's concern for the moral status of the nobles to a concern for their economic welfare. His moral considerations did lead him to political ones, but he only alluded to their connection with economic matters. The principal challenge to the fronde theory is that, without the separation of personal and service values, the opposition of the nobles' interests to those of the state does not arise. Sumarokov set the standard of consistency for the nobles so that their way of life would correspond to, not be in conflict with, that of a civil ruler. All the more damaging to this allegedly irreconcilable conflict between the throne and the nobility was Sumarokov's lifelong conviction that his political ideals could and would be realized only by trusting and relying on the throne.

—— 10 ——

Sumarokov's ideals remained apart from his political loyalties until the late 1750s. At that time he changed the format of his literary works: he stopped placing general statements of principle in the mouths of fictional rulers of distant realms and began making specific comments on contemporary politics. In the 1750s he was not closely associated with Elizabeth but probably could have won her favor. Elizabeth was well disposed toward him and supported his literary efforts with funds and encouragement until her death in 1761.[88] Yet Sumarokov wrote very few odes to Elizabeth. In 1755 he did compliment her for her restraint in refusing to yield to any temptation for territorial expansion.[89] When Elizabeth did yield and became involved in the Seven Years' War, Sumarokov interpreted her policy as a reluctant and defensive one, an unavoidable reaction to the Prussian King Frederick's aggressive ambitions and military provocations.[90] Sumarokov's literary silence in the years immediately preceding Elizabeth's death is evidence of the great difference between him and Lomonosov. Sumarokov was willing to commit his principles to the service of a particular ruler.

Sumarokov's silence was due primarily to the nature of his ties to his patron, A. G. Razumovskii (1707–1771), the empress's lover and a leading court figure during the 1740s.[91] Razumovskii had been impressed with the odes, psalms, and songs Sumarokov had written as a student in the Infantry Cadet Corps in St. Petersburg. He arranged for Sumarokov's appointment as his personal adjutant after Sumarokov's graduation from the Cadet Corps on April 14, 1740. Sumarokov's early tragedies were produced with Razumovskii's encouragement and support. The playwright's first tragedy, *Khorev,* was first presented at the Cadet Corps where it won Razumovskii's enthusiastic approval. Razumovskii then arranged to have the play reproduced at court in the presence of Elizabeth. Thereafter Sumarokov's rise was meteoric. He was called upon frequently to write tragedies and comedies for the pleasure of the empress. When the Russian Theater was to open in 1756, his good standing with Elizabeth and the intercession of Razumovskii in his behalf led to his appointment as director of the theater.

Razumovskii, unlike some other patrons, expected services from his client that were not confined to the world of belles lettres. His influence with the empress was contested in 1749 and lost by 1751 to Ivan Shuvalov. At that point Razumovskii turned to Count A. P. Bestuzhev-Riumin (1693–1766) for aid in discrediting Shuvalov and restoring his own lost prestige. Razumovskii found a willing ally. Bestuzhev-Riumin was an ardent advocate of a foreign policy that would join Russia, Austria, and England against the perceived threat of French aggression. His personal preferences matched his diplomatic policies: he was notorious in court circles for his Francophobia. During the early and mid-fifties Bestuzhev-Riumin witnessed with dismay the deterioration of relations with England—the empress repeatedly delayed signing the Anglo-Russian subsidy treaty before finally approving it on February 12, 1756—and her preference for tying Russia to France as well as Austria to counter the presumed ambitions of Prussia. Bestuzhev-Riumin's control of foreign affairs declined with the rise in influence of the pro-French Shuvalov brothers. Their policies were ratified by the famous Diplomatic Revolution of 1756, the reversal of alliances in which Russia set aside its traditional enmity with France and Austria and joined these two powers in opposing Prussia. The consequence was a war that was indecisive, expensive, exhausting, and unpopular. Bestuzhev-Riumin was eager to avail himself of Razumovskii's services not because the two had common ideas on foreign policy—Razumovskii's preferences on this score were of no significance— but rather because he found in Razumovskii an ally for his own schemes to discredit the policy that had led Russia into a disastrous military involvement. Bestuzhev-Riumin and Razumovskii recruited into their conspiracy Grand Duchess Catherine who claimed she also disagreed with the government's pro-French policies and was eager to make use of Bestuzhev-Riumin to arrange her affairs with Poniatowski and Saltykov.[92]

The conspirators seized the occasion of Elizabeth's sudden illness on September 8, 1757, when she suffered a serious convulsion and her death seemed imminent, to try to prevent the accession of the empress's legitimate heir, the future Peter III, by changing the order of succession to the benefit of Catherine. As early as October 28, 1756, Catherine had sent word to General Apraksin in command at the Prussian front that the advance of Russian troops should be delayed as a mark of his loyalty to her rather than the empress.[93] No appeal was made by the conspirators to the regiments of the Guards, the agent of so many palace revolutions in the eighteenth century. Bestuzhev-Riumin and his colleagues planned to wait for Elizabeth's death before taking any action against Peter. The empress, to the dismay of the conspirators, survived. She learned of the intrigue,[94] and Bestuzhev-Riumin was arrested. Razumovskii's precise role in this sequence of events is not clear. Whatever his activities were in 1758, they sufficed to earn him the hatred of Grand Duke Peter. In the initial days of Peter's rule, Razumovskii was forced to retire rather precipitously.[95]

The political tangle is not as important as the fact that Razumovskii required his aides to join him in the intrigue. One of his adjutants, Ivan Perfil'evich Elagin (1725–1794), was exiled.[96] Sumarokov had acted, voluntarily or not, in the political interests of his patron, for he fell under suspicion for some unspecified activity and was "subjected to much unpleasantness and many inquiries."[97] The details of this investigation are lacking. It might well have been an unavoidable political commitment for, as Razumovskii's adjutant, he could hardly have served him and remained apart from the fray. Whatever his part in this conspiracy, Sumarokov was hereafter a political partisan whose services were committed to promoting the interests of his patron and his associates. Sumarokov had been expected to serve Razumovskii in a manner quite unlike that required of Lomonosov by Shuvalov. The role of the poet as impartial observer of political events was recast to one of the littérateur as participant.

Sumarokov did not match his commitment of personal services with any engagement of principle. After the succession crisis, Razumovskii had no chance of recovering his lost prestige. Even Catherine, who came to power in June 1762, respected Razumovskii for his support in 1758 but considered him very much an individual from Elizabethan times. Power at Catherine's court was no longer decided by his palace intrigues against the Shuvalovs but was now contested between the Panin brothers, Nikita (1718–1783) and Peter (1721–1789), and Grigorii Orlov and his four brothers. Razumovskii was considered a somewhat quaint figure in the last years before his death in 1771, recognized more for his past service to the empress than for his current influence on her policies. Sumarokov was aware of his patron's waning prestige and, to protect his position, sought the favor of Nikita Panin sometime during the 1760s.

As a supporter of Panin, Sumarokov had the opportunity to align his principles with those of his patron. Under Razumovskii's protection Sumarokov had been in the position of advocating consistency in politics while being sheltered at court by a man whose influence resulted from imperial favor. In the sixties his patron was not a favorite but a career statesman—a leading diplomat and "senior member" of the College of Foreign Affairs. Sumarokov could have sustained his personal campaign for consistency in politics with the assurance of support from a patron with political opinions similar to his own. Yet when Panin's political fortunes were associated with his proposal of 1762[98] to establish an Imperial Council, Sumarokov wrote nothing about his belief in the advantages of a council for curbing an abusive monarch. He was consistent in his political involvements and values but there was no consistency between his ideas and commitments.

———— 11 ————

Although Sumarokov was not interested in protecting his political ideals by linking conviction as well as career to the fortunes of his patrons, he made an exception in the case of Catherine. After the succession crisis of 1758, he was willing to commit his principles as well as his services to her cause. In January 1759 Sumarokov founded a new journal, the *Industrious Bee,* to give public notice of his enthusiasm for the grand duchess. The publication of the *Industrious Bee* opened a new chapter in the story of the relations between the Russian throne and its men of letters. The journal now came to replace the ode, the tragedy, and the essay as the literary mode most frequently used by literati to convey their political message. The audience was no longer limited to a few people at court but also included the "public." Though the number of its subscribers was surely small, the very appearance of a journal served to arouse, inform, and influence the political opinions of the public.

The *Industrious Bee* was the first Russian periodical to give some consideration to the tastes of a reading public.[99] Rather than serving as a government-sponsored medium for publishing official works, the *Industrious Bee* accepted articles written by private writers on a broad range of topics. Its staff was composed of the literary wing of its competitor, *Monthly Compositions.* The academician Müller edited *Monthly Compositions* and was disposed to accept articles written in his own fields of interest. His editorial policy gave preference to scientific topics, and literary pieces were considered of secondary importance. Müller even placed the literary section of *Monthly Compositions* at the end of each number,[100] a practice that provoked some of his collaborators to start a purely literary journal. In 1759 this group moved to the press in the Cadet Corps and reorganized as the staff of the *Industrious Bee.* Contributors to the new monthly included Mikhail Kheraskov (1733–1807), later the author of the well-known epic poem *Rossiada,* Ivan Dmitrevskii (1734–1821), famous among his contemporaries in the last half of the eighteenth century as an actor, and Grigorii Kozitskii (1724–1775), later Catherine's secretary. These and other individuals wrote articles on a wide variety of topics, ranging from the philosophy of Locke or the history of Moscow to a linguistic analysis of the dialects on the Kamchatkan Peninsula. Selections from Lucian, Cicero, and Ovid were printed. Contemporary writers were represented by Voltaire, Corneille, Swift, and Holberg. Many of the pages of the *Industrious Bee* were reserved for Sumarokov, and this proved to be the ruin of the journal. He clashed continually with the censors at the Academy of Sciences. By December 1759 these difficulties had become sufficient to close the journal. In the December issue Sumarokov wrote an article, "Parting with the Muses," blaming the government apparatus for forcing him to stop publishing the journal.[101]

During its year of publication the *Industrious Bee* was used by its editor to publicize his support for Catherine. He dedicated the first issue to the grand duchess, favorably comparing her qualities to those of Peter the Great.[102] This dedication was an act of political boldness. The astute reader readily perceived the implied slight to Elizabeth and Grand Duke Peter. Catherine's friendship a year after the crisis of 1758 was of questionable political value, and she had few allies. Sumarokov's involvement in the politics of court parties led him, as if inexorably, to commit his political ideals to the service of a partisan political cause. The littérateur as participant was soon the political writer as advocate.

His expectations of Catherine were initially no more than a general association of her with his ideal of a civil ruler. In the final issue of the *Industrious Bee,* his "Dream of a Happy Society" envisioned a utopian state "ruled by a great man . . . with the help of his chosen assistants." [103] These aides were organized in a state council (*gosudarstvennyi sovet*) which had the right of initiative, appointed judges, codified the laws, and was the highest court of appeal.[104] Membership in the state council was open only to those of honorable and reasonable conduct.[105] Sumarokov emphasized that the functions of this council included the supervision of military affairs. The army was controlled by a war council which, in turn, was directly subordinate to the state council.[106] Wars were to be fought only for defensive purposes, which implied that the council mechanism served as the potential check on rulers with warlike ambitions.

The significance of Sumarokov's utopia is readily exaggerated on two counts. His support for a council composed of men of rank and merit might suggest, as was implicit in Gukovskii's argument, an appeal to Nikita Panin, who was to espouse these very causes during the 1760s.[107] The "Dream" has been taken to represent the public expression of the political hopes of Panin, and a signal of the political opposition to the policies and person of Elizabeth. But the link is only one of similarity: there is no evidence Sumarokov knew anything at all about Panin in 1759. Though Sumarokov did curry Panin's favor in the sixties, the "Dream" was written while Panin was still the ambassador in Stockholm where he had been for the past eleven years.

Second, although the reliance in the "Dream" on a council to restrain the military was potentially of great importance, this reference to a council proved to be unique in Sumarokov's writings. The contrast of civil and military rulers, present in the tragedies of the early fifties, had seemingly led Sumarokov by 1759 to endorse a specific institutional check on belligerent monarchs. The ideal of a council might well have served as the first instance of Sumarokov's definition of the *modus operandi* of a state acting as an agent of legality and interceding between the ruler and ruled. Yet the appearance of the council is curious. Sumarokov could not have meant his ideal council to be literary testimony to the need for an actual one. On March 14, 1756, Elizabeth had already established the Conference as an advisory body of ten to supervise plans for Russia's engagement in the Seven Years' War. Nor could Sumarokov have been promoting Razumovskii's interests. After the debacle of 1758, there was no realistic chance that Razumovskii would be appointed to any council. Moreover the Conference was dominated in 1759 by M. L. Vorontsov, the man whose intrigues had compelled Bestuzhev-Riumin to surrender control of foreign affairs. The article's alluring vision of a utopian government was published at a time when it brought its author no immediate advantage and did not reappear in the sixties when it might have served a purpose.

Sumarokov irrevocably committed his services and ideals to Catherine at the time of the palace revolution of June 28, 1762. He chose to view with enthusiasm the overthrow of a legitimate ruler, regicide, and its condonation by the new monarch, for he saw in these events the accession of his ideal civil ruler. In an ode written to commemorate the coup he avoided mention of the odious particulars. He attempted to justify Catherine's seizure of power and celebrated her accession as marking the end of a period of unparalleled debasement of honor, faith, and wisdom.[108] Her initiative saved the Russians from Peter III, whose policies were determined by force, not law. In another ode greeting the new year in 1763, Sumarokov again stressed the lack of laws (*bezzakonie*) and the evil actions (*zlodeistvo*) typical of Peter III and extolled the virtuous and honest character of Catherine.[109] His zeal was still unabated in 1766 when he praised the palace revolution as an event signaling an end to the diplomatic policies of Elizabeth and Peter III which committed Russian troops to disastrous European involvements.[110] He lauded the new empress's recognition of her duty "to give us . . . . a peaceful century, and remove those days [of war] from us; man is not born for that!"[111] Peter III was described as a military ruler, the new empress as the embodiment of the civil monarch. In return for his support, Catherine rewarded Sumarokov at the time of her coronation with a promotion to the civil rank of state councilor, fourth class on the Table of Ranks.[112] (The Table of Ranks was a system established in 1722 to rationalize civil, military, and court positions. Each category was divided into fourteen classes, the first being the highest.)

When the court traveled to Moscow in 1763 for the coronation ceremonies, Sumarokov participated in the pageant of "triumphant Minerva," a street festival organized to glorify Catherine's accession to power. He used the occasion to reaffirm his image of the empress as the embodiment of his ideal ruler. The presentation was intended to convince the common people that the empress was a virtuous monarch. A series of scenes portraying such moral failings as deceit, ignorance, vice, and modishness was wheeled on carts along the streets of the city, proclaiming the new era of virtue and peace under Catherine.[113] It would be idle to speculate on what the average Muscovite thought as these carts passed in review; he or she would not have had the slightest notion of the apparently grave social danger of, say, modish conduct. Sumarokov wrote the chorus accompanying each section.[114] In one of these, he celebrated his confidence in Catherine: "Blissful times have begun, they radiate throughout Russia the ray of truth. . . . You have begun hopefully a golden century for Russians."[115]

Sumarokov's praise for Catherine, however effusive it seemed, was primarily a matter of calculation. His odes publicized the similarity between his image of the empress and her description of herself as sovereign. Catherine provided her interpretation of the events of June 28 in an imperial manifesto signed on July 6, 1762.[116] She contrasted the reign of Peter III to the intentions of her own government. When her husband was crowned, she claimed, Russia became subject to a man of unbridled passions, oblivious to his primary role as God's custodian over the well-being of all Russians. Peter's decisions were arbitrary, and he was devoted to selfish gain rather than the common good.[117] The new empress's supporters, she promised, could count on a virtuous sovereign who would labor for the welfare of all and do whatever was in her power to prevent the recurrence of government by whim. "Autocracy unrestrained by good and humane qualities is such an evil in a sovereign as to be the immediate cause of many pernicious consequences."[118] To protect her subjects against the threat of another Peter III, Catherine promised "to legislate such official regulations . . . that . . . each governmental position has its limits and laws . . . and by this we hope to preserve intact the empire and our autocratic power."[119] The coup was necessary to eliminate Peter's abuses and install a ruler who could act virtuously and abide by laws. At the same time Catherine let it be known in public what she wrote in private on the very day of the coup: "Our intention was and now is to use every method of achieving general peace in Europe; . . . the tranquility and prosperity of our throne demand this immediately."[120] In short, Catherine wished her contemporaries to think of her as a virtuous sovereign who would rule with restraint, abide by the laws, and not pursue military chimeras.

Catherine carefully chose the words of her manifesto to attract the attention of many audiences. She wanted to win the support of experienced government officials like Nikita Panin whose interest was in curbing the arbitrary power of the ruler. She was appealing to the *philosophes* in Western Europe whose approval her vanity and regard for European public opinion demanded. Catherine was also mindful of her standing with her own subjects, whose enthusiasm she aroused by playing on their distaste for the Seven Years' War. As it happened, her public pose was consistent with the political ideals conveyed by the characters in Sumarokov's tragedies and the descriptions of the monarch in his odes. Catherine's manifesto of July 6 allowed Sumarokov to curry favor with the empress and promote her version of the significance of her accession without retreating from his own ideals of the 1750s and early 1760s. Sumarokov was not coopted in 1763 but had the best of all possible worlds: his political principles coincided with those of the ruler.

The significance of his relation to Catherine can be gauged by comparing his mental and literary image of the empress with that of Lomonosov. For both writers she was virtue incarnate, a military defender rather than aggressor, and the embodiment of each man's hopes for a government more orderly than that of Peter III. Lomonosov's ideals were, however, no more or less applicable to Catherine than they were to any other monarch. He wrote only two odes to her, neither of which was distinguished by its literary artistry or particular in its terms of support for Catherine.[121] Lomonosov had several opportunities in 1763 to praise the empress: the anniversary of her accession, the celebration of the new year, and the festival of triumphant Minerva. Yet he withheld any poetic comment on these occasions. Where Lomonosov was impartial toward the ruler, Sumarokov took the stand as her advocate. He dispensed with Lomonosov's moral criteria in favor of legal standards that could serve to evaluate and define what he expected of Catherine. His position vis-à-vis the empress posed for him both a dilemma and a challenge. Should she at some point take belligerent or extralegal action, he could lose his status as a man of political conviction or, should he stand on principle, his position as a writer in her favor. Since Sumarokov engaged his political convictions with commitments to Catherine alone, he made it possible to lend his political allegiances a theoretical basis and, thereby, cherish what was to prove to be only an illusion—that he was not entirely dependent on the throne. He was, in fact, less dependent than Lomonosov. Sumarokov tried to maintain his image of the ideal ruler and resolve the problem of reconciling his conception of a civil monarch with Catherine's conduct during the mid and late 1760s, which was increasingly that of a military ruler.

———— 12 ————

The empress's policies during the first six years of her reign gave Sumarokov no reason for concern. Nevertheless, he became something of an annoyance to her, and his credit suffered accordingly. Sumarokov had an abrasive temperament, provocative and easily provoked. He could drive his associates to extremes of rage and exasperation. When he was editing the *Industrious Bee,* his tantrums and brusque conduct toward his assistants became at one point literally unbearable to them with the result that every single article in the May issue was written by Sumarokov. This volatile temper was usually expended on other writers and was of little consequence to the throne. In 1766, however, it caused an incident that became a public scandal. Sumarokov's father died that year, and the inheritance became a matter of legal dispute. When Sumarokov sensed the legalities were favoring his mother, he tried to resolve the squabble by silencing her, transforming a routine case into a *cause célèbre.* When Catherine learned of Sumarokov's action, she reacted angrily and intervened directly to prevent any recurrence of his antics.[122]

In the same year the empress had an opportunity to show her displeasure with Sumarokov. She was to appoint a director of court music and theater, and Sumarokov was a prime candidate for the post. He had established the Russian Theater in St. Petersburg in 1756, supervised its presentations until 1761, and clearly had the credentials and prestige for the directorship. Catherine passed over Sumarokov, appointing in his stead Elagin, his coconspirator in 1758.[123] Sumarokov persuaded her to reverse the decision and give him the post in 1769, but his success was illusory. His appointment brought about the circumstances that furthered his decline.

Sumarokov expected the court theater would serve as the setting for plays written in the classicist mode. Though classicism was no longer dominant on the European stage, its influence continued to prevail in Russia until the late 1760s. At that time classicist tragedies and comedies had to contend with a rival in the form of the *comédie larmoyante,* a play written in the style of Diderot and Lessing in Western and Central Europe. Diderot dispensed with the strict separation of genres common to classicist plays and with classicism's deference to tragedies as a more prestigious literary form than comedies. He allowed for serious drama that had elements of both comedy and tragedy. The classicist interest in the study of the human personality, removed in time and space from the audience, was replaced by what were essentially homely situations in which the particular problems of the characters could readily arouse the empathy of the listeners. This epochal change in literary values was initially evident on the Russian stage just at the time that Sumarokov became the director of court music and theater.

On May 18, 1770, Beaumarchais's *Eugénie,* a play in the new style, was presented. Sumarokov reduced a fundamental change in literary standards to a personal insult. The chief Russian advocate of classicism, his zeal had even led him to compose in 1747 *Two Epistles,* revisions of the credo of European classicist writers, Boileau's *l'Art Poétique.* He was recognized by his contemporaries as, in Nikolai Karamzin's words, "our Racine, Moliere . . . [or] Boileau." [124] Forced now to preside over the presentation of a work that violated the very rules he had imposed on himself and other Russian playwrights, he wasted little time in responding. He wrote a statement censuring *Eugénie* in the introduction to his own *Dmitrii the Impostor* (1771). His terms were more personal than literary. He condemned the play in the scolding, bitter, and sarcastic words of a mentor unappreciated by his own disciples.[125] Then, in a display of bad humor and with a glaring lack of common sense, he appealed directly to Catherine, imploring her to intercede in his behalf. She, predictably enough, ridiculed his claims to be the unquestioned literary authority. Her sarcasm was expressed by a play on words in Russian which retains some of its derisive tone in English: "Sumarokov is and will be mad [*Sumarokov bez uma est'i budet'*]." [126]

These incidents did not suffice to override the harmony of interests between the autocrat and the poet. Sumarokov's eccentricities were occasionally annoying to Catherine but could hardly be of serious consequence to her. Catherine's actions may have given Sumarokov cause for dismay, but his image of her political personality remained unchanged. His difficulties even served to remind him that he could ill afford to tamper with his own portrayal of her as the ideal ruler. When his threats to his mother lowered his standing in Catherine's eyes, he was quick to compensate for the embarrassing episode by writing an ode in praise of Catherine's virtues. He did temporarily recoup his stature with her but at the price of having to reconfirm her credentials as a civil ruler.

Sumarokov's ability to maintain both his allegiance to the empress and steadfast adherence to his political ideals was tested in 1768. At that time Catherine made a key decision that called into question Sumarokov's expectations. The outbreak of the Turkish War discredited the diplomatic policies the empress had established in 1762 and was to lead to a reorientation of Russian foreign policy away from restraint and toward expansion at the expense of the Turks and Poles. When the exigencies of the Seven Years' War had compelled Catherine to withdraw Russian troops, Sumarokov had been able to see her action as compatible with his ideal of a civil monarch. During the Turkish War, however, her policies were similar to those of the military ruler of Sumarokov's tragedies as well as those of Elizabeth in the late 1750s. The poet was confronted with a political circumstance that might readily have shaken the principles he had steadfastly advocated during his long literary career.

When hostilities began, Russian forces engaged and defeated the Turks at Khotin. The victory provided Sumarokov with an event as rich in symbolic importance as the battle against the Turks in 1739. He wrote an ode on the Khotin battle but one quite unlike that composed by Lomonosov in 1739. Sumarokov's ode was not a paean to the valor of the Russian troops and the glory of their monarch. Khotin was not significant because of the military prestige accruing to the victors. There was no reason to take pride in the fact that the Russian triumph instilled fear in the Turks. Rather, it was an example—and a horrifying one—of the human cost of military victory. The Russian armies succeeded at an unacceptable price in terms of individuals killed, homes ruined, and buildings destroyed.[127] In this initial ode on the war, Sumarokov had remained true to his opinions about foreign policy.

As the war continued, the poet's objections to the war changed. He edged toward justifying the campaign. However detestable Russian aggressiveness was in general, an exception could be allowed in the case of a greater evil, the tyrannical and barbarous Turkish state.[128] This opinion succeeded in being both a qualified condemnation and a qualified endorsement of the war. It masked Sumarokov's reservations, indecisiveness, and perplexity. After the ode of 1770 he fell silent, withholding comment as he had in the late fifties. When next he commented on the war, he reversed his apparent readiness to justify the war. In an ode written in 1774, he interpreted Russia's commitment of troops as a defensive necessity imposed on a reluctant belligerent.[129] During these four years, when Sumarokov seemed to be reconsidering and then reaffirming his principles he was, in fact, in disarray, futilely trying to reconcile his ideal of a nonbelligerent ruler with the policies of a monarch who was very much the military ruler of his tragedies. The ode of 1774 was followed in 1775 by an ode that cast aside every hesitation he had harbored about the war: he offered Catherine an unrestrained paean to her military success.[130]

Sumarokov's varied and hesitant reactions to the Turkish War were those of a man beset by personal as well as theoretical perplexities. The war was popular and successful and, unlike the Seven Years' War, did not readily lend itself to criticism on conveniently reconcilable grounds of principle and opportunism. To make matters worse, Sumarokov's stock in Catherine's eyes was declining. He could not criticize her war policy while he was hoping to win the appointment as director of court music and theater or, after he was awarded that post, to gain her assistance in his confrontation with the disciples of Beaumarchais. Sumarokov had many reasons of direct, practical importance to his career and very livelihood that undermined his interest in making a stand on principle against the Turkish War. The immediate difficulties in his life can be measured by his changing opinion of the war. He did not revise his viewpoint in consistent fashion but wavered between approving and condemning the campaign against the Turks. During the course of the war he could not extricate himself from his difficulties. His final ode was written after hostilities had ceased. By then he allowed loyalty to the empress to prevail over principle. In accommodating himself to her in 1775, Sumarokov did not shield himself from the harsh realities of Catherine's actions and take comfort in the solace of illusion. He cast aside his ideal of a civil monarch and accepted the rationales for a military ruler cited in the Khotin ode, not his of 1769 but Lomonosov's of 1739.

Why did Sumarokov not do in the early seventies what he had done in the early fifties in his tragedies and the late fifties by his actions, namely brand a military ruler as a tyrant? Simply stated, he could not afford to do so. He had never reconciled his convictions about an ideal ruler with his position at the court. When imperial diplomatic policies changed and were at variance with his own preferences, he could not be expected to modify his loyalties to Catherine as he had, in similar circumstances, to Elizabeth in 1758. His conduct in that year was prompted by his allegiance and service to his patron, Razumovskii, rather than reservations about the ruler's policies. Even when Nikita Panin—among Catherine's advisers the prime sponsor of a policy of restraint in foreign affairs—was Sumarokov's benefactor, the poet sought his favor not to win the protection of someone of a common mind but simply to be safeguarded by the favor and influence of a powerful man. Razumovskii and Panin were, in Sumarokov's mind, one and the same type, patrons whose power might be beneficial. If he had worked to promote Panin's diplomatic plans and engaged his own literary talents to publicize Panin's cause, Sumarokov might have become a political as well as literary client of Panin. This status would have afforded him protection when he lost the favor of the sovereign. Sumarokov was willing to forgo this means of ensuring his personal fortune. When forced to reckon with a monarch whose policies were not in accord with his ideal of a civil ruler, he was not prepared to propose institutional guarantees against an abusive ruler. Sumarokov brought himself to an impasse. His ideals could be entrusted to Catherine only so long as his principles did not conflict with the empress's reading of the best interests of state.

—— 13 ——

Lomonosov and Sumarokov were key figures in Elizabethan Russia. Their writings show how German natural law was treated by men of letters. Lomonosov cared little—if at all—for the ideal of the legal ruler. If the policies of Russian rulers were to be at all intelligible to him, he had to divest their authority of its claims to theoretical legitimacy. The very monarchs who would embody the political ideals of German natural law jurists could be recognized only if these theoretical pretensions were ignored. When the legal dictums of Pufendorf and Wolff became the acceptable premises for political discourse, contemporary Russian thinkers could dispense with an image of the monarch composed of mythical symbols and conceive instead the legal ruler. Sumarokov's works were abundant evidence of his attempt to redefine the image of the utopian monarch in a way that emphasized his own version of the legal ruler. The emergence of the concept of a legal monarch in the minds of mid-eighteenth-century littérateurs led to its refinement and ever-increasing approximation to the utopian ruler of German natural law. In this respect the writings of both men adumbrated the direction political thought was to take during and after their lifetimes.

This progression led Sumarokov to a major dilemma, which was to confront all those interested in adapting German political ideals to the realities of Russian politics. The more he committed his ideals to a single Russian monarch, the more he became dependent on the ruler's intention of following policies consistent with his ideals. Yet the more elaborate the portrayal of the legal ruler, the more Sumarokov was equipped to evaluate and pass judgment on the theoretical legitimacy of those policies. As his anguished reactions to the Turkish War proved, he had the capacity to speak out when the empress violated his political code but reason to be reluctant to exercise that power. A man with a career as well as principles, he was buffeted by the political storms of his day and did not allow himself recourse to safe harbor.

Though Sumarokov and Lomonosov had different notions about the proper functions of the monarch, their images of the utopian ruler shared a static quality, and their ideas depended on the beneficence of the ruler. These characteristics mark them as writers of Elizabethan Russia and set them apart from political commentators of Catherinian Russia. Neither man based the strength of his political convictions on the firmer grounds that were taken by their successors in the 1760s; neither man sought to derive political principles from personal values, valid by assent of conscience and independent of the decisions of the throne. This basis would have set aside Lomonosov's impartiality toward his monarchs and given Sumarokov's commitment of principle to political loyalty a new element of vigor and advocacy. When political considerations of ideals and involvement originated in the personal moral values of the commentators, a dynamic element would be introduced, which would overcome Lomonosov's and, ultimately, Sumarokov's fascination with the person of the ruler. A moral impulse would impel its advocates to reform contemporary Russian politics and society. Their endeavors would not, however, free them from the dilemma Sumarokov had faced in the late 1760s. Rather, moral zealousness would serve to revise the terms of the dilemma: Sumarokov's painful choice between loyalties and principles would become his successors' need to decide between career and sense of self.

The Moral Fraternity of the Early 1760s

—— 1 ——

Lomonosov was quite accurate in predicting that he would have successors. For in fact the political ideals developed by the Fonvizin group in the 1760s were based on those of Elizabethan writers. The Fonvizin group did not simply refine the original lines of thought, however, but changed the bases on which these political principles rested. The three men's primary interest was ethics, not politics. They sought before all else a sense of personal moral integrity and in so doing discovered that the ethical order they cherished for their personal lives entailed their commitment to the social and political worlds around them. As their involvement became steadily more extensive, they imposed on themselves the obligation to sort out and define the proper dimensions and priorities of their engagements. Though the men felt compelled to venture out into the world of political and social facts, their search for personal moral tranquility remained the wellspring of all their associations.

Contemporary politics gradually interfered with the Fonvizin group's moral deliberations. The group was first forced to recognize the links between its ethical concerns and political issues during the years at Moscow University. Reality intruded most forcibly at the time of the coup of 1762 in St. Petersburg. The accession of Catherine the Great required them, if they were to be true to themselves, to relate their political ideals to the new empress immediately, and they responded with the sureness born of moral conviction. Fonvizin and his colleagues modified Lomonosov's and Sumarokov's political ideals to allow for their own sense of personal moral integrity. When in the 1760s they confronted the same difficulties that had caused Sumarokov to forfeit any claims to principle, they could strengthen their political convictions with the force of their moral idealism.

—— 2 ——

The Fonvizin group first met at Moscow University in the 1750s. The opening of the university in 1755 drew to Moscow young men interested in following a course of studies in either the university itself or one of its two boarding schools. The two schools, one for nobles and one for nonnobles, were responsible for preparing students to pursue the university curriculum. The three men were among the first students to enroll in the nobles' boarding school and the university.

Each one in the Fonvizin group came to Moscow from a home heavily influenced by traditional patriotic and religious values, which gave the group its first bonds of union. Ippolit Fedorovich Bogdanovich was born on December 23, 1743, in the small town of Perevolochna in the Ukraine.[1] His early education was personally directed by his father, who instilled in him both nationalist and uncomplicated religious values. As he later reported, "I am ready to admit that I was brought up with a love for my fatherland. . . . The age, religion, and customs imbued in me a view of the world that remains with me to this day."[2] While still living at home, Bogdanovich developed a passionate love for reading and exhibited a talent for painting, music, and poetry.[3] Like all Russian noblemen, he had to enter state service. When he was enrolled in the Justice College in 1754, its president, G. Zheliabuzhskii, misread Bogdanovich's interests, assumed they were scientific, and assigned him to the mathematics school affiliated with the Senate.[4] Here his inclination for drama first attracted attention. In 1758 he simply presented himself to Mikhail Kheraskov, soon to be director of the Moscow Theater, and requested that he be made an actor. Although Kheraskov denied this petition, he arranged for Bogdanovich's transfer from the mathematics school to Moscow University and even gave him lodging in his own home.[5] This was Bogdanovich's entree into the social and literary circle around Kheraskov.

The same path from a traditional home to the enlightened environment of Moscow University and Kheraskov's salon was followed by Denis Fonvizin. Fonvizin's father, Ivan Andreevich, was a military serviceman whose ancestor, a Baron Peter von Wiesen, a knight of a Livonian Order, joined the Russian service nobility in the sixteenth century after being captured by Ivan IV's armies in the Livonian Wars.[6] Ivan Andreevich eventually attained the rank of state councilor in the bureaucracy.[7] He supplemented his government salary with the income provided from a considerable number of "souls," that is, serfs. This wealth did not bring on the profligacy and eventual indebtedness that were typical for the wealthy few among the nobles. His eldest son Denis[8] noted with some pride and perhaps exaggeration: "I must say to the honor of my father that he owned no more than 500 souls [and] . . . had to educate eight children, but was able to live and die without debts. In society's present condition this ability is not at all familiar to anyone."[9]

Ivan Andreevich played a key role in his son's education. Usually a young Russian noble was brought up by parents who were illiterate and made no effort to acquire any basic skills. They remained devoid of intellectual interests and generally suspicious of the corrupting effects of education.[10] Denis Fonvizin was more fortunate. Ivan Andreevich did not hire a tutor for his son but assumed the role himself, listening to Denis's reading, coaching and encouraging him. By the time Denis was sent to Moscow University and registered in its boarding school for nobles, he was well prepared for his studies. Ivan Andreevich also served as an influential moral example to his son: "My father was a man of substantial intellect but did not have the occasion . . . to enlighten himself by studies. He read all Russian books, of which he particularly liked ancient and Roman history, the discourses of Cicero, and other good translations of moralizing books. He was a virtuous man and a true Christian. He loved the truth and refused to tolerate lies to such an extent that he always blushed when anyone was not ashamed of lying in front of him."[11] Fonvizin explicitly admitted he wanted to emulate his father,[12] and as a mature writer he endowed the protagonists in his later plays, the *Starodum* figures, with the same moral and patriotic qualities he so admired in his father. When he went off to Moscow in 1755, he was fortified with the aspiration, as much psychological as moral, to identify himself with the ethical ideal represented by his father.

Nikolai Novikov's family history was similar to Fonvizin's. Novikov's ancestors first appeared in Russia in the sixteenth century. Because of the family's service to the Russian throne during the sixteenth and seventeenth centuries, the Novikov name was included in the family registers collected after the destruction of the *mestnichestvo* system, the books of ranks and social precedence burned in Moscow in 1682. Novikov's father, Ivan Vasil'evich, was a successful career serviceman who held an appointment in the Naval College under Peter the Great and posts in the civil bureaucracy under Anna and Elizabeth. He retired at the rank of state councilor. Novikov's parents were financially independent. They had 700 souls and a house in Moscow,[13] which would place them in approximately the upper three percent of the nobility.[14]

Although Novikov's family could probably have afforded to pay for his education, his only teacher until he arrived at the boarding school of Moscow University in 1755 was a church sexton. "I learned to draw letters on paper while still a child. I say draw since I learned how to read and write Russian from a sexton who did not even know any rules and had not heard of grammar."[15]

In a revealing comment Novikov remarked that "God was my first tutor."[16] His education and upbringing were guided by religious values before all else. A young nobleman was, like Novikov, usually first taught at home by a domestic or minor church official who emphasized the study of church customs and faith, to instill in the boy a belief in God as well as a respect for church rituals and books.[17]

Novikov's characterization of his own youth would also serve for Fonvizin and Bogdanovich: "I was born and reared in the womb of the fatherland. For this I am obligated to serve it by my labors and to love it."[18] The young men were well prepared by their upbringing and by parental example to serve the Russian state. Though they were not fabulously wealthy, they were clearly better off than the typical Russian noble, forced by economic necessity to live in a style quite similar to that of his own serfs. The literary interests of Fonvizin's and Bogdanovich's families reinforced the distinctiveness of their social position. These were clearly not the boorish, provincial noblemen so frequent in the pages of eighteenth- and nineteenth-century Russian literature. When the three men enrolled in Moscow University, they emerged from the "womb of the fatherland" to be trained for the life of service. There was every reason to assume that their careers would be similar to those of their parents and no reason to suspect they would become anything other than well-trained, loyal servants of the throne.

In their first classes at Moscow University were several people with similar interests. Denis Fonvizin was accompanied to Moscow by his younger brother Paul (1745–1803). Paul was enrolled in the university in 1755 and remained until 1762.[19] The Fonvizins' close friend Sergei Gerasimovich Domashnev (1742–1796) entered the nobles' boarding school shortly after Elizabeth exiled his mother to Moscow in 1754 for attempting to bewitch the empress.[20] Alexander Grigor'evich Karin was sent to the university by his father and was listed on the student rolls of the same boarding school in 1756.[21] Vasilii Dem'ianovich Sankovskii (1738?–?) became a student at the university in the 1750s, though the year of his matriculation is not definite.[22] These men are not significant because of their writings as students or their later careers as bureaucrats, but because of the light they cast on what made the Fonvizin group distinctive. From similar backgrounds and with similar educations, these men followed different routes after the early 1760s. Their literary and bureaucratic careers will be referred to often as points of comparison to the Fonvizin group.

—— 3 ——

The Fonvizin group's formal education in the boarding school and lecture halls of Moscow University is significant because the young men studied in circumstances that set them off from the world outside the classrooms. The university was handicapped by the lack of a secular school system. Few young men were prepared for matriculation in the 1750s. To compensate for this, the government dragooned many candidates from the seminaries, the one institution housing young people qualified to begin a university education.[23] Unfortunately, these students were schooled in Latin, not Russian. The erudition of the *latinniki* marked them off, both in the seminary and the university, from the lay public. When it was decided to deliver classroom and public lectures only in Latin, the distinction was reinforced. In addition to speaking in a foreign language, the students were further removed from the world around them by their attire. Required to wear a green uniform with a bright red collar, a student was readily detected on the streets of Moscow. Set apart by manners, speech, appearance, and education from everyday life in Moscow, each student had to find meaning for this exclusiveness and form his own sense of identity by reference to the small community within the walls of the university.

Furthermore, the organizational structure of the institution put the students under the continued, direct, and intense influence of their professors. Fonvizin and his peers were housed and schooled together. Their daily routine was strictly monitored by the administrative officers of the nobles' boarding school, the inspector and rector. These two posts were always staffed by professors from the university, who acted *in loco parentis,* checking the students' activities, academic and otherwise. Regulation was extensive, obliging the two officials to oversee even the minutiae of their wards' everyday lives. The professors' presence was felt even more strongly because there were so few students in the late 1750s and early 1760s. Although dormitory facilities were available for 164 residents, the university accommodated no more than 100. There were few students in the nobles' boarding school; no one graduated until 1759.[24] When Fonvizin, Novikov, and Bogdanovich were students in the university itself, there were many more professors than students, and classes could be quite small. Fonvizin remembered one course with only three students.[25] Moreover, the young nobles were taught in the university by the very same men who had directed their studies in the boarding school.[26]

These circumstances are important because most of the instructors were hired on the recommendation of Gerhard Friedrich Müller, the academician, historian, and publisher. Müller, a graduate of Leipzig who arrived in Russia in 1725, relied on the suggestions of former colleagues and acquaintances at the most prestigious German universities. At this time Leipzig, Halle, and Tübingen were intellectual centers of the German Enlightenment, and consequently Müller's nominees were scholars familiar with the important German theorists of natural law, Christian Wolff and Samuel Pufendorf. Ioannes Matthias Schaden, a graduate of Tübingen in 1756, was a persuasive interpreter of Wolff's philosophy in his courses on moral philosophy and on Greek and Roman history.[27] Heinrich Philipp Dilthey had been one of Pufendorf's students before he was invited to Moscow in 1756 to teach history and law.[28] A majority of the new professors—Reichel and Kellner from Leipzig, Rost from Göttingen, and Froman from Stuttgart—had been similarly schooled within the general framework of the ideas of the German Enlightenment.[29] Although obviously the faculty's common philosophical persuasion did not mean the students would necessarily come away imprinted with the ideas of Pufendorf and Wolff, there is sufficient reason to assume that the position of the professors and the nature of their influence disposed the young men toward accepting the teachings of the German Enlightenment.

The ethical philosophy typical of the writings of German enlighteners was, as Marc Raeff has demonstrated, quite distinct from that advanced by British and French thinkers. Where one spoke in England or France of emancipating man from the slavish bonds of tradition and freeing the individual to determine his own destiny for himself, German enlighteners emphasized each person's duties to his fellow man. "The individual was never seen in isolation and independently from the group; he was not endowed with absolute and equal rights. The German philosophers and jurists of the *Aufklärung* always conceived of the individual within the context of a community, with rights being conferred on him only in return for the fulfillment of his obligations to his fellow-men and to the group." [30] The individual was to rely on his rational faculties to come to know the terms of this service. Reason was the instrument enabling the individual to perfect himself. As Pufendorf explained, "He will fulfill his duties toward others more satisfactorily as he exercises himself with greater care for his own perfecting." [31] Self-perfection educated the individual's mind to "matters which concern his duty . . . that the impulses of the mind be regulated and governed by the rule of right reason." [32] Reason also made known to all men their absolute duties to one another. In general terms, the ethical message of Pufendorf and Wolff was that before all else each man must recognize his obligations to his fellow man.

The instruction in German natural law introduced the students to the fundamental terms for debate of moral issues. The question was how a virtuous life was to be led. Natural law in its contemporary German form put a premium on an active life, that is, one devoted to the cultivation of moral and intellectual values and the practice of wise and virtuous conduct. The individual was to cherish these qualities as desirable traits of the heart and mind. As their validity was not dependent on circumstances external to his person, his pursuit of an active life aroused and freed him from the world of immediacies. An active life does not by definition necessarily entail any relations with other individuals. One's ideas and values could be ends in themselves. However, the ethics of natural law emphasized that an active life could only be achieved by directing the moral regeneration within oneself to focuses external to oneself. The inner self could be fulfilled only by seeking its image in the social self. Moral imperative compelled the individual to extend the bounds of the moral kingdom within himself into the world of social and political phenomena. He was to seek in that reality an identity with his inner moral personality that would validate his personal self. For all their lives the members of the Fonvizin group sought the completeness that was the promise of this moral idealism.

The urge to participate in the affairs of man was intensified by the influence of neo-Stoicism. The revival of this philosophy in Western and Central Europe in the sixteenth and seventeenth centuries emphasized the ethics and politics of Stoicism rather than its metaphysics and epistemology. In eighteenth-century Russia, neo-Stoic thought was popular for the spirited tone of its ethical and political ideas as much as for the ideas themselves. Stoicism was mentioned frequently by the students at Moscow University.

They usually did not refer directly to the works of European neo-Stoics. The only neo-Stoic writer singled out for attention was the Dutch scholar Justus Lipsius (1547–1606) whose books, particularly *Manuductio ad Stoicam Philosophiam* (1604) and *Physiologia Stoicorum* (1610), aroused the interest of many European contemporaries in neo-Stoic ideas.[33] In the Russian journals of the sixties neo-Stoicism was reduced to a single set of terms that were standard and recurrent: the individual was created to perfect himself; society was the proper forum for this endeavor; each man was required to benefit others lest he fall prey to selfishness and mar his own moral integrity.

The appeal of these key tenets of Stoicism lay in the stress on voluntarism. The disciplining of the will to attain moral perfection was what the students repeatedly singled out for praise.[34] The legend of a Greek philosopher whose life was continually beset by tragic occurrences was a good example of this ideal.[35] When his home was destroyed and his children murdered, he refused to mourn for his children. "For the loss of my children and estate cannot truly be termed a privation as long as my life remains uncorrupted by vice and free of any taint of dishonor." [36] When his wife died, he did not allow himself to be overcome with grief. She was destined to die at a time appointed by God, not human expectations. To bewail her death was to challenge God's authority. The philosopher was asked by Athenian citizens if a man deprived of his political freedom and forced to obey a tyrannical government should submit. The philosopher was quick to reply: each man can be bound only by vices within his own character. A person who was ridden with vice should be considered a prisoner of his own conscience even if he lived in an ideal state.[37] This legend was important in two respects. The voluntaristic spirit clearly implied the duty to fulfill one's obligations to oneself, whatever the obstacles or personal hardship. More important, this goal might even entail giving up one's relations to others. The active life of Stoic thinkers was always subject to conversion to the contemplative life.

Save for this ultimate eventuality, neo-Stoicism reinforced the emphasis in German natural law on the extension of the personal self into the affairs of the political and social worlds external to it. This obligation compelled the individual to seek not only a series of images of his personal self in the different domains of reality, but also to recognize the moral unity of these images. The voluntaristic element in Stoic and natural law philosophy led the Russian students to assume that there was a unifying principle to the particulars of the social and political worlds. In the midst of disorder was a moral order. However unmanageable and even bewildering the phenomena of the actualities external to each of them, they could take comfort in the constancy of this moral realm. This assumption was to be important to the students because it allowed them a potential escape from a world that did not conform to their moral expectations. They could withdraw into a moral kingdom and ignore contemporary politics.

—— 4 ——

The students' initiation to Moscow University was assisted by Mikhail Matveevich Kheraskov. He acted as the young men's patron during the early 1760s and was the single figure outside the classrooms who shared their moral concerns and encouraged them in their study and appreciation of these issues.

Kheraskov's family, Wallachian by origin, entered the lists of the Russian nobility during the reign of Peter the Great.[38] His father was a member of the middle nobility, who had only a modestly successful career in the army and was a major at the time of his death in 1734.[39] Mikhail Kheraskov's future was assured when his widowed mother remarried within a year, this time to the famous Nikita Trubetskoi. Trubetskoi's wealth and influence provided his stepson with the means to pursue a bureaucratic career that could be prestigious, undemanding, and tolerant of literary aspirations. In 1743 Kheraskov entered the Cadet Corps in St. Petersburg. Though the school was originally designed, as its title would suggest, to prepare minors for military service, it also came to provide training for careers in the civil bureaucracy. For Kheraskov as for Sumarokov, the Cadet Corps was one of the few available means to be introduced to the world of contemporary European and Russian culture and to be allowed to develop particular cultural interests.

At the Cadet Corps Kheraskov joined a literary circle, the Society of Lovers of Russian Literature. The circle was organized in the late 1730s by the young Sumarokov. Several of its members became notable literary or political figures in the 1760s, namely Elagin, Peter Panin, and P. A. Rumiantsev (1725–1796).[40] Little is known about this circle. Unlike some nineteenth-century literary circles, it was not an exclusive organization, meeting in secret. These men met, according to S. I. Glinka, "on holidays and in [their] free time to read to one another their early compositions and translations."[41] They also founded a theater in the Cadet Corps whose performances merited several visits by Empress Elizabeth.[42] The circle was not central to

Kheraskov's life. He was only ten years old in 1743, and the circle's leading, not to say overbearing, figure, Sumarokov, had graduated in 1740. The Society of Lovers of Russian Literature was important to Kheraskov as a model for the one he organized himself at Moscow University in the early 1760s.

His circle was formed after his appointment in 1755 as director of the university's press. Only six years later Kheraskov was put in charge of the university theater and, also in 1761, was named acting director of the university. Kheraskov opened his home to the many young nobles then attending the university and came to be a moral as well as an official figure in their lives. He was respected for his humility and the simplicity of his manners.[43] A witty conversationalist, he appealed to the students with humorous, if involved, remarks on the events and personalities of the day.[44] Kheraskov was also quite attentive to his charges' complaints and anxieties. For the students, most of whom were in their late teens, a receptive audience in the person of the university director, himself only in his late twenties, was both welcome hospitality and intellectual stimulation. Kheraskov's lavish soirees attracted many students, some of whom he encouraged to form a literary fraternity. In this way Kheraskov protected and encouraged many young nobles while maintaining a loose control over their intellectual and literary activities.

Kheraskov groomed, according to Gukovskii, as many as twenty-three writers. Bogdanovich, who, as we have already mentioned, had become a ward of Kheraskov at their first meeting in 1758, was among them. Fonvizin joined the circle by 1761. Kheraskov's periodical *Useful Entertainment* published Fonvizin's first contribution to the journal in November 1761.[45] All of the minor figures associated with the group were also members of Kheraskov's circle. Sankovskii, Domashnev, Karin, and, of course, Paul Fonvizin attended its meetings and published articles in its journals. Kheraskov also drew into his literary camp several writers who were not students at Moscow University, the most prominent being the Naryshkin brothers, Semen (1734–1807)[46] and Aleksei (1742–1800).[47] Semen Naryshkin was more generally attached to St. Petersburg than Moscow. Older than Fonvizin and his peers, Semen Naryshkin also differed from them in literary status and experience. His younger brother led the typical life of a rich young nobleman with an avocation in belles lettres. The Naryshkins were steady contributors to both the *Industrious Bee* and *Idle Time Used for the Good,* a weekly published at the Cadet Corps from January 1759 to June 1760. Their articles also appeared regularly in *Useful Entertainment.* Aleksei Andreevich Rzhevskii (?–

1804) also worked for both the St. Petersburg and Moscow journals.[48] His position in the Kheraskov circle was identical to that of the Naryshkins. Kheraskov also attracted the interest of Dmitrii Sergeevich Anichkov (?–1788) and Nikolai Popovskii (1730–1760), the noted philosophers and first native Russians to hold chairs at Moscow University.

These writers were like-minded in their willingness to publicize the moral and philosophical arguments currently being debated at the university and at Kheraskov's soirees. They were eager to criticize and to praise each other's ideas, thereby strengthening their morale. This interest (and Kheraskov's control of the university press) provided the impetus for the circle's principal activity between 1760 and 1764—the publication of four journals.[49] All four journals were characterized by a striking sameness of views, a consensus that accounted for the moral coherence in the majority of the articles.

The most successful of the four was *Useful Entertainment*. It was edited by Kheraskov himself, a role he believed was ordained by fate. *Useful Entertainment* surpassed the others in the range of its interests and the quality and quantity of its articles. Written in the style of a "moral weekly," [50] the journal referred frequently to classical authors and included translations from Ovid and Socrates, Cato's famous speech to the Roman Senate denouncing Cicero as a tyrant, selections from Horace, and Lucian's *Dialogues of the Dead*. A few contemporary writers, especially Rousseau, were also represented. The Russian students themselves contributed a great many poems—odes, elegies, and sonnets—distinguishing *Useful Entertainment* from its predecessors as the first journal giving poetry equal status with prose.

The journal's fate, however, did not depend on its quality, but on the fact that it supported Peter III. Kheraskov allowed his collaborators to print several odes to the tsar, and *Useful Entertainment* was never published after the revolution of June 28, 1762. The writers around Kheraskov had not expected the journal's sudden end,[51] and the June issue had included a note indicating that one article would be continued in future numbers.

The quality of *Useful Entertainment* was never again matched, but it was taken as a standard by the three other periodicals. In January 1763, Bogdanovich published the first issue of the new monthly *Innocent Exercise,* which was to provide "a mixture of the humorous with the useful," [52] that is, useful entertainment. His colleagues refused to sign their articles and were known only as "certain young authors." [53] However, they were probably the same individuals who had previously worked with Kheraskov.[54]

Innocent Exercise was unique among the journals of 1759–1764 for its philosophical orientation. Translations of Helvetius, selections from Leibniz, and Bogdanovich's translation of *Le Poème sur le désastre de Lisbonne* were supplemented by passages from Pythagoras, Socrates, Lucian, and Cicero. Bogdanovich's periodical also included detailed, though quite superficial, analyses of Racine, Molière, Milton, Addison, and Steele as writers whose works should be emulated by contemporaries.[55] Many other articles were dry, abstract pieces on man's eternal vices and follies. Typical were timid exercises proving the value of virtue, constancy, and the like. Only a few pieces contained any social comment, and of these only a few satirized topics particular to Russian society. Most of the entries in *Innocent Exercise* were prose, though each issue included a few epigrams or madrigals and occasionally the beautiful love verses of Bogdanovich.

Innocent Exercise was closed after only six issues. The June number carried an open letter from the editors to society at large (*obshchestvo*) which announced that the journal was closing because of "many disgusting obstacles."[56] One of these obstacles was the return to St. Petersburg of Catherine and her court after a ten-month stay in the old capital. The periodical lost some of its audience as well as those members of its staff who were in service at the court. *Innocent Exercise* also became politically suspect when its most active supporter and patroness, Princess Dashkova (1743–1810), the priggish confidante of the empress, became physically and politically incapacitated in the late spring of 1763.[57] When coupled with the usually short life span of moral weeklies, these factors were sufficient to account for the closing of the journal in June 1763.

A second journal edited by Kheraskov, *Free Hours*,[58] was issued at the same time as *Innocent Exercise*. Published monthly at Moscow University, *Free Hours* was staffed by the same writers who had written for *Useful Entertainment*. Both of Kheraskov's journals were similar in their zealous crusading against man's eternal vices. But *Free Hours* also contained articles critical of certain superficial characteristics of Russian society. Its brief satirical attacks on French fops were the prelude to the extensive commentary in the periodicals of 1769–1774. *Free Hours* closed after one year for unspecified reasons.[59]

A third successor to *Useful Entertainment* appeared in January 1764. *Good Intention* was a monthly published at Moscow University under the editorship of Sankovskii. The staff was composed primarily of the *Useful Entertainment* writers. Sankovskii, Karin, and Paul Fonvizin contributed most of the signed articles. Their works were supplemented by the writings of men who had not written for the other journals. Several of these new men, including

Aleksei Vershnitskii, Ivan Slotvinskoi, and Vasilii Petrov, were students at Moscow University.[60] Both the members of the original coterie and the new writers tried to follow the example of *Useful Entertainment*. The appeal to antiquity was made in the form of Sankovskii's translations from Ovid and a speech of Marcus Aurelius. Yet the journal lacked any direct reference to contemporary enlightened thought or any satirical themes relevant to Russian society. The poor quality of *Good Intention* perhaps accounted for its closing with its December issue, indicating as well that by 1764 the enthusiasm, energy, and commitment aroused four years earlier by the opening of *Useful Entertainment* had been lost.

— 5 —

The most remarkable feature of these journals was their very occurrence. Their appearance was a signal event in the development of Russian social opinion. The intense, if brief, effort of the students to cultivate the ideas and tastes of a small audience in Moscow was an episode in Russian journalism with few precedents, principally the St. Petersburg journals *Industrious Bee* and *Idle Time Used for the Good,* and many successors, especially the famous satirical journals of 1769–1774. The significance of the student periodicals makes it important to account for their publication. Clearly they were organized to serve as forums for debating the ethical issues raised in the classrooms of Moscow University and discussed at Kheraskov's soirees.

Whether Kheraskov's or the professors' influence was stronger is a matter of dispute. Gukovskii, Zapadov, Serman, and Ryu argue the accepted opinion: Kheraskov dominated his circle.[61] His influence with the students was so pervasive that there was a virtual identity between his moral standards and those of the students. Kheraskov's power over the young men was direct; the authority of their professors was so removed as to be diffuse. Leaving aside for the moment the questionable interpretation of the professors' influence, this reading rather casually assumes that the values of the patron of the circle must have been shared by each of its members. Since there were no contributors to Kheraskov's journals who were not both students at the university and participants in his circle, his influence on the ideas and writings of his protégés can best be seen by comparing their works to his.[62]

Kheraskov charged his writers with a task that was at once noble and ennobling: they were to publish *Useful Entertainment* so as "to encourage those who would defend virtue, expose vice, and entertain society." [63] For his part Kheraskov assumed that his intent to remake society had to be preceded by his own attainment of inner harmony (*tishina* or *pokoi*). When the individual sought a sense of quietude for his personal self apart from worldly concerns, he was confronted with the most essential questions. What was the purpose of life? Why did God create him? If there is a divine purpose, how was he to make his own life accord with God's plans? Kheraskov was genuinely bewildered by his own questions. He was wont to avoid his perplexities by dwelling on the transitory quality of life.

> As a single drop cast into the deepest ocean,
> As a single leaf swept into the thickest woods,
> So is this world in the infinite universe;
> In the turmoil of this inscrutable age,
> I have lost sight of the individual.
> When this globe which is our birthplace,
> Is recognized as but a tiny particle in the universe,
> How can we possibly think well of ourselves,
> For we are so utterly insignificant?
> How can we possibly bestir ourselves
> When we are nothing at all? [64]

In less despondent moods Kheraskov would assume that, even if God's order was unknowable, the Creator surely intended the individual to embody the ideals of virtue and reason (*razum*). Kheraskov was anything but a rigorous thinker. He did no more than accept the fashionable premise that the use of one's reason to cultivate virtues and curb passions would ensure one's serenity.

He feared that his inner sense of quietude was endangered by his commitments to others. The threat came from those in capital society, that is, those in the social worlds of St. Petersburg and Moscow, who frequented the balls, played cards at extravagant stakes, and were consumed with the desire for promotion in rank.[65] His distance from the decadence of capital society can be measured by his attention to the corrosive effect of wealth on the individual's capacity to act rationally and virtuously. He warned the readers of *Useful Entertainment* that "gold captivates the rational faculties of everyone and leads only to tears and sorrows." [66] Gold could buy splendor and luxury and attract the company of those similarly afflicted. Kheraskov was primarily interested in wealth, not luxury, in the threat to the tranquility of the inner self, not the consequences of disorder in the social self. To shield and maintain his personal moral equilibrium from the malignant corruption of high society in the capitals, Kheraskov carefully circumscribed the extent of his involvement with others and withdrew into a sheltered world.

His decision to leave society was explained in his *Friend of the Unfortunate*,[67] a sentimental drama in which Kheraskov resorted to quite conventional stage imagery. The heroine, Milana, though impoverished, was still hounded for the debts she owed Zelit. The latter was a "godless hypocrite,"[68] corrupted by the money he had acquired, no doubt by illegal means, while Milana was the epitome of virtue unrewarded. Her cause found a champion in Prechest', who consoled her but could not eliminate her difficulties. Milana was eventually rescued from the clutches of Zelit by the sudden appearance of her long-lost father, Svedon. He explained to his daughter why he had forsaken her. At the time of her birth he succumbed to a fit of self-indulgence, followed the lure of capital society, gambled recklessly, and lost the family fortune. Victim of his passions, he left the city in disgrace. Svedon's return and payment of Milana's debts enabled her to marry Prechest'. Urban wealth was opposed to the unappreciated virtue of Milana while its attraction temporarily overcame Svedon's ability to master his passions.

As to what was to be done, Kheraskov only hinted in the play at what he described in some detail in several of his poems. He contraposed the decadence of the cities—where virtue was in a hostile environment—to an idyllic image of the countryside, where virtue could find a hospitable haven. Kheraskov often contrasted the enviable simplicity of the shepherd, innocent of the troubles of urban life, with the woes of the urban sophisticate, beset by dangers to his inner tranquility.[69] This withdrawal to the countryside was a standard literary device, used by Kheraskov in an ordinary and uncomplicated way to convey what he perceived to be the moral dangers of life in the capitals. The image could not, however, serve as an aid to the real-life problem of defining the limits of engagement that would not threaten his own sense of quietude.

Kheraskov was certainly not prepared to retreat to the countryside himself. The extent of his involvement with others was a problem that recurred throughout his life. In the early 1760s, his social self was engaged only with the Fonvizin group and the other writers staffing the student journals. His charge to these men, quoted above, was accompanied by his reluctant admission that the task of correcting society was one he did not expect to be immediately successful. He consoled himself with the thought that, however incorrigible the many, he at least was associated with the virtuous few.[70] After these students left the university, he never again extended himself to trust others as he had the Fonvizin group. In the introduction to the *Storyteller or the Unknown One,* he wrote that he found safety for his inner sense of serenity only in isolation.[71] It was, to be sure, a mental not a physical state of isolation. In the *Storyteller* he continued to bewail the moral degeneration of capital society and ask himself the same basic questions about life's purpose that he had posed to his circle in the early 1760s. The book was written in 1803.

Reassured by the notion that quietude could be preserved only in solitude, Kheraskov dismissed all commitments to others. This limit, which was set independently of the actual circumstances in his life that might endanger or be hospitable to his sense of quietude, was never reconsidered. Kheraskov lacked the intellectual discipline that could have enabled him to find personally satisfactory solutions to the problems that troubled him for so long. His notions about the need for rational, virtuous conduct and personal withdrawal were static; his expression of his moral convictions lapsed occasionally into terms that were no more than fashionable formulas. Yet if his reflections and moral imperatives furnished little personal satisfaction and did not lead him to expect the reform of others, why did he write what he did?

His works were, in part, quite self-serving, an ode to get the attention of Catherine, a verse to curry the favor of a courtier or, in the case of *Rossiada,* an epic poem to return him to the good graces of the empress. He lauded each of his subjects equally as exemplars of the ideals of reason and virtue. To be sure, the timing of his opportunism was not very astute politically, for he wrote the last of a series of odes to Peter III for *Useful Entertainment* only a few weeks before the coup of June 28. Kheraskov did not see any contradiction between his moral convictions and his desire for promotion. His lack of interest in defining in rigorous fashion the relationship between moral concerns and service advancements suggests that he did not think of himself as being subject to his own ethical demands. Even though he claimed to have withdrawn to a solitary retreat in which his quietude was protected from the tumult and decay of capital society, he did not really live in that moral realm.

Kheraskov's unwillingness to abide unequivocally by his own moral standards proved to be intolerable to the student journalists in his circle. To the *Kheraskovtsy* his inconsistency was laxity, his opportunism delinquency. Their voluntaristic bent did not allow for any qualification to what they considered to be ethical imperatives. The Fonvizin group and its peers never acknowledged any intellectual indebtedness to Kheraskov despite their extended and intensive contact with him. His role in the students' lives was as patron, organizer of the journals, and overseer of their literary standards.[72] He was not a primary intellectual force in the formation of their values and priorities. The activities of his circle grew out of the influence exerted on his protégés by their professors at Moscow University. The publication of the journals was a means of publicizing the ethical norms taught the students at the university. Kheraskov's moral interests, however conveniently and inconsistently pursued, left one clear, enduring mark on the Fonvizin group's own ethical concerns. He first defined the problem that was to be a constant and primary characteristic of their own writings, namely how one can live in a world hostile to virtue and still broaden the dimensions of one's social commitment without endangering one's personal serenity.

6

The students in grappling with the problems that so bedeviled Kheraskov at first accepted his terms for the debate. The available moral alternatives were described by Semen Naryshkin. He suggested that the group's concern for ethical questions led to a choice between two modes of individual behavior, the useful life and the merry one.[73] For those who lived in a hedonistic style, life would be overabundant in luxury and splendor but would eventually come to be wearisome to the individual and finally leave him remorseful, poor, and in tears.[74] The attractions of the useful life were not immediately obvious, and "sound men" had to sacrifice immediate advantages for eventual rewards. Without specifying the characteristics of the useful life, Naryshkin did hold out to useful men the prospect that, however trying the circumstances they could expect to endure, they would be fortified by the promise of eventually achieving inner quietude (*pokoi*).[75] Naryshkin's article was typical of the Fonvizin group in its interest in moral questions to the virtual exclusion of purely intellectual ones. The goal common to the members of the group was the same one Kheraskov had so vainly sought to attain. They were all interested in working out a set of standards that would give order and integrity to their personal lives. They were all intent on finding in this moral code a context for its potential use. They insisted that the personal self had to be coupled with the social self, the former being fulfilled only by means of the latter. It was in the balance struck between personal and humanitarian duties that the students and Kheraskov parted ways, and that made all the difference.

In the May issue of *Innocent Exercise* an article signed by "your faithful friend" recorded the writer's attempts to work out his own values.[76] "After examining my soul and all the thoughts that I allowed myself to entertain, I found that I had passed from one system to another without becoming at all knowledgeable. I had, however, succeeded in calming my spirit and restraining desire so that I could recognize the value of reflection and the orderly disposition of my thoughts. . . . As yet I have not perfected that order."[77] The "faithful friend" did not provide readers with any specific details of this arrangement. The writer (Princess Dashkova, perhaps?) did mention the proper criteria for attaining this order. "If one is to have order in one's thoughts, one must have an appreciation of each thing and know its worth, not as determined by fashionable opinion, but its true worth. Then one must order one's thoughts to accord with these evaluations and in dependence on them."[78] The reader was instructed to act not by what was venerated or disparaged by social convention but by the dictates of his own judgment. How was one to trust one's own faculties save by self-knowledge?[79] Know thyself, one member wrote, drawing on the Socratic dialogue, for without knowledge and mastery of oneself, one was not able to comment on others without falling prey to pride and self-delusion.[80] The call for the analysis, evaluation, and perfection of the individual's moral personality was an affirmation that one's inner harmony had priority over everything else. The emotional vigor and potential moral rigor of this assertion distinguished it sharply from similar prescriptions in Kheraskov's writings.

Braced with an ardent moral idealism, the Fonvizin group embarked on a moral quest for the discovery of personal values that would properly guide the individual's conduct. The group's venture was no doubt both exalted and exalting to its participants. Nevertheless, it was undertaken on terms that were quite common to the literature of eighteenth-century Europe. The group's investigation in the realm of the individual's inner qualities led to the discovery of the passions and their claims to influence a person's behavior. In a short poem composed in 1761, Bogdanovich described his recognition of the fact that human nature was innately inclined to do evil, a disposition that, if unchecked, resulted in the dominance of the passions and the sway of vice.[81] Dismayed, he admitted quite reluctantly that man was constantly prey to the illusion that he could satisfy the insatiable demands of his passions. But Bogdanovich was philosophically optimistic, for he assumed that God did not consign man to a lifetime of futile exertions. Rather, God gave the individual the tool of reason (*rassudok*) to harness the cravings of his passions, direct his life, and, in so doing, distinguish himself from an animal.[82] Man's rational faculties were the means by which he could regulate his actions and strike the balance between the rational and the emotional that would assure his inner tranquility.

In an unsigned article in *Idle Time Used for the Good*, the author likened the inner self to a ship which would be buffeted by the winds of passion and lost at sea unless the vessel was captained by reason and able to use the winds to bring it into safe harbor.[83] Where reason was dominant, the influence of vice would decline, and an individual could lead a virtuous and useful life.[84] The contest between virtue and vice could not be resolved until reason had won out over the passions. The dominance of reason made possible the cultivation of virtue and was necessary if the individual was to achieve an inner moral equilibrium.

The validity of the principle of rationality as a personal, regulative norm was, however, challenged by the prevalence of vice. To account for the existence of vice, a phenomenon that seemed to have genuinely perplexed many of the students, an anonymous contributor to *Innocent Exercise* recalled to his readers the voyage to hell made by the philosopher Elifer. Elifer's purpose was to find out if the gods really punished the vice-ridden and rewarded the morally constant.[85] One of the condemned complained to the traveler that he lacked the food and clothing that were once his on earth. The voyager's guide, Socrates, informed him that a life full of excesses obscured the path of rational activity and took man away from the true route to happiness.[86] A coquette was encountered who had been cast into hell for attempting, unsuccessfully, to seduce a man who "was training himself in the art of self-perfection . . . and was not to be tempted by the lure of beauty, transient no matter how perfect."[87] A hypocrite was uneasy with the serious tone of his conversation with the voyager when the guide, now Virgil, interrupted to reprimand him. The hypocrite was so used to the vacuous distraction of idle chatter that he failed to recognize the merits of serious and informed discussion.[88] After these and similar encounters, Elifer admitted to himself that vices, whether the deceit of the hypocrite, the flattery and vanity of the coquette, or the arrogance and excess of the superfluous man, were indeed punished by the gods.

Sincerity, constancy, modesty, and moderation resulted from the proper use of reason to maintain moral order in one's life. The more one acted rationally and avoided the emotional turmoil caused by disorderly desires, the less one would be prone to act according to the single characteristic that betrayed the faulty functioning of one's inner moral mechanisms, namely arbitrariness. An individual who acted arbitrarily was described in *Anything and Everything*, a journal issued in 1769 under the general supervision of Catherine herself, as a person lacking reason "who obeys more his desires than the established rules. . . . Desire without rules is caprice [*prikhot'*]; caprice brings harm to oneself and near ones, but rules in life serve as a control on harmful whims." [89] Rationality was accepted by the Fonvizin group as the personal standard that made possible a virtuous life. Rationality in personal affairs was understood as the opposite of arbitrariness and attested to the soundness of one's moral equilibrium. Rationality also made it possible to link one's behavior to that of others. The students' commitment to rationality was not lightly made. It carried with it a responsibility they willingly accepted. Failure to abide by the norm was, as Elifer declared at the end of his voyage, not to be attributed to the sternness of the ethical standards, the vagaries of fate, or any other agent, but directly and solely to the individual himself.[90]

The call for reform of self aroused in a few cases the doubts of the skeptic rather than the enthusiasm of the idealist. One writer contributed an unsigned article in which he argued that human nature was basically unchangeable. "I am of the opinion that a very small part of the human race becomes more and more intelligent, but the remainder becomes more and more ignorant, and the more stupid they become the haughtier they are." [91] As proof that human nature was not malleable, the anonymous writer cited the example of the young Russian dandies who affected a preference for all things French. The differences between their tastes and those of traditional nobles were only superficial, concealing the same ignorance and arrogance that the French fops supposedly overcame.[92]

Both this hesitation about the commitment to reason and the students' support for the value of rationality could be found in the writings of many contemporary Europeans. Yet the similarities are potentially misleading. To compare Fonvizin and his friends to the mature, sophisticated thinkers of the salons in Paris and Berlin is to exaggerate the stature of the Russian students. However much they might see themselves as participants in the European-wide debate about the ideal of rationality, they were nonetheless young men whose intellectual experiences were limited. The fact that some did not support the standard of reason was as much testimony to their theoretical immaturity as to their diversity of opinion.

Rational, virtuous conduct was an ideal that the members of the Fonvizin group retained, unaltered, for the rest of their lives. Rational, virtuous conduct provided their assurance of inner harmony and tranquility. This quietude was a permanent refuge into which Kheraskov had withdrawn; for his protégés it was to be a safe harbor from which they sallied forth. The ethical core to their ideas was a constant, but they had to determine how they were to expand the periphery of their interests without yielding to self-delusion or upsetting their moral equilibrium.

—— 7 ——

The figures in the Fonvizin group considered any commitment as cautiously as had Kheraskov. They shared his opinion of capital society as the sanctuary of the socially decadent and railed at the corrupting influence of wealth. The three men's opinions brought them to the same question Kheraskov had asked himself: could a virtuous man live in such a morally contaminating environment? In their search for the right balance between personal and social self, the three men benefited from several commentaries written by other students.

Two friends of the group, Denis Fonvizin's brother Paul and Aleksei Rzhevskii, deliberated the advantages of solitude in the pages of *Useful Entertainment* and *Good Intention*. Rzhevskii was tempted to find in solitude the only sure guarantee of inner moral purity. He cursed the "evil men" and "slanderers" who dominated capital society and fled Moscow to the seclusion of one of Kheraskov's estates. When he returned, he announced to his peers that his period of isolation was enriched by his discovery of the joys of isolation.[93] "In you [that is, isolation] I found consolation beyond compare. My spirit was not troubled by the turmoil of civil [*grazhdanska*] concerns; blessed simplicity [reigned]."[94] According to another writer, solitude "frees one from the turmoil and confusion ensuing from the disorders . . . in society; it allows one to be in command of oneself, to appreciate fully the benefits of feelings and to reflect on one's well-being. . . . Were a man to be a recluse, he could becalm himself and enjoy the freedom that comes from communion with his own soul. . . . When I say he could be untroubled I mean that he would possess the order and proper disposition of his soul."[95] Paul Fonvizin occasionally lapsed into moments of despondency similar to those that enveloped Kheraskov. A life of solitude in the countryside was not, Paul Fonvizin warned his peers, an escape from capital society but still another lure in one's search for true contentment. Its blessings were no less illusive than the advantages of involvement in that society.[96] One's inner harmony could not be safeguarded by the exertion of the individual but was dependent on the vagaries of fate. "Fata viam invenient." [97]

Resignation to the inevitable seemed inconsistent with the call for self-perfection. While Rzhevskii and Fonvizin were not directly rebutted, their mood of acquiescence contrasted with the strident assertion of self made by many writers in the student journals. Typical of those entries was an unsigned article in *Innocent Exercise*.[98] Solitude was no longer considered a haven for the virtuous from the contaminated environment of the city. Rather it was the refuge of those who sought a cure for their immoderate involvement in capital society by an equally immoderate escape to isolation. The flight was in vain because solitude induced "a gloomy pensiveness" that gradually undermined one's sense of virtue and ultimately ruined it.[99] The search for self-perfection without social involvement was nothing more than self-exaltation. "What can be expected of a man, whether he be born a noble or peasant, who has made himself immune to moral improvement and heeds only his own predilections as if they were the sole measure of what is good and truthful?" [100] Solitude, now the solace of the immoderate and selfish, denied the individual the necessary complement to his virtuous self. "In solitude a man, even the most virtuous of men, is in no position to demonstrate and proffer his virtues. He lacks the means to benefit people and thereby perform the service that would come from his presence." [101] Quietude without commitment to others was not honorable. Those individuals who remained in society and cared for the well-being of others were to be recognized as "honorable men" (*chestnye liudi*).[102] This designation, rich in significance for the students' later commentary on politics and society, was initially employed with reference to questions of ethics. Their priorities never changed.

The moral injunction against a life of withdrawal is a clue to the key distinction between their moral works and those of Kheraskov. They disavowed any flight from an irretrievably corrupt society as a facile solution enabling the individual to avoid dealing with the morally troublesome activities in that society. Unlike Kheraskov, the students subjected themselves and their activities to the dictates of their own values. They charged themselves, whatever the peril to their inner tranquility and whatever the decadence of capital society, with the duty to venture into that society resolved to correct its moral deficiencies. During their university years they assumed that personal contentment was inseparable from their obligation to their fellow man.

The young writers accepted a series of commitments to individuals and associations external to their own personalities. The circles of their engagement broadened steadily during the 1760s and 1770s and came to include a sense of responsibility for the welfare of all of society and government. This extension of their personal selves continued as long as the integrity of their personal moral values was maintained. During the early sixties the students kept to themselves any doubts they may have felt about the rationality of man or the obligation to involve oneself with others. Were any serious threat to their inner moral equilibrium to arise, as was precisely the case in the early 1770s, the balance struck between personal and social selves would be disturbed. At such a time the students would be compelled by the logic of their own ethical principles to seek once again morally acceptable extensions of the personal self. Their reconsiderations would return them to the conceptions of personal and social duties that were unconvincing in the early sixties. The group entered society[103] with the assumption that "others" would conform or be persuaded to conform with the students' own values. They did not expect that their moral consistency and advocacy might well encounter opposition.

The students' extensions of self began with other members of their own circle. They praised the virtues of each other's company and exalted their ties into a cult. "There is nothing excelling or more binding than the friendship that unites honorable people [*chestnye liudi*], men of common moral conviction, with the bonds of mutual affection." [104] They likened themselves to Damon and Pythias in their friendship for one another and readiness to make the same sacrifices for their friends. "Life would be unbearable without friendship." [105] Their union protected them from the social evils assumed to be rampant in the world surrounding the university. This attitude, born of naiveté as much as ignorance, lent to the moral purpose of their friendship an added emotional bond. For Bogdanovich, "true happiness is not to be found in this society, but there is within it an association which is welcome. . . . Love, of course, is what sustains it." [106]

The students' common moral bond was not solely an emotional one. Though Bogdanovich's psalms and Kheraskov's poems anticipated the sentimentalist literature of the late eighteenth century, their contributions were no more than the initial glimmerings of that literary style. The primary quality shared by all the students was a sense that their union had to have an ethical purpose. Witness the complaint of an anonymous contributor to *Innocent Exercise*: "No longer are people united by any common endeavor. . . . It is appropriate in these times to remember Aristotle's lament: 'Oh! my friends, there are no longer in society those who could be called friends.' "[107] The students looked upon themselves as more than members of a literary circle; Kheraskov's soirees were never directly mentioned. They elevated their regard for one another into a brotherhood whose members were knights on a mission into society. This sense of belonging to a moral fraternity allowed the students to extend themselves to one another without endangering the validity of each one's personal values. The confidence they drew from these friendships served to strengthen their resolve to remedy the ills of the society outside the university.

The students' conception of society had little to do with the particular character of Russia in the early 1760s. They commented on a utopian order that had the characteristics of their own student association. Above all, in the ideal society the moral equality of all members was recognized. "All mortals are equal; they differ only in the masks they wear."[108] Each person was considered a creature of God to be equally rewarded and punished by the Divine. "God in his wisdom created us for society and imparted to our nature desire, reason, and passion; he allotted us days of joy and days of sorrow. . . . In this way each man is equal, and God has made us parts of one and the same symmetry of things."[109] The equality of each man implied the existence of an unchanging moral order. Sergei Domashnev admonished the readers of *Useful Entertainment* to remember that equality and freedom were opposites, not complementary qualities. "The love of freedom [*vol'nost'*] is oftentimes so harmful to people that it deprives them of what they so cherish, namely equality. . . . Slavery is the natural condition of man. All one's efforts to surmount it, no matter how strenuous, serve only to confirm one's slavery."[110] Social inequality was the accompaniment to moral equality. This assumption was rendered readily acceptable to its advocates by their idealized image of the socially disadvantaged classes, especially the serfs. An anonymous writer in *Innocent Exercise* presumed that the peasants actually benefited from a lifetime of poverty and labor. They were not burdened by the complexities of capital society. "They spend their nights in blissful sleep and in tranquility [*pokoi*]."[111] This bucolic image of the serfs was not marred by reference to the social and economic conditions of their lives. These considerations were irrelevant to the students. They were concerned with the moral welfare of the peasants to the exclusion of their social well-being. The students felt no class or ideological compulsion to contrast their idealized version of society with the actual particulars of Russian society. Their moral convictions served as a prism through which they perceived the real conditions they so zealously wished to rectify. The angle of refraction was reduced, never eliminated, as the students came in the mid-sixties to have opinions on many social issues. Throughout their lives, the image of society as an association of moral equals remained their primary assumption, transcending any specific social concerns.

Later, when the students tried to integrate their ideal moral version of society with actual social and economic conditions, they did so according to the ideas they had developed in the early sixties. Their commitment to "society" was to expand or decrease depending on whether the realities of the social world reinforced or conflicted with their ideal image of that society.

The students distinguished a special place for themselves in this moral order. Those who were favored by God with rational faculties were equipped with the capacity to serve and benefit their contemporaries. The privileged few had a special debt. "The advantaged must instruct the disadvantaged; the latter must obey the former." [112] As Aleksei Rzhevskii reminded his friends, a man who recognized his duty to improve his own ethical standards was ultimately obliged to recognize that he had a responsibility to tame the savageness inherent in his fellow man.[113] Rzhevskii was led by his own consistency to dimensions of commitment that were as grandiose as they were binding. If the individual violated this set of obligations, he was bonded in a moral rather than a legal sense. He was enslaved (*nevol'nik*).[114] All the premises the students accepted as their own were just as valid for all others, an inextricable link binding the young men to recognize the full extension of their obligation to others and, more important, to act on it.

—— 8 ——

The final sanction to the group's moral order was, of course, God. The young men sought a personally satisfactory relationship with God as the final extension of their inner, moral selves and validation of their commitments to others. Rationality would necessarily become the primary feature of their image of God. Yet the students discovered that their attempt to have their personal values serve as religious standards reactivated the same hesitations and disagreements that originally arose over the validity of rationality as a personal value. These difficulties were recorded in the exchanges of Aleksei Rzhevskii and Aleksei Naryshkin.

On the pages of *Useful Entertainment* Rzhevskii despaired of meriting salvation. Society was a hostile environment, he cried out, ill-suited for an individual's search for a virtuous course of action.[115] "There is no happiness in this society [*svet*], no matter how one lives, there is no happiness . . . no peace for the soul. Anyone who calls himself happy is wrong; we are all beset with troubles."[116] How could one, Rzhevskii asked, possibly live a virtuous life and achieve the merit necessary for salvation? He made no mention of reason or what it could accomplish. Man was a dependent creature whose individual efforts to achieve divine rewards were doomed.

Naryshkin responded in the next issue of *Useful Entertainment* and criticized Rzhevskii's failure to consider the power of reason.[117] "How weak is the mind [*um*], our R[zhevskii]! sunk in vices, to blame matters on others without understanding oneself. Is it not better to take note of one's vices and strive virtuously to correct them?"[118] Why, if not for this, did God give man rational faculties? "He [God] gave us reason so as to direct them [the desires], so that the goal of the passions was only virtue."[119] Naryshkin linked his idea of rationally restrained behavior with his conception of God. He did not, however, allow this association to lead him to a rational image of God. Naryshkin recognized only a divine sanction to the individual's efforts to follow a rational, virtuous course of action. He counseled Rzhevskii that he need not endure vice as an unalterable characteristic of society. An individual "tries to free himself of [his own] vices. As each would thus correct himself, society would be corrected [and] all evil uprooted. . . . One is in this world by the will of the Supreme Creator of all the universe for a life in . . . society. Together with everyone [else], each is created for a use . . . each should try to eradicate evil in society."[120]

Rzhevskii responded immediately and was apparently persuaded by his friend's admonitions. He was now ready to accept Naryshkin's explanation of the need to curb the influence of the passions. If reason was dominant, then "because of this, your life was useful, everyone was useful to you; [and] you were useful to society [*obshchestvo*]: life was pleasant to you, and society was acceptable to you."[121] If the passions were checked, then one could be both personally virtuous and useful to others; "preserving the happiness of all preserves one's own."[122] This reappraisal of the worth of individual initiative did not lead Rzhevskii to revise his notions about the Divine. In a subsequent contribution to *Useful Entertainment*, he appealed for God's intervention, not impartiality: "To you, my Master and God, I cry out. . . . On you alone I rest my hope. Through your will I have this life . . . through it alone I hope to be saved from [my] cares. I see myself surrounded on all sides by enemies; . . . but you are [my] defender." [123] Clearly Rzhevskii had either not realized or not accepted the connection Naryshkin had made between personal and religious values. While Rzhevskii came to admit that the individual was not necessarily corrupted by society and had, in fact, the capacity to direct and improve his conduct, he did not alter his pessimistic opinion that man was entirely dependent before God.

This debate was only one example of the Fonvizin group's hesitation to extend its personal standard of rationality to its religious values. Consistency required that the men's image of man as one who could rely on his reason to restrain his conduct and direct himself to lead a virtuous and useful life accord with their image of God. But this correspondence was not easily attained. The men in the Fonvizin group came from homes in which assumptions about human nature were formed according to traditional Orthodoxy, and man was understood as depraved and dependent. The God of their youth was the ominous, threatening, and vengeful God of the psalms of David. It was quite typical for a young nobleman to be required to study the Book of Psalms, at times memorizing them verbatim. [124] A straightforward fear of God was instilled in the three young men, which remained in their minds after they arrived at Moscow University and even after they had begun to speak so optimistically of the potential in human nature. During their university years Fonvizin, Novikov, and Bogdanovich to varying degrees broke with the God of their youth and sought to refashion their individual images of the Divine to accord with their personal ethical values. Later in their lives, however, they returned to the original Davidian image. Novikov had remarked that "God was my first tutor," but for all three men God was their last tutor as well.

Fonvizin's thoughts best reflected this hesitant reappraisal of religious ideas. His "Epistle to My Servants Shumilov, Vanka, and Petrushka," written in the early 1760s, [125] was meant to investigate the basic questions of why God created man and how man was to live in society. Fonvizin asked each of his servants: "Why is this society created? And how am I to live in it, give me your advice. . . . Say, I ask you, why are we created?" [126] Shumilov, an elderly servant, could only say that his existence was justified by his obedient service to his master. Vanka explained that "I consider all of society as nonsense. . . . And every single thing in society, it seems to me, is nothing but an annoyance. Here I notice foppery, and there I see avarice; wherever I turn, I see stupidity. . . . Everyone understands that contemporary society is depraved, but nobody knows why it exists."[127] Petrushka believed that "all of society . . . is a child's toy; it is only necessary . . . to know how best . . . to play with that toy. . . . That is how society turns around. But why it is so, neither a wise man nor a fool knows."[128] The three servants suspected that their master did not himself believe that man's purpose in society could be served by traditional, submissive attitudes, pessimistic complaining, or sarcastic fatalism, but was concealing the answers to the questions he had asked them. "Do not hide secrets from us; reveal to us the wisdom of your judgment, solve . . . the problem for us!"[129] The master simply responded in conclusion that "I myself do not know why this society is created."[130] Clearly Fonvizin's skeptical attitude toward life's fundamental questions implied that he was casting about for answers that would satisfy him.

For Fonvizin the questions posed to Shumilov, Vanka, and Petrushka were eventually answered by deism, though first he displayed a brief interest in what he feared was atheism. He joined a circle at Moscow University which was dominated by Prince F. A. Kozlovskii, a minor poet. Details about the membership in this circle are few. What was important to Fonvizin was that he was appalled for the rest of his life by his association with the Kozlovskii circle. As he admitted in his confessional memoirs, "I entered a society which I cannot remember hitherto without fear. For the best [way of] passing time consisted of blasphemy and irreverence. . . . At this time I composed the epistle to Shumilov in which certain verses reflect how wrong I was then, so much that from the work, many took me as an atheist."[131] Fonvizin's revulsion was born of time as much as conviction. His memoirs were written in the years immediately before his death in 1792 when he was anxious to reassure himself of his chances of salvation. He was quick to dismiss with horror his interest in the Kozlovskii circle as a whimsical episode, brief and best forgotten, in his experiences as a student. Nonetheless, the poem was one of several similar works he composed during the early sixties, a literary effort that is inexplicable if he was not reconsidering his religious beliefs.

Fonvizin, who discovered in deism the explanation for his own existence and role in society, may first have learned of it at the university, where the theories of Lord Shaftesbury were taught.[132] When Popovskii's translation of Pope's *Essay on Man* was published in 1757, it provoked the fury of the ecclesiastical authorities, who tried unsuccessfully to prevent its publication. The controversy may have attracted Fonvizin's attention though there is no direct evidence of this. He definitely was introduced to the basic tenets of deist thought by his close friend G. N. Teplov (1720–1770). Teplov advised him to read Samuel Clarke's *Proofs of the Existence and Attributes of God*,[133] a defense of the existence of God by a mild Christian rationalism. Clarke's image of God was as both an omnipotent unfathomable God and an intelligent "Governor of all things." At least one of his famous contemporaries, Anthony Collins, believed Clarke's religious ideas were decidedly more traditional than modern. Collins expressed only disdain for Clarke's deism. In responding to the latter's charge that Collins believed "too little," he remarked that Clarke "neither *believes too little* nor *too much;* but that he is perfectly, and exactly, Orthodox and in all likelihood will continue so." [134] Clarke's tempered deism certainly did not shock his contemporaries, and its mildness may have made it easier for Fonvizin to accept it. Fonvizin was delighted with Clarke's ideas, reading and rereading the book. He even proposed to translate it though eventually he wrote only a summary.[135] Viazemskii noted correctly that this interest in deism was not just a fad, as Fonvizin's own memoirs suggest, but a lasting characteristic noticeable in his later writings.[136]

Fonvizin made his first public comment on his deist beliefs in 1761 in a translation for *Useful Entertainment*.[137] In a short piece entitled "The Just Jupiter," he described a universe managed by an enlightened, beneficent ruler. Jupiter was not a god who intervened regularly to mete out vengeance or rewards but a detached observer of the world's evolution, the Voltairean not the Davidian god. His stance drew the criticism of some individuals. "Jupiter was finally enraged by the complaints that the human race so often lodged against him, . . . [particularly those from men] who were considered the wise ones. . . . How much more perfect society [*svet*] would be if they were Jupiters! Since they did not yet dare to challenge him [that is, Jupiter] and deny his existence, they tried to destroy the respect due him by a very dangerous method." [138] These unspecified "wise ones" sought to persuade the human race that Jupiter's impartiality was really the negligence of a "tyrant." Provoked by this charge, he decided to intervene in worldly affairs a single time to prove that individuals cannot rely on divine help but must discipline themselves for what fate will bring.[139] He granted the human race one wish, which proved to be to "give us [that is, the human race] that which will enable us to bear our burden. Give us the gift of knowing our fate in advance." [140] When the illusory attraction of this desire quickly became apparent, the people "attributed all of their unhappiness to Jupiter. Must we suffer more, they cried, from the knowledge of the evils that await us?" [141] This time Jupiter paid no heed to their "unreasonable" complaints and resumed his posture of benevolent neutrality. The futility of tampering with the universe's evolution was clear, as was the duty of believers to prepare themselves for their appointed fate. Rational and virtuous behavior was in accord with the operation of the mechanistic universe of "The Just Jupiter."

Unlike Fonvizin, Novikov did not accept deism in any clearly expressed, thoroughgoing manner. Always a believer, Novikov never recorded in print the precise character of his religious sentiments. He was quite disparaging of atheists. His disdain for them prompted him to translate in 1772 a book, *Contemporary French Philosophy*, that was, in part, an attack on atheism. [142] Strict Orthodox traditionalists also fared poorly at Novikov's hands. Consider an unsigned article he accepted in 1772 for his journal, *The Painter*, [143] which was written in the form of a letter to a young man from his uncle. The uncle cautioned his nephew against abandoning the sacred books for the sake of secular ones. "Why do you study these [that is, secular] books? Do you doubt the faith that is the only means of attaining salvation?" [144] The uncle urged his nephew to draw himself back from the brink of damnation by throwing himself at the mercy of God. "Do you know that God does not punish every sin, but, knowing our complete feebleness, demands only a contrite soul and penance?" [145] The uncle's image of God was the ominous God of David in the Book of Psalms, but neither this traditional image nor the position of the atheist was as acceptable in the 1760s as a rational image of God.

Bogdanovich understood the need in theory to realign his religious beliefs to fit his personal values. He was willing to accept religion as the means to confirm social tranquility and pass judgment on personal virtue, [146] but he was unable to proceed from this point to refashion his image of God. As the editor of *Innocent Exercise* in 1763, Bogdanovich accepted unsigned articles offering the broadest possible religious viewpoints. The journal usually described God in terms of being the ruler or creator, *povelitel'* or *sozdatel'*, both of which have deist overtones. The journal even included a lengthy article, probably written by Princess Dashkova, that implicitly endorsed Helvetius's philosophy. [147] Yet it is quite probable that Bogdanovich's own ideas remained unchanged. His "Spiritual Odes," written in 1760, drew on the psalms from David and reflected the traditional view of the omnipotent, vengeful God.[148] The only intimation that he was influenced by differing religious ideas was his rather facile and fashionable discrediting of fanatically superstitious religious practices.[149] Bogdanovich was aware of the need to correlate his personal with his religious values, yet his responses were ready solutions, well short of any basic changes. His lack of resolution showed that, like Fonvizin, he was confused about religious questions, but he lacked Fonvizin's intellectual discipline.

The character of the group's religious beliefs was clearer for what it was not than for what it was. Fonvizin and his associates readily identified both atheists and superstitious believers as religious extremists. They opposed in quite straightforward, uncomplicated terms the dominance of reason and the acceptance of deism against the uncontrolled influence of the passions and fervor for atheism or superstitious practices. Both atheists and superstitious persons failed to understand the motive force behind the universe. The atheists were guilty of pride, self-interest, and malice by assuming the world had no divine, guiding hand; superstitious individuals erred by not realizing that superstitions were characteristic of primitive societies in which reason was not yet mature. Neither side grasped the evolution in the universe toward societies in which the prevalent personal and religious values were rational. Sumarokov phrased this common opinion quite succinctly. Who erred more, he asked rhetorically, atheists or superstitious people? His answer was that both were equally wrong.[150] The students dwelt in an uncomplicated religious universe that did not require of them sustained attention to metaphysical or teleological explanation. Their need was to draw in their own minds a mental picture of a God whose primary feature was readily recognizable as similar to that of their own inner selves. They wanted the assurance that came from a conception of God that served to reinforce and validate their personal values.

The extension of self to God created a circle of commitment within which each man's duty to perfect himself was not threatened. The image of the Divine may have remained constant, but its presence varied over time. As students, their concern with fitting the image of God to the one they cherished of themselves gave their experiences with the Divine a sense of immediacy. They sought to perfect themselves by, in part, perfecting their relationship with God. This personal communion brought the supernatural close to their human concerns. Their bonds to God gradually slackened as they made other extensions of their personal selves during the early and mid-1760s. As they became interested in the political and social problems of the day, they reached a point in the mid-sixties when they almost never mentioned the Divine. Only after they were confident of their links to God could they allow themselves to be impelled by the force of moral imperatives into the arena of social action. Only after they tested the validity of their personal ethical values against the characteristics of contemporary society did they need to return to the security and serenity of an intense and immediate relationship with their God.

—— 9 ——

The dynamism of the students' ethical commitments was the fundamental element that distinguished their moral ideas from the notions and moods that pervaded Kheraskov's works. That there were similarities was not surprising. Kheraskov was a prestigious literary figure at a time the members of the Fonvizin group, still in their teens in 1762, were earning their credentials as writers. Yet Kheraskov's prestige came more from his official positions at the university and his status in capital society than the caliber of his literary talents. He cannot be credited with any significant originality of theme. He took what was for him a firm stand on principle when he chose to favor reason over passion and virtue over vice. Obviously his preferences were shared by innumerable contemporary writers. His condemnation of the malignant influence of wealth came several decades after the theme was stated in Pososhkov's famous *Book on Poverty and Wealth* (1724) and had already become standard in Russian publicist literature. Kheraskov's resort to the countryside as the environs suitable for a virtuous life and his less than zealous advocacy of rationality provided points of continuity with the sentimentalist writers of the late eighteenth century. His writings introduced the students to some of the main themes of eighteenth-century Russian literature. Nonetheless, their articles, poems, and essays were written for quite different purposes than those of Kheraskov. The students were not really interested in rationality or virtue as independent values. They had no desire to condemn the influence of wealth or to indulge in any type of literary ruralism. They were acutely interested in the principle of rationality as the criterion for defining their relationship to others, whether their peers, society as an abstract moral entity, or their God. What prompted the students to honor their duties to their fellow man was not what they learned from Kheraskov but from their professors at Moscow University. The ethical dictums of German natural law provided the moving force that impelled the students to seek an identity of the personal self in a series of extensions of the social self.

What had been for Kheraskov a rather listless, futile quest for the answers to life's most basic moral questions was transformed by the students into an active quest for moral fulfillment. German natural law lent the group's moral concerns a systematic, philosophic base that was not available to Kheraskov. Nevertheless, he and they recognized the priority of the inner self over all extensions of the social self. In that one respect, the works of Kheraskov and the Fonvizin group, however distinct in sophistication and complexity during the 1760s and 1770s, found common ground in the mid-seventies and thereafter.

The ethical questions that preoccupied the Fonvizin group during the early 1760s were, of course, not dwelt on *in vacuo*. Fonvizin, Novikov, and Bogdanovich were attending Moscow University to prepare for service careers in the civil or military bureaucracy. The code of personal ethics that they applied to themselves was soon to be inseparable from the demands of service. Since they accepted the priority of their personal self before all else and imposed on themselves the obligation to fulfill the dictates of the inner self, they were putting service on an ethical basis. Service was not only a question of loyalty to the ruler or faithful allegiance to the state. It was also a means to an ethical end, one that was defined before entering service and, initially, independent of both the tsar and the government. The Fonvizin group was forced by the logic of its members' convictions to work out criteria for service that the men could reconcile with their inviolate moral standards. While still students, they began to set down the ethical terms that permitted "honorable men" to work in harmony with the purposes of the state.

Their endeavors were complicated by the encroachment of the phenomenal world on their moral kingdom. They had to cope with the political realities of the early 1760s. As was the case with religion and society, politics was regarded as an involvement of the social self, one that was morally acceptable only as long as it reflected the image of the personal self. As they fashioned their political ideals, the Fonvizin group became immersed in the events leading to the palace revolution of 1762. The men committed themselves and their convictions to the service of Catherine the Great soon after the coup. When their politics and principles led them to contend with the very same difficulties that had undermined the validity of Sumarokov's ideals, their esteem for the assertion of the social self enabled them to consider the associations they made as, cumulatively, constituent parts of a fictional entity, not dependent on the authority of the ruler.

— **III** —

Political Ideals and the
Revolution of 1762

— 1 —

As the Fonvizin group prepared to leave the university, the sanctuary where reason and virtue were assumed to prevail, its members were resolved to join the imperial bureaucracy where they fully expected to display and test their moral virtues. Bureaucratic service was to be an appropriate arena in which to encounter individuals who embodied the very flaws of personality its members so righteously denounced in its journals and in which to promote their cherished ethical standards. The young men were not just men of words, but lived by their own ideals and worked to make them intelligible and acceptable to others. As men of fixed moral purpose, the members of the group imposed on themselves the obligation to work out political values that could be aligned with their personal and religious standards. For this reason the periodicals of 1760–1764 featured articles that argued for the advantages of rationality in political affairs. The students' political ideals of the early 1760s came to coincide with those claimed by Catherine II at the time of her accession in June 1762. For the students, politics was the means by which they would move out of Moscow University and into the offices of the central administration and the court of Empress Catherine. At the same time politics remained the means to ratify their moral expectations not only of themselves but of Catherine as well.

— 2 —

The students' first political writings were quite circumscribed. Their age and inexperience ruled out any possibility that they would speak to questions requiring detailed knowledge of the intricacies of the bureaucratic apparatus. From a vantage point within the walls of the university, their view of politics was all but exclusively focused on the person of the monarch. The students became interested in depicting a fairly precise image of an ideal ruler, one whose personal behavior and political decisions were regulated by rational and virtuous standards. In so doing, the students often described a monarch similar to that depicted by Elizabethan writers. This utopian monarch shared with its counterparts in the literature of Lomonosov and Sumarokov a dominant presence that precluded any distinctions between the state and the throne. Before all else, political questions were concerned with the integrity of the sovereign's character. This attention to the monarch, myopic in its focus, varied in degree. Lomonosov never overcame his fascination with the personality of the ruler, while the Fonvizin group's political ideals gradually became less reliant on the role of the sovereign. Their initial descriptions of the ideal ruler were phrased in terms quite similar to those employed by Sumarokov. The members of the Fonvizin group were seemingly putting themselves on the same path that led Sumarokov to the disappointments and disgrace of his final years.

The students spared themselves the indignities visited upon Sumarokov. They drew on intellectual resources not available to him, namely the political principles they were taught at Moscow University. The young men described the monarch according to their understanding of German natural law and neo-Stoicism. This intellectual lineage was not clear-cut, and several caveats are in order. Many of the students' articles about the utopian ruler contained descriptions that were bland and general. The influence of German natural law and neo-Stoicism cannot at times be distinguished from that of many other contemporary political philosophies. Even where the students were specific in detail, their references to neo-Stoic or German natural law politics were selective and indirect. Moreover, their comprehension of these philosophies was not immediate but a process that was to continue throughout the 1760s. The students of the early 1760s—and state officials of the mid and late sixties—portrayed an image of an ideal ruler that only gradually came to approximate the utopian monarch of neo-Stoic and natural law thought.

It would be useful at this point to describe the primary characteristics of the sovereign as portrayed by the neo-Stoics and German jurists. Reference will be made to the issues of political authority that attracted and maintained the Fonvizin group's interest for a decade, specifically questions about the nature of sovereignty, the proper functions of the ruler, and the legitimacy of popular resistance to an illegitimate monarch. The dominant political opinions among German philosophers were those of Pufendorf and Wolff. According to Holborn, Pufendorf's "influence prevailed in academic political thought" in early modern Germany.[1] Both Pufendorf and Wolff were concerned with defining the characteristics of a legal ruler, one whose status was validated by the nature of his services to the state and by the terms of his possession of sovereignty (*imperium*). Pufendorf found in the person of the monarch the source of political legitimacy. He was quite definitely opposed to any separation of governmental powers. Sovereignty was possessed solely by the monarch. The rights of the ruler were virtually unconditional, subject only to God.[2] A government that divided political sovereignty was "simply a case of *respublica irregularis;* and a state of that kind is a diseased or 'perverted' state." [3] Separation of powers was favorably considered in a single reference to the understanding that a monarch's rule could be ultimately limited (*imperium limitatum*)[4] by the assent of the citizens. This rather startling and potentially contradictory statement was, however, an exception.

Wolff, on the other hand, pursued the possibilities of limited sovereignty. "Supreme sovereignty [*imperium summum*] is originally with the people, and it remains the property of the people, even if it shall have been transferred completely to the ruler of the state as regards substance." [5] These rights were not exchanged when the people or nation (*gens*) formed civil society (*societas*) or when civil society submitted to a ruler.[6] As a guarantee of these rights, a governor should be accepted only with conditions. These stipulations, termed fundamental laws, were unconditionally binding on a monarch. "It is incumbent on him to govern the State well. . . . *Consequently he must not allow his sovereign authority over the state to lapse into personal arbitrariness. He has the obligation to know quite thoroughly the nature of his rights as ruler and their legitimate exercise.* . . . Similarly, he must be well-versed in the fundamental laws—if there are any—which he is duty-bound to honor." [7] Wolff seemed to revise Pufendorf's absolutist opinions in favor of popular sovereignty, a change significant for its potential implications for political opinion in the German states and Russia.

This element of Wolff's political theory was tested when he attempted to define what type of fundamental laws best served the nation. Laws establishing absolute popular sovereignty were dismissed as readily as those providing for absolute royal power.[8] The proper balance between popular sovereignty and royal power was defined only in somewhat circuitous, inferential fashion. In describing the relations between the throne and state, Wolff cited distinctions among what he considered three types of monarchical government. The "royaume hérile" was one in which "the King has the same rights over his subjects and their property as the master has over his slave;" [9] the "royaume Lacédémonien," one in which the ruler was obliged to execute the will of the "people" or "magnates," and, third, the "royaume légitime," one in which the monarch governed according to "fundamental laws." [10] Although the monarch's obligation to observe the fundamental laws was unconditional, his obligation to make his policies and actions conform to the positive laws of the kingdom was imperfect. This came about because the civil laws were not promulgated until after the original contract between the individuals-then-citizens and the ruler had been made.

The striking feature of Wolff's reliance on laws lay not in the content of the laws, which necessarily varied with circumstances, but in their attributes. Pufendorf ascribed to laws intrinsic moral qualities (*entia moralia*) that modulated an individual's conduct.[11] These qualities were autonomously recognized by each person, and this perception was at once described and confirmed by the civil statutes. In Wolff's case the relative import of the moral and technical senses of laws was changed. Laws were no more than directional in nature: "A *law* is defined as a regulation with which we are obligated to accord our actions." [12] Wolff considered the moral element but defined that as a derivative of acting in conformity with the law, both positive and natural.[13] He imposed on rulers the duty to represent the highest moral ideals.[14] Yet Wolff understood that conduct to be consequent to the monarch's observance of laws which, after the original convention vesting him with sovereignty, he could himself legislate. While Wolff's intention was to contain the monarch's activities within the framework of the laws of his state, the ruler's legal obligations did not have the potential to make the distinction between the monarch and the state anything more than artificial. Wolff's opinions on sovereignty attested to his essential agreement with Pufendorf that absolutist rulers, unhindered by any limitations, were preferable.

The ideal ruler of the German jurists was restricted not in his possession of sovereignty but in his exercise of it. The functions of a sovereign were commonly defined by Wolff and Pufendorf in relation to the goals of civil society. *"The purpose of society is* (1) *to provide the necessities of life,* . . . (2) *to maintain social harmony* so that it remains free of any fear of injury or violation of its rights, . . . (3) to protect *the security* of its members from the threat of violence from the outside. In sum, *the well-being of civil society consists in the possession of what is required for its sustenance, tranquility, and security."* [15] This understanding of the public welfare determined the acceptable functions of the ruler.[16] A monarch was to preserve the security of his citizens by neither insufficiently nor excessively guarding against wars. The ruler was allowed to go to war only on the very carefully specified bases of defense, a legitimate claim against another monarch, an irreparable wrong inflicted by one sovereign on the other, or the threat of an irreparable wrong.[17] Wars begun for any other reason were the consequence of rulers blinded by a passion for glory or revenge. "In every period the more civilized nations have recognized that unjust belligerents are to be classed with robbers, invaders, and bandits, . . . unjust war is not only opposed to the personal glory of the ruler of the state, but also to the glory of his nation, for which he ought to care." [18]

A monarch was capable of avoiding unjust wars and fulfilling his obligations to the common good if he cultivated the ideals of reason and virtue. A sovereign whose conduct was rationally regulated could resist any abusive implementation of his power. Without this "purity of mind," [19] a monarch is prey to his own passions and consequently is "devoid of the arts of reigning, and unconcerned, or insufficiently concerned, for the state, and prostitutes it to be rent asunder by the ambition or avarice of unworthy ministers; or . . . dreaded for his cruelty and proneness to anger." [20] A monarch should act with the same concern for security and order within his own state as he does in his relations with other states.

If the monarch violated his expected functions, did individual citizens have the right to question his legitimacy? Could citizens assume an adversary relationship toward the ruler? The German jurists analyzed this possibility by referring to the issue of just resistance. Pufendorf's writings were virtually unqualified in reaffirming the subjects' duty to obey a ruler no matter what. "Upon the subjects, indeed, there rests the perfect obligation of doing the bidding of the prince, and . . . the prince has ground for action against the disobedient. . . . But upon the prince . . . it is merely an imperfect obligation, for the reason that it merely binds him by the force of the law of God and the law of nature, but not as by the force of some civil law." [21] The sovereign's power overrode any evaluation of his conduct by his citizens. A citizen should resist his ruler only if the sovereign commanded obedience to a civil law that violated divine laws or if the monarch no longer protected the citizen but treated him as an enemy.[22]

This very narrow basis for just resistance was broadened somewhat by Wolff. The ruler had a perfect duty to obey his obligations to his citizens. "The sovereign has no right whatsoever to issue any order that is contrary to the fundamental laws. . . . *Should he do so there is no obligation to obey him any longer . . . and it is even permissible to resist the sovereign and curb his powers.*" [23] Citizens were not bound to obey a monarch who "tyrannized" and abused his authority.[24] But who was to judge a ruler's abuse of power? Popular opinion was dismissed as unreliable.[25] The only other assessor of royal conduct was the sovereign himself. Wolff's opinion led him to admonish subjects to obey a ruler whatever his qualities.[26] Wolff changed the bases for considering just resistance from a reliance on the quality of the sovereign's authority to the agreement establishing that power. Nonetheless, this contractual and potentially reciprocal premise was not as important as the more general agreement on the question of legitimate resistance. Pufendorf and Wolff provided virtually no theoretical bases for opposing the policies and authority of a monarch.

The two jurists' ideal ruler, restricted in his exercise of sovereignty but not his possession of it, was one who found a testy ally in the utopian monarch of neo-Stoicism. The ethical imperatives of Stoic thought imposed on every man, king or commoner, a duty of service. Politics was not a constant flux of purposeless actions and people, but one means of promoting the moral perfection of all men. When the individual detected this political purpose amid the seemingly chaotic course of everyday events, he recognized his duty to serve its cause. In politics as in ethics the first step toward recognizing this transcendent unity was to be taken within each person. Reason and virtue calmed the individual and equipped him to resolve the dissensions present in the political affairs of his time. Neo-Stoicism, in its high estimate of civic virtue, was more in the tradition of the great Roman Stoics, Seneca, Epictetus, and Marcus Aurelius, than in that of their Greek predecessors. Politics was an arena in which to demonstrate one's personal virtue and serve as a responsible citizen with an interest in furthering the common good. These obligations were particularly binding on the monarch. He was to represent in his person a model of self-control and the cultivation of virtue. His political status was similar to that of the utopian ruler of German natural law, but his power rested on a different base.

The neo-Stoic monarch's right to wield political power was conditional, not absolute. Subjects were to obey their rulers unless a monarch's policies were disruptive and injurious to the commonweal. A ruler's military victories were to be applauded unless they threatened the very existence of the enemy. Most important, the subject's right to condemn and resist an unworthy sovereign was not dependent on the quality of the monarch's authority or the fundamental laws. The power of recall was reserved for the moral judgment of the individual. Neo-Stoicism was primarily a reaffirmation of the ruler's authority to govern and his subjects' obligation to obey and serve.

Yet neo-Stoic ideas carried the potential to limit and undermine the validity of the political ideals of German natural law.

The relationship between these two philosophies was clearly illustrated not on the pages of the student journals of the 1760s but in the sculptural artistry of Etienne-Maurice Falconet (1716–1791). His stay in Russia (1766–1778) was the occasion for his famous statue of Peter the Great. Falconet's masterpiece portrayed the tsar as a heroic figure urging on his charger and with outstretched arm appealing to his people. Falconet's choice of imagery was quite deliberate. He modeled his Peter on a statue of Marcus Aurelius in Rome.[27] The tsar who enshrined German natural law as the official ideology of the state was lent the face of the emperor who was the epitome of Roman Stoicism. The Russian monarch who sought to embody legality as the instrument of social order was astride his steed encouraging observers to join him in a common endeavor to bring about by laws an ethically beneficial order. Peter engaged his civil servants in the administration of the state and rewarded loyal service with promotions in rank; the bronze horseman served as a notice to bureaucrats that service was an honorable calling as long as position and advancement were not achieved at the price of sacrificing the morally good. The tsar represented the politics of German jurists who allowed virtually no legitimate cause for opposition to a ruler, no matter how delinquent his person or policies; his statue was a visual message to its beholders that they were common members of humanity as well as subjects of the Russian government. The tsar's authority derived from his own claims to legality and his subjects' decisions of conscience. The power of the state was ratified in the quiet world within the individual as a mark of the indivisible link between the inner moral self and the political world external to him.

The potential impact of both German natural law and neo-Stoicism depended on the ability of the students at Moscow University to comprehend these political ideals, not as a body of political theories to be accepted or rejected in toto, but as a set of theories to be adapted to the circumstances of Russia in the early 1760s. Fonvizin and his associates could not possibly maintain the German ideals with the comprehensiveness and elaboration typical of the original German works. They were not philosophers but university students with limited intellectual experience. Nevertheless, the young Russians assigned themselves the ambitious task of interpreting the political principles of the German Enlightenment and adapting them to the realities of Russia in the early 1760s.

— 3 —

This process of refinement and assimilation has served in recent scholarly literature as the benchmark in assessing the political significance of the students' writings. Famous nineteenth-century publicists, such as V. Belinskii, N. Chernyshevskii, and N. Dobroliubov, created the historiographical bases which were continued and put in their most complete form by several Soviet scholars. Pigarev, Makogonenko, and Gukovskii readily characterized the cult of the ideal ruler in the journals of the early 1760s as the origins of a constitutional movement in Russia similar to those of mid-seventeenth-century England and late-eighteenth-century France.[28] The students were fired with the zeal of converts to a new faith when they were introduced by their professors at Moscow University to the political ideals of the Enlightenment in Europe. Alarmed at the despotism of the regime in the late 1750s and early 1760s, they were of common resolve in publicizing the image of a ruler whose regard for legality allowed for the establishment of "fundamental laws" or a "constitution." Convinced of the need for such reforms, Fonvizin, Bogdanovich, and Novikov tried in 1762 to win Catherine's endorsement of their ideals and were, apparently, successful. The basis was set for a later stand on principle against a monarch whose public image was unmasked and proved deceitful by her opposition to any limitations on her powers. For Gukovskii, Fonvizin and his associates were "constitutionalists" on the order of Sumarokov, that is, *frondeurs* who sought in legality a means of ensuring their own positions against the menacing power of the central government. For Pigarev and Makogonenko as well as Gukovskii the students were men of political principle. Their constancy of conviction made them the first of many whose resistance to the despotic powers of the sovereign culminated in strict sequential fashion in the Decembrist Revolt of 1825.

The analyses of Makogonenko, Pigarev, and Gukovskii remove the members of the Fonvizin group from the realm of purely literary figures, the role in which they were cast by non-Soviet literary and political historians. Moreover, by arguing that Fonvizin and his peers were "gentry constitutionalists," an invaluable focus is placed on the question of sovereignty, that is, on the students' opinions about the proper relation between the ruler and the ruled. What is not persuasive is the way Russian political ideals are integrated with those of contemporary European theorists. "Constitutional" ideas and references to "fundamental laws" were indeed parts of the political vocabulary of

English, French, and German philosophers and were frequently employed in their treatises. Yet little regard is given to the specific origins in European political theory of the students' "constitutional" opinions. Makogonenko stated in the introduction to his biography of Fonvizin that Russian writers' "ties with the French and German Enlightenment have not been fully discovered." [29] Nevertheless, he did not hesitate to categorize his subject as an enlightener and therefore a constitutionalist and necessarily an opponent of any autocratic regime. General references to contemporary European thinkers obscure the differences in the political character of the Enlightenment in each state.

"Constitutionalism" and "fundamental laws" were code words for a political philosophy in the German states that was markedly different from that in France.[30] The individual as a political creature was not isolated and alone, left to resist the encroachments of the state. He was considered a member of a political community whose common interests were protected by the governing body. In politics as in morals, the individual was obliged to serve the representative and guarantor of his social self. As the references to Pufendorf and Wolff demonstrate, the Fonvizin group could be considered constitutionalists only in the sense that a well-ordered government—one whose processes were regulated by laws—confirmed and strengthened the powers of an absolutist state.

—— 4 ——

The Fonvizin group should not be removed from undeserved affiliation with French and English enlighteners only to be categorized as the bearers into Russia of German political ideas, unaltered in content and understanding. The young men were not passive agents of contemporary European political ideals, German or otherwise. They were able to extract from the writings of German enlighteners their own version of the ideal ruler. The features of this image provide clues to the character of the students' relationship with the ruler.

In the student periodicals, the young littérateurs made repeated attempts to describe the necessary qualities of their version of the ideal monarch. This utopian image was best outlined by Sergei Domashnev,[31] who recounted his dream of a trip up a high mountain path. His escort explained that the path was one of false glory nourished by pride and vanity. Its travelers failed to master their passions. The author recognized Alexander the Great along the way and asked the guide the reason for this ruler's presence. His guide responded that *"Alexander* is called *Great* because he more than others is blinded by pride."[32] Alexander failed to realize that the glory he desired to satisfy his pride and vanity could not be attained by military victories but only by the betterment of his own citizens' prosperity.[33] Domashnev noted that "it seemed very strange to me that the name of Hero is given to people who surpassed others only in lawless actions [*bezzakonie*] and became famous by bloodletting, laying waste to lands, and causing countless calamities for the human race."[34] When, later in the dream, the author climbed a second mountain, following the path of true fame, he met fewer rulers. He encountered Marcus Aurelius, Augustus, and Peter the Great. The characters of these men were witness to the dominance of reason, cultivation of virtue, and more concern for benefiting their subjects than for waging unnecessary wars.[35] Domashnev's "dream" stressed the monarch's duty to act rationally by restraining his passions and avoiding "lawless actions."

Domashnev's criticism of warlike rulers was expanded and made more detailed by many of his peers. Belligerent monarchs, whatever the state or century, were individuals whose political standards sufficed to raise doubts about the validity of reason as a personal value, the very same apprehensions that were part of the debate over rationality as a relevant value for religious convictions. These doubts, born perhaps of cynicism or despair, were ultimately based on pessimistic appraisals of human nature. In a partial translation of Swift's *Tale of a Tub,* the translator chose a selection satirizing man's peculiar capacity to support large armies for mutual destruction.[36] Rulers whose conduct was not morally regulated were reminded that they had been commissioned by God to be the impersonal executors of his intentions.[37] Sovereigns were oblivious to this mission if they arrogated wealth, territory, and credit for victories. A monarch should remember that "those and only those are favored and acceptable to God who love peace and virtue."[38] A ruler who violated his expected role was threatened with God's revenge.[39] Monarchs who waged unnecessary wars and pursued expansionary foreign policies risked God's intervention, violated divine stewardship, and lacked the necessary rationally controlled conduct.

This concern with rulers who failed to fulfill their proper functions can be ascribed, to a certain degree, to the similar interests of Pufendorf and Wolff. Yet what accounts for the stress on this single part of the German jurists' political philosophies, particularly in comparison to the attention paid to the two other cardinal points of sovereignty and just resistance? The Russian students expressed no interest in deliberating on the nature and possession of sovereignty; the potentially provocative references to Pufendorf's *imperium limitatum* and Wolff's *imperium summum* were not pursued. Similarly, the very limited bases for just resistance were not described in print, let alone challenged. Even if the students were to be credited for being selective in their reference to the political ideas of Pufendorf and Wolff, the ideal monarch of the journals was not one whose qualities were directly derived from the model ruler of the German jurists. The striking feature of Domashnev's "dream" was not the clear presence of natural law ideals but the fact that they were almost never mentioned.

The students' portrayal of the ideal ruler was influenced less by the legal dictums of natural law politics than by their own interest in determining the ethical dimension to political authority. Dmitrii Anichkov returned in *Useful Entertainment* to the figure of Alexander the Great and described his encounter with "one reasonable man." [40] Alexander was warned to cease all hostilities. His love of war betrayed the aimless course of his life. Unless he repented, he was doomed to await the revenge of God.

Alexander could rescue himself from certain disaster if he realized his lack of self-knowledge. "Glory can never be attained by the slaughter of the innocent. . . . It has long been in the common knowledge of mankind that a good government is one in which the sovereign punishes the evildoers and rewards those who are good." [41] True glory is reserved "not for one who spends his whole life in constant wars but for a ruler who dies at peace with his world." [42] A "good" monarch controlled his political conduct by relying on the advice of councilors who were virtuous and reasonable men.[43] Their example demonstrated to their subjects that self-perfection was not a matter of riches and transient fame but of submission to the will of God.[44] Each man was to discipline himself to practice restraint and avoid aggression. The model of the king was followed by each subject as all joined in a common endeavor to attain individual and collective self-perfection. United by common resolve, "those in positions of responsibility are obliged to train those still unprepared, and these individuals must obey those in authority." [45] Alexander, at first delinquent in his personal and political conduct, was transformed into one whose self-reform set the standard for a moral regeneration of the social and political order. Anichkov's vision was the first glimmering of an ideal version of politics, one in which morality dominated concerns for legality.

For the students' purposes it was more useful to refer not to their trials with Alexander the Great but to their affection for Marcus Aurelius. The statesman-philosopher enjoyed a marked popularity in eighteenth-century Russia. His *Meditations* were reprinted in five editions between 1740 and 1798.[46] For the young men at Moscow University he served as the champion of Roman Stoicism and the embodiment of the moral sense they expected in a ruler. One contributor to *Good Intention,* a minor writer, A. Vershnitskii, provided the most extensive record of the emperor's merits. He was portrayed as a model of virtue and simplicity.[47] "Why do we mortals need to reside in opulent homes and magnificent palaces!"[48] Rulers require only virtue, wisdom, and moderation. A virtuous monarch governed with the willing assent of his "good" subjects and the fearful obedience of his "evil" subjects.[49] A worthy sovereign took advice from morally sound assistants and shunned the company of sycophants.[50] Vershnitskii put his praise for Marcus Aurelius in terms so general it was clear his work did not derive directly from the emperor's *Meditations* or other works. Vershnitskii implied a comparison between, on the one hand, virtuous rulers, morally sound advisers, and "good" subjects, and, on the other hand, monarchs in lavish palaces, flatterers, and "evil" people. He supplied the first details of the ideal political order outlined in Anichkov's article and intimated later refinements.

The political ideals of German natural law and neo-Stoicism were reduced by the students to a single set of constants.[51] They phrased their descriptions in such general terms that it was easy to compare their ideal ruler to the utopian monarch in the literature of many European political theorists and publicists. The Fonvizin group was undoubtedly influenced by the example of the utopian ruler described in Fénelon's *Les Aventures de Télémaque, Fils d'Ulysse.* Fénelon, like the students, imposed his political principles on the figures in his works. Fénelon's Telemachus recognized that he was invested by God to serve as the instrument of public happiness, a mission that required him to subject his passions to reason. Telemachus's rival, Pygmalion, disclaimed the values of reason and virtue and relied on force and an insatiable desire for ever more power. At one point Telemachus was asked by the Cretans to choose between a warrior-king or a peace-loving monarch. His answer was unqualified: a warrior-king's military aggressiveness was the product of personal ambition and brought only disorder and economic ruin to the conquerors while inflicting misery and suffering on the conquered.

Seven editions of Fénelon's book were published in eighteenth-century Russia. Versions of the original appeared in four different translations. The book was probably known to the students in the Fonvizin group. In fact, in

1769, Fonvizin referred to his translation of Paul Jérémie Bitaubé's *Joseph* as similar to *Telemachus* (*Telemak*), though presumably he meant the verse translation published in 1766 by Trediakovskii rather than another earlier translation of the French original.[52] The figure of Telemachus set in sharp relief those very same features that were prominent in the ruler imagery of the German jurists and neo-Stoics. Fénelon's volume publicized political ideals that were conducive to the formation of the students' own political opinions. His specific influence on them was, however, limited. He lent the prestige of his person to the political ideals of his time but phrased his statements of principle in terms so general as to coincide with those typical of several political philosophies, including the theories of German natural law. Fénelon's volume did not add to or alter what was contained in the works of the jurists of natural law. His book could be taken by the students as a testament to the validity of the ideals they had already made their own. Their model of a utopian monarch was a theoretical construct shaped to be in general accordance with specific points in Pufendorf and Wolff. The ideal ruler in the works of the German jurists served as the prototype for the students' version. It served time and again in the 1760s and 1770s as the referent to reconsiderations of the locus and exercise of sovereignty. Fénelon's book was not a source for the students' political ideals; rather it corroborated them.

The members of the Fonvizin group did not simply subscribe to contemporary European political ideals. Nor could the intellectual origins of their utopian monarch be directly located in a single source, whether German natural law or neo-Stoicism. The students were quite unwilling, in the early 1760s or at any later time, to adopt uncritically the ideal ruler of the German jurists and neo-Stoics. The young Russians were to prove reliant on natural law and neo-Stoicism primarily in the refinements they made to the image of the ideal ruler in the mid and late sixties and seventies. Then, as in the early 1760s, they were selective in their references to the political ideas of the German philosophers and the neo-Stoics because of contemporary Russian politics.

—— 5 ——

The students ventured away from the literary imagery of an ideal ruler and into the world of politics at the time of Peter III's accession to the throne. The tsar was the subject of many panegyric odes in the student journals. In

January 1762 Bogdanovich expressed the common opinion by praising the emperor as one who would "console the Russian lands, / and frighten her enemies."[53] His subjects should be grateful. "Virtue triumphs now, / Insidious malice is scattered by the wind: / Ours is a happy fate, / when PETER rules us."[54] Confident of the virtuous character of the new monarch, Russians could also rely on Peter for military protection. "Subduing destroyers of the peace / By the power of his own hand: / Who can take up arms in battle / Against the Russian Hero?"[55] Bogdanovich hoped Peter would personify in his character and programs the qualities of the ideal ruler.

Poetic language and political reality were more closely aligned in an ode published by Aleksei Rzhevskii in the March issue of *Useful Entertainment*.[56] Peter III was again portrayed as the defender of his people and the embodiment of virtue. Rzhevskii's hopes in Peter were confirmed by the manifesto of February 18, 1762, releasing nobles from obligatory state service, except in time of war. He praised the emperor's initiative as demonstration of his regard for his subjects.[57] "You are virtue incarnate, / Fear is not your power over us; / Love is the hallmark of your reign, / He is not considered great, / Whose rule is based on fear alone."[58] Similar remarks were made by Aleksei Naryshkin in the February and March issues of *Useful Entertainment*.[59] The students' odes to Peter III were their first comments on specific personalities and policies of the 1760s. They sought the utopian ruler of their ideals in the person of the actual monarchs of their day.

The students' commentary on the political realities of the day is striking because of their willingness to laud in verse someone like Peter III. Many of his contemporaries had a low estimate of the tsar and described him in terms that became historiographical commonplaces in the works of many nineteenth- and twentieth-century historians.[60] The emperor is consistently portrayed as a disreputable character whose official policies were ruinous to the integrity of the Russian state. Though Peter ended Russia's alliance with Austria in the Seven Years' War, he forfeited the credit due him from that decision when he was ready to dispatch units from the Guards regiments to recover a patrimonial claim to the duchy of Schleswig from Denmark. Rather than being a ruler who abided by the law, Peter was often unmindful of routine administrative processes. His government was dominated by personal cronies, notably Holstein relatives and German military officials. The return from exile of Münnich and Biron lent the regime unavoidable associations with memories of Anna's unpopular government.[61] Given these particulars about the tsar and the generally unfavorable regard for Peter in the scholarly literature, there is apparently sufficient reason to assume that the students' praise for him was, at best, a sign of their political innocence and, at worst, clear proof of their opportunism.

There is, however, reason to doubt this arrangement of the facts. The emperor succeeded in withdrawing Russian troops from their protracted commitment to Austria in the Seven Years' War. As Aleksei Naryshkin and Aleksei Rzhevskii noticed, releasing the Russian nobility from obligatory service was a popular measure among the nobles. His actions on other counts belie the conventional interpretation of his reign. Peter abolished Elizabeth's security police on February 21, 1762; he granted a measure of religious freedom to Old Believers on January 29 and released them from fear of the persecution they suffered at Elizabeth's hands; his reforms, particularly the decree of January 17 reducing the price of salt, dealt with issues important to the common people. If Peter was unpopular at the time, his problems were with those at court who did not benefit from his decisions and looked to Catherine to recover their own fortunes. Peter's reputation suffered in part because he lacked the ability to write his own rebuttals to contemporary critics. He never enjoyed the services of an apologist of high personal repute and established intellectual reputation. His wife could draw on the services of many defenders of considerable literary skill, the foremost among them being Catherine herself. When the students praised Peter in *Useful Entertainment,* they stated publicly expectations that were shared by many outside the court. The poems were reliable witness to the students' increasing interest in contemporary politics.

The students appealed to the tsar as the embodiment of their utopian ruler. He was to bring about the ideal political order whose characteristics were suggested by Anichkov and Vershnitskii and rephrased to refer to Peter by Bogdanovich, Rzhevskii, and Aleksei Naryshkin. Their idealism was tempered only by their naiveté. The students were novices in the world of politics and were not always well informed about current events. They were taken quite unawares by the coup of June 28, 1762. When the new regime stopped publication of *Useful Entertainment* after the June issue, the young contributors were genuinely surprised. In their first attempt to use the medium of the ode as a means of moving from the literary model of an ideal ruler into the world of the politics of their day, the students foundered seriously.

The palace revolution of June 28 and Catherine's accession to power were received by the Fonvizin group on terms that were consistent with their comments on Peter III. The new empress was the subject of odes by Bogdanovich, Karin, and Domashnev, each enthusiastic in praise of her, each careful to contrast the hopes in Catherine with what were now considered the disappointing characteristics of her husband's reign, and all, cumulatively, portraying an image of the new ruler as a law-abiding, peace-loving monarch.[62] A complete description was provided inferentially in one of Denis Fonvizin's first works to be published after the coup. The article was an extract from his translation of Jean Terrasson's *Séthos, vie tirée des monuments de l'ancienne Egypte.*[63]

Terrasson described an Egyptian ruler who "fulfilled faithfully all the duties for which she was obligated to the gods. . . . Her concern for the general welfare and zeal shown in that regard clearly demonstrated that she preserved the divine laws immutably and that they directed her heart." [64] Conscientious in observing her obligations to her own subjects, the monarch also "mastered external enemies by her bravery and her inviolate word." [65] The ruler "did all this with true virtue, respecting with good reason the fulfillment of her duties and the purpose of the general welfare. She did not use sovereign power for the satisfaction of her passions; but determined that the tranquility of her domains depended on the tranquility of her soul." [66] This description of a dispassionate ruler, careful to fulfill her duties—to defend her subjects and observe the laws—was an unmistakable sign of trust and confidence in Catherine and a restatement of the standards of official conduct expected of her.

The Fonvizin group did not merely write about the *coup d'état.* Several of them were actually caught up in the events of June 28, 1762. In the early morning hours of that day Catherine was awakened in her quarters in Peterhof, an imperial resort near the capital along the southern coast of the Gulf of Finland, and informed that her plans to depose Peter had been discovered. She set out immediately for St. Petersburg. Upon her arrival she went directly to the barracks of the elite Izmailovskii regiment. Its leader, Count Kirill Grigor'evich Razumovskii, ordered his men drummed into formation and put them at Catherine's disposal. She then moved past the quarters of the Semenovskii and Preobrazhenskii regiments, welcoming their hurrahs, and receiving their pledges of loyalty. Within the day Catherine won the support of the principal military commanders in the city as well as that of the senior officials of the civil bureaucracy and church. While all these parties gathered in the Kazan Cathedral to proclaim Catherine as autocrat, her husband was still not fully aware of the misfortune that had befallen him.

Peter retreated to Oranienbaum, another resort on the gulf a short distance west of Peterhof. In the evening of June 28 Catherine led a column of troops toward Peterhof and Oranienbaum. Peter surrendered without a fight, and his wife returned in triumph to the capital.

Novikov and possibly Karin and Domashnev were stationed in key military units and able to prove their allegiance to Catherine on June 28. Novikov and Domashnev were on the rolls of the Izmailovskii regiment. Novikov, a member of the unit since January 1762,[67] saw the future empress for the first time while on guard at the bridge that Catherine crossed to reach the barracks of his regiment. What he did subsequently is not clear. He may have marched to Peterhof and back[68] or simply been on duty at regimental headquarters when Catherine returned from the resort.[69] The role of Sergei Domashnev is also vague. He was on the rolls of the Izmailovskii regiment as of February 12, 1760,[70] and may have witnessed the coup. Similarly, Alexander Karin was involved to some unspecified degree. His biographer noted only that Karin "took an active part" in the events of June 28.[71]

The literary efforts to attract the empress's attention and favor were successful, though for reasons quite independent of the ideals expressed by the students. Catherine wanted to portray her husband as an arbitrary ruler given to needless military initiatives and create for herself a public image of a virtuous monarch, intent on ruling according to the laws and unwilling to pursue belligerent military policies.[72] Catherine's own attempt at ruler imagery was made most clearly in her declaration of good intentions proclaimed in the manifesto of July 6, 1762. The pose she wanted to strike coincided in its particulars with that of the ideal ruler publicized in the student periodicals.

The empress was disposed to reward the littérateurs by giving them their first appointments in the government service. In October 1762 Denis Fonvizin was transferred from Moscow University to the College of Foreign Affairs at the rank of lieutenant, tenth class on the Table of Ranks.[73] Bogdanovich began his service career on October 29, 1761, with an appointment "to supervise classes" at Moscow University at the rank of ensign, thirteenth class. In May 1763 he was transferred to the War College as a translator for Peter Panin.[74] Nikolai Novikov was promoted to the status of a junior officer.[75] Three other writers received promotions and ranks in the military soon after June 28. Paul Fonvizin was given a position in "the lower ranks" of the Semenovskii regiment of the Light Guards.[76] On August 3, 1762, Alexander Karin was rewarded for his commitment on June 28 as well as for his endorsements in print, by an appointment to the Horse Guards at the rank of cornet, twelfth class.[77] The promotions were quite modest tokens of imperial favor. The once-students-now-public-servants were favored by Catherine to a degree that fairly accurately assessed the benefits she derived from the literary commentary written at the time of her accession and, in a few cases, from the students' personal involvement in the events of June 1762.

These initial bureaucratic and military assignments, however modest, put the young writers in a vulnerable position, exposing them to charges of opportunism. The journalists might well be no more principled than Kheraskov; their interest in a utopian ruler could be perceived as no more than an elaborate use of political ideals to win the attention of the monarch. To be sure, the students were well aware of the advantages of currying imperial favor as they were about to leave Moscow University and enter the bureaucracy. Career advancement does not, however, suffice as the sole explanation of their concerns. The students were consistent in their support for their own conception of the ruler's proper functions. Public criticism of belligerent, delinquent monarchs served the writers well during the initial period of Peter III's reign but led them away from the course of political events in the early summer of 1762. The students' political writings were not simply prompted by the dictates of expediency, but by the imperatives of political idealism. Their descriptions of the ideal monarch were bold statements of conviction. Each was moved to appeal to the throne and act as "one reasonable man" speaking truth to power. When Catherine portrayed herself as a monarch whose policies would approximate the qualities of the ideal ruler, her public image enabled the students to seek her favor without violating their principles. They could support her on the basis of political conviction and, at least for the early years of her reign, reconcile political preferences and the promotion of their careers.

—— 6 ——

The young bureaucrats were, however, engaged in a contest with Catherine that was the same as Sumarokov's and had the same potential consequences. For, however selective the students were in the features they attributed to the utopian monarch and however harmonious the relationship between their politics and principles, their image of the ideal ruler remained in many ways not much different from that of Sumarokov or Lomonosov. The focus on the throne was not broadened sufficiently to identify as separate fictional entities the ruler and the state. Concerned only with the person of the sovereign, all the writers from Lomonosov to Fonvizin were primarily interested in the functions of the monarch. Sumarokov, with his call for rationality and consistency, had added the grounds for determining the legitimacy of the monarch's official conduct, but he was reluctant to question the bases of a sovereign's authority. He invoked the term for an illegitimate ruler, "tyrant," only in passing references rather than in a systematic bill of particulars. Even then, Sumarokov could brand as tyrants only the fictional rulers of his literary works rather than the Russian monarchs of his day.

The students adopted Sumarokov's ideals regarding the monarch and used the same vocabulary of political terms. These similarities of principle and language veiled significant differences. The premises behind the students' appeal for a legal ruler were quite foreign to Sumarokov's thinking. For the students and, among them, the Fonvizin group, opposition to belligerent rulers and arbitrary monarchs was not based on the failure of these sovereigns to act rationally and consistently. Rather, their inability to conduct themselves with restraint violated their functions as defined in German natural law and neo-Stoicism. The group evaluated a ruler's policies not by a literary standard, independent of philosophical bases, but by criteria whose validity depended on their ultimate derivation from comprehensive political and moral philosophies. The theoretical potential was available to the Fonvizin group to define the legitimacy of the monarch's rule. A ruler judged legally wanting could be cited for violations of "the fundamental laws" and denied the bases of his authority.

Conflict between the throne and the students was a most unlikely prospect in 1762. The two sides were hardly equals. When Catherine gave her subjects reason to expect her policies would be peaceful and within the law, she provided the students with a most welcome opportunity: they were able to reconcile their political ideals with the demands of service to the state. Their support for the empress was a case of a coincidence rather than an identity of interests. The students did not lend their voices to her cause only to be drawn, as Sumarokov had been, into the vortex of court politics and ultimately deprived of the principled basis of support for Catherine. They served the empress because this loyalty did not violate their interpretation of the political dictums of German natural law and neo-Stoicism. If she changed her plans for governing by laws and with peaceful intentions, her young supporters retained the option of withdrawing their support from the monarch. They could make their political loyalties dependent on the demands of their convictions rather than the interests of state. This possibility was forecast in 1762 by none other than Catherine herself. The imperial manifesto of July 6, 1762, implied what Sumarokov suggested and Wolff claimed, namely that the legitimate exercise of sovereignty was inextricably linked to the right to possess it.

The Fonvizin group came to terms with this problem quite haltingly, impelled by the logic of the members' convictions yet reluctant to accept the political consequences. Over the course of the 1760s and 1770s the students made various adaptations in German natural law and neo-Stoicism to fit the politics of Catherinian Russia. The political idealism of the early sixties was not uniformly maintained. For most of the students the tension between idealism and ambition proved to be too great and was resolved by placing careers before conviction. But for some among them, namely the Fonvizin group, steadfastness of principle was more important than bureaucratic advancement. The politics, policies, and personalities of the 1760s and 1770s were to sort out the characteristics unique to the Fonvizin group and distinguish its members from their former classmates at Moscow University.

The Fonvizin group's later political commitments and references to natural law and neo-Stoic ideals were to rely on the same moving force that originally brought its members as students to define their ideal ruler. They wanted to arrange a political order that corresponded to the one they had constructed in the realms of religion and personal morals. They continued to give their personal values pride of place over their replication in the various dimensions of reality. Given this priority the students' ideal ruler was in preliminary form the embodiment of their personal values extended and exalted to correspond to the status of the monarch. As they expanded and refined their interest in politics, they assumed that their moral values held sway over a broadening range of political interests beyond the ruler. The group's support for Catherine in 1762 was based on a rationale that allowed a gradually more sophisticated understanding of the state, their fellow man, and themselves.

Politics and Principle:
Commitments to the Panin Party

— 1 —

The members of the Fonvizin group left Moscow University for posts in the bureaucracy during the early and mid-sixties. As public servants rather than students, their comments on the ideal ruler were supplemented by specific remarks on contemporary reform proposals. Their opinions on politics acquired a level of sophistication and scope of interests that led them to defer consideration of a rational, virtuous monarch and talk instead of a rationally administered government. The impetus for this change in their thinking came from the assignments they received in their new posts. Their duties, in turn, required that the Fonvizin group refer back to the texts of German natural law for guidance, information, and theoretical maxims. In so doing the young men not only carried out their bureaucratic chores but also worked out an idealized conception of the proper duties and operations of the state. They were not simply obliging servants of the state but bureaucrats whose ideals and *modi operandi* were potentially independent of commands from the throne and the policies of their bureaucratic superiors.

— 2 —

All the members of the Fonvizin group were bureaucratic clients of Nikita Panin. Their first jobs were with Panin or one of his associates, and subsequent transfers were all from one member of Panin's party to another. Given this record of service, what the three men were to write about politics is fully understandable only by reference to the composition, political values, and reform proposals of the Panin party.

In eighteenth-century Russia parties were not organized along lines similar to their seeming counterparts in contemporary England. Russian political parties were "familial and personal patronage networks that dominated the court and upper administration. These 'parties' constituted the main sphere of policy development, supervised the recruitment and training of personnel for high office, and supplied the organization that made for effective policy implementation."[1] The Panin party was composed of individuals who worked their way to positions of influence via service in the colleges and Senate. As a consequence they acquired the means to manipulate the levers of power in the main institutions of the state apparatus. They allowed themselves to assume that their abilities—in terms of experience and knowledge of the management of the central administration—stood them in good stead in contrast to those of their chief rivals, the clientele system led by Grigorii Orlov and his brothers, Ivan, Aleksei, Fedor, and Vladimir. Grigorii Orlov was a former artillery officer in the Guards regiments stationed in the capital. In the months before the coup of June 1762, he used his position to win over these elite units to the side of Catherine and summoned them to action on the night of June 28. Grigorii also enjoyed the singular power of one with whom Catherine was quite genuinely in love. For the Orlov party, the loyalty shown the new empress and the services rendered on June 28 were sufficient bases for the influence they believed was their due. The Orlov and Panin parties were not the only ones at Catherine's court, but they were the only ones contending for political dominance. For the first ten years of the empress's reign the Panin party regarded its opponents as no better than parvenus, inexperienced and unfit for positions of great power. In its turn the Orlov party recognized the experience of the Panins, but attributed it to the privilege of the well-born, not the merit of the competent.

Despite each side's claims to worth and political power, the struggle between the dignitaries, as Panin's party might be labeled, and the favorites, as the Orlovs' faction was known to contemporaries, was no more than a rivalry between two contenders for imperial favor and bureaucratic influence. The goals of both groups were similar, namely to gain control over the patronage and policies of the imperial bureaucracy. Each party tried in 1762 to get "in" and keep the other "out." The scholarly literature on this bureaucratic struggle exhibits a clear preference for the Panin clique. Possibly, this bias is due to the fact that some early commentators on Catherinian politics were on the staffs of members of the Panin party, for example Denis Fonvizin himself. Possibly, many nineteenth- and twentieth-century historians were attracted by the Panins' alleged "constitutional" schemes.[2] The conflict between the dignitaries and favorites was not even particular to its own time. Peter the Great, for example, was as interested in establishing in the Table of Ranks a set pattern for bureaucratic assignments and promotions as he was willing to circumvent this process by suddenly elevating favorites like Alexander Danilovich Menshikov (1673–1729) to positions of great power. The Orlovs and the Panin party could find ample and equal justification for their positions by reference to the Petrine tradition.

Nikita Panin was the chief advocate of the view that merit and experience should be the prerequisites for government service. His reliance on these criteria was justified in his own mind by his successful diplomatic career. He was appointed Russian ambassador in Copenhagen in 1747. Soon thereafter he was transferred to Stockholm, where he served for twelve years before his return to St. Petersburg in the late spring of 1760. While in service at the Swedish court, Panin was informed of his appointment as *oberhofmeister* to Grand Duke Paul. He was informed of his new duties, according to Ransel, no later than November 1759 and assumed them upon arrival in St. Petersburg.[3]

This position at the Russian court was the vantage point from which Panin witnessed the final days of Elizabeth's rule and the short reign of Peter III. The latter's administration came to represent, in Panin's own words, the worst consequences of a government not managed by men of merit: "[Peter's] favorites were fools or traitors. He indulged himself with them in the most dissolute debauchery of drunkenness. His mistress, Mlle. Woronzow [*sic*], was ugly, stupid, annoying, [and] offensive. Peter believed it was fashionable to have a mistress. . . . All minds, except those which were as depraved as Peter's, were therefore alienated from him; no one was satisfied with him; they wanted another sovereign no matter what trouble it would bring."[4] Repelled by Peter as a person and a ruler and threatened by the tsar's apparent disdain for the routine bureaucratic and legal processes, Panin joined the conspiracy that brought about the overthrow of the emperor.

The nature of the threat Peter seemed to pose must be precisely understood. It was not simply that the tsar paid no heed to men of merit and experience. Panin was not primarily concerned with representing those who worked their way up the bureaucratic ladder only to be scorned by the emperor. After all, his own career began with an ambassadorial post at the age of twenty-nine, an appointment that, despite his claims to the contrary, was hardly typical or a matter of personal merit. He meant to represent those individuals who acquired experience in the bureaucracy and also belonged to the leading families, prestigious by blood or marriage, that had risen to positions of influence under Elizabeth. As Ransel noted:

It was precisely in the senate and other leading administrative bodies of the empire, where positions were monopolized by the leading families, that these older officials saw an effective guarantee for their continued security, retention of their wealth and status, their last line of defense against autocratic caprice. They had spent twenty years building the authority and independence of these institutions and were loath to see them destroyed by a new ruler. They wished rather to extend the authority of these institutions, regularize their functions, and define their relationship to the sovereign in such a way as to reduce the charismatic, personal, and ultimately capricious aspect of autocracy. . . . These changes would affirm the bureaucratic service hierarchy rather than imperial favoritism as the main upward route to political power.[5]

Regularity in the formulation and implementation of policy was the standard against which to measure Peter III and the favorites of any reign. It also marked the standard held up by Panin in 1762 first to Grand Duke Paul and, when his accession was barred, to Catherine as well.

The political principles of the Panin party corresponded to those contained in the imperial manifesto of July 6 and, in particular, Catherine's announced intention of legislating "governmental regulations." Panin himself wrote that section of the manifesto.[6] Within the month he submitted to her the proposal that served as the specific means of carrying out the general policy directions of the July 6 manifesto and as the key statement of the political interests of the Panin party. The proposal was the famous plan for the institution of an Imperial Council (*Imperatorskii sovet*).

In a memoir accompanying the proposal, its sponsor provided the historical background to justify his "reform." He described the effects of the Seven Years' War on Russia in terms of the depletion of resources, economic disorder, and excessive demands on the state treasury. Panin phrased these points quite succinctly in a talk with de Breteuil, the French ambassador. According to de Breteuil's report to his government in October 9, 1762, Panin told him that "the interests of Russia require that she occupy herself for many years only with the general reestablishment of all the parts of her internal administration which is in such a state of disorder as to demand prompt remedies."[7] Why did the Russian government impair its own internal order for the sake of extensive and extended military involvements abroad? Panin's answer was clear: because of a breakdown in the institutions of government. Elizabeth attempted to rule with the assistance of a personal cabinet, composed of court favorites. The results were no less than a disaster in terms of the efficient management and proper order of the bureaucracy. "Capricious favorites abused the cabinet, corrupting the form and good order of government; from everywhere business was transferred to the cabinet, and the cabinet's prejudiced decrees and orders resulted in matters never being settled. . . . [The favorites] created their own governmental procedures and ruled through them. . . . Favor and seniority became everywhere the basis for assignments; nothing was left to talent and merit. Arbitrarily and by means of court intrigue everyone was grabbing and taking possession of the section of government he expected to be of greatest convenience in defeating his rival or for combining with others against a third." [8] When Elizabeth came to rely on a formally instituted Conference (*Konferentsiia pri vysochaishem dvore*) during the final years of her reign, this body could not successfully contend with the favorites nor stem their abusive practices.

The Conference was abolished by Peter III on January 29, 1762. The tsar then authorized by an edict of May 18, 1762, the meetings of a new council, not even titled, and staffed it with his cronies from Holstein. The council's place within the government was not strictly defined. Moreover its members derived their power from their personal relationship with the tsar. Panin was appalled by its example. Without legal position in the apparatus or duties defined by statutory law, Peter III's favorites were given great power, but no responsibility. They were put in a position in which they were able—and did so successfully in Panin's view—to take advantage of the debilitated conditions of the central institutions, particularly the Senate, and usurp the monarch's power.

Panin's memoir carried his own interpretation of the reigns of Elizabeth and Peter. Panin was no more impartial in his comments on Peter than Catherine herself. As coconspirators in the coup of June 28, 1762, both had an obvious stake in portraying Peter III in dismal terms. His reign was to stand in unenviable contrast to the splendid days of Catherine's rule. Panin's own account arranged the historical detail in a way that benefited a specific political goal: the creation of a new institution that ensured regularity in the processing of official business and protected the principal governmental institutions against rule by the arbitrary power of favorites.

To rectify past abuses of institutional order, Panin proposed the creation of an Imperial Council, an advisory body with official legal status and well-defined functions.[9] The council was to be composed of six to eight members who deliberated on "everything that is to serve the autocrat personally in his efforts at increasing and improving the state." [10] Questions of foreign or internal affairs were handled by the appropriate collegial office, routed to the council for final review, and then submitted to the ruler. The plan was to institute a method of government operation that would prevent any interference in the routine handling of affairs by the favorites. Panin urged that as a twin to this council the Senate be made into a primarily judicial body, reorganized to regain the capacity to manage its duties. If both institutions were reformed, Panin assured the empress in the preamble to the proposal, it would "secure on an indestructible basis the forms and procedures by which—under imperial autocratic power—the state will always be governed." [11]

Panin's arguments for the Imperial Council in terms of political principle are tenuous. It is doubtful that the military engagements and economic difficulties of Elizabeth's final years can be accurately attributed to the faulty functioning of the mechanisms of government. Even if that were the case, why did Panin, once in power by October 1763, lose interest in some version of a council project? [12] Panin's proposal was not born of circumstances peculiar to Russia in the late fifties. His plan had several precedents. During the reign of Catherine I, the influence of the current favorite, Menshikov, was curbed by the establishment of the Supreme Privy Council (*Verkhovnyi tainyi sovet*), created in February 1726 and abolished in 1731. Anna's favorite, Biron, was limited by the Cabinet (1731–1741). In 1747 Chancellor A. P. Bestuzhev-Riumin, then the dominant voice in the bureaucracy, resisted the efforts of M. L. Vorontsov to check the chancellor's power by forcing him to make decisions in concert rather than on his own authority. Bestuzhev in turn used the same tactic in 1756, when he was losing power to the Shuvalov brothers and sponsored a "secret Military Council" as a means of regaining his former influence.[13] Panin's proposal of 1762 was but one more episode in the history of eighteenth-century Russian bureaucratic "reforms" proposed by one court faction to stay in power when challenged by another clique or, if not in power, to get there. Panin offered his Imperial Council to Catherine as a purely bureaucratic reorganization to ensure his superiority over the Orlovs.

—— 3 ——

Panin's tactics and motives were surely not known to the young public servants in the Fonvizin group. They could readily detect in his reading of the reigns of Elizabeth and Peter III apparent similarities to their own criticisms of utopian rulers, reckless in their involvement in unnecessary wars and disdainful of the established legal processes. The similarities belie the considerable difference between Panin's version of the reign of Peter III and the students' own accounts. The young men were as enthusiastic about Peter as they were about Catherine. They were innocents amid the factional maneuvering and political events of the first half of 1762. Panin's court politics were quite removed from the abstract moral statements of the students.

After the Fonvizin group was assigned to bureaucratic posts under Panin or individuals in his party, his political opinions served as guidelines to redirect the group's own thinking. The idea that regularity should govern the decisions of the throne was extended to apply to the operations of the central institutions of the state. Concern for the moral welfare of all Russians was redefined in terms of the economic and financial conditions necessary for the well-being of the Russian people. Because Panin and the Fonvizin group quite coincidentally shared certain general opinions, the new public servants were able to maintain the political ideals of their student days and refine these principles by referring to the particular reform projects of their bureaucratic superior. Their idealism was sheltered by their position. They could afford to be consistent in their political ideals because they benefited from the protection afforded them by their status. This harmony of theoretical and bureaucratic interests was sustained as long as the group's moral concern for political issues was not challenged by Panin's tactical interests. After all, when the Fonvizin group worked for enactment of Panin's reform proposals, the men were hardly acting as Panin's equals. However consistent and true to principle they were in political issues, they were beneficiaries of Panin's good will only as long as his calculations of court politics happened to represent or appear to represent their political principles. Panin's favor protected and encouraged their steadily increasing reference of personal moral principles to ever-widening spheres of governmental and economic affairs. His influence with each of them induced the young bureaucrats in his offices to view these issues through his eyes.

The members of the Fonvizin group worked not just for Nikita Panin, but for several key individuals in his party as well.[14] Princess Dashkova was a close associate of Panin, so close in fact that she once, in typically mischievous style, called Panin "either my lover or father."[15] She persuaded Panin in 1760 to cooperate with Grand Duchess Catherine.[16] The princess was also instrumental in winning the loyalty of her uncle, Mikhail Vorontsov, the chancellor and director of foreign affairs after Bestuzhev-Riumin's loss of influence in 1758.[17] Nikita Panin was himself responsible for winning the support of Kirill Grigor'evich Razumovskii, the commander of the Izmailovskii regiment of the Guards in 1762.[18] Ivan Perfil'evich Elagin at first worked with Panin because of his hatred for the Orlovs, known and reciprocated, not because of any belief in Panin's political schemes. Elagin later came to admire Panin, describing him in his own *Memoirs* as "the perfect benefactor for the human race." [19] Nikita Panin's younger brother Peter distinguished himself by his leadership during the Seven Years' War and, soon after the revolution of 1762, was put in charge of the Russian armies still deployed in Central Europe. Catherine appointed Peter Panin to the Senate and valued his candid, not to say blunt, criticisms of her policy.

As described in the last chapter, Denis Fonvizin began his service career at the College of Foreign Affairs in the fall of 1762. The court had traveled to Moscow the previous month for the coronation ceremonies, and there Vice Chancellor A. M. Golitsyn had arranged for Fonvizin's appointment. Fonvizin's credentials were, before all else, a working knowledge of Latin, French, and German.[20] His facility with language stood Fonvizin in good stead, for he was soon translating "very important" papers directly for the chancellor, Mikhail Vorontsov. In December 1762, the young translator was sent abroad to bestow the ribbon of the Order of St. Catherine upon the duchess of Mecklenburg-Schwerin.[21] After his return he published a translation of Voltaire's *Alzire* and caught the attention of Elagin. Fonvizin's favor with the confidant of the empress led to his reassignment on October 7, 1763, as Elagin's secretary and promotion in 1764 to the rank of titular councilor, ninth class in the bureaucratic hierarchy.[22] Since Elagin was part of Catherine's entourage, he and his new secretary accompanied the empress wherever she went. More important, Fonvizin's duties now included preparing petitions for Catherine's review as well as writing, though infrequently, précis for reports to the empress.[23]

These contacts, surely a heady experience for a twenty-year-old recent graduate, brought Fonvizin many advantages but also forced him to work with Vladimir Ignat'evich Lukin (1737–1794), Elagin's other secretary and a literary figure in his own right. Lukin and Fonvizin became such bitter personal enemies that Fonvizin wrote his family on June 26, 1766: "I swear by God to you that it is impossible to imagine all of the maliciousness, all the idle cunning that he [Lukin] used to discredit me in the mind of Ivan Perfil'evich. . . . . Despite the fact that I am poor and must seek happiness by my service, he did this so that I would be forced to leave the service." [24] Fonvizin was easily put in a dither. Whenever Elagin gave any sign of preference for Lukin's literary or bureaucratic talents, Fonvizin was likely to be thrown "into despair." [25] These clashes with Lukin were resolved only when Fonvizin left Elagin's service.

On December 9, 1769, Fonvizin was promoted to the rank of court councilor, seventh class, and transferred back to the College of Foreign Affairs to work directly under Nikita Panin. Their cooperation on political and diplomatic plans led to a personal friendship which lasted until Panin's death in 1783. Fonvizin became a trusted worker who could be assigned weighty, even politically sensitive, tasks. The minister gave Fonvizin supervision over the correspondence between the ministry and several important Russian ambassadors, Zinov'ev in Madrid, Bulgakov in Warsaw, Musin-Pushkin in London, Obreskov in Constantinople, and Osterman in Stockholm. When Peter Panin was rather quickly retired from the Turkish War in 1771 and ordered to live on his Moscow estates, Fonvizin was given the task of keeping him informed of political events in St. Petersburg. These assignments, telling indications of the Panins' trust in Fonvizin's integrity and abilities, also included his participation in their project of the 1780s to establish permanent laws to "reform" the administration of government.

This clientele network provided the means for many young public servants to rise through the ranks and achieve advantageous service posts.[26] Bogdanovich was appointed on May 3, 1763, to the College of War and assigned on May 26 to work as a translator for Peter Panin. This position was arranged by Princess Dashkova, then Bogdanovich's colleague in *Innocent Exercise*.[27] There is no direct evidence as to how Bogdanovich fared with Peter Panin. Within one year, however, he was transferred to the College of Foreign Affairs to work with the older Panin.[28] Here Bogdanovich remained for almost twelve years as a translator, except for a brief appointment at the court in Saxony. He was promoted to the rank of collegial assessor, eighth class, with duties in the Senate on March 23, 1776.[29]

The posts Fonvizin and Bogdanovich occupied in the College of Foreign Affairs were rich in prestige and rewards in terms of ranks and duties. Obviously, they did not come by these positions because of the force of their political convictions. They benefited from government policy toward the personnel of the college. A potential public servant usually joined a college at the lowest rank as a *iunker,* fourteenth class, and worked his way up the bureaucratic ladder. Only the College of Foreign Affairs was allowed to hire new men at a rank determined by particular abilities, such as knowledge of foreign languages.[30] The College of Foreign Affairs along with the other "primary" colleges (War and Admiralty) also had the power to evaluate and promote their own employees without reference to the service lists in the Heraldry Office.[31] Moreover there were advantages in terms of salary levels. Troitskii noted that rank holders in the primary colleges were paid higher salaries than those allotted officials in the other colleges.[32] These benefits were still again augmented by the prestige and visibility of jobs in the College of Foreign Affairs. Fonvizin and Bogdanovich enjoyed the special status that came to individuals frequently in the company of the Panins or, occasionally, of the empress. The young men did not have to share that notice with many others. The College had only twelve staff members in 1779,[33] so that all its officials enjoyed prominence as members of the government elite.

Only Novikov was willing to forgo climbing the rungs of the bureaucratic ladder so as to devote himself to literary interests. He remained on the rolls of the Izmailovskii regiment, which was under the command of K. G. Razumovskii. There are reports that in 1768 he resigned from the regiment at the rank of lieutenant. Thereafter Novikov's bureaucratic relations with the senior members of Panin's faction are not as clearly delineated as is the case with Fonvizin and Bogdanovich. Novikov could not have legally resigned from the Izmailovskii regiment in December 1768,[34] since he was prohibited from leaving the service when Russia was at war, and hostilities with the Ottoman Empire had begun before December 1768. There is one report that he transferred from the military to the civil bureaucracy and received an appointment in the College of Foreign Affairs shortly after 1768 with duties as a translator working directly for Nikita Panin. Makarov noted in 1839 Panin's familiarity with Novikov's writings, though this may well be no more than a hint of Panin's reading habits.[35] Even if the official bureaucratic link is not clear-cut for the post-1768 period, Novikov's writings are compelling evidence that politically he remained a client of the Panin party. His works contained opinions of both the dignitaries and the favorites similar to those of Fonvizin and Bogdanovich.

Were this similarity only a casual one it would not suffice to sustain Novikov's credentials as a member of the Fonvizin group. Compare his example not to Fonvizin and Bogdanovich but to his former university colleagues. Sergei Domashnev left the university to join the infantry company of the Izmailovskii regiment. By the time of the outbreak of the war against the Turks, Domashnev had risen from the ranks to a position on the regimental general staff. During the war he sought Grigorii Orlov's favor and was part of Orlov's retinue at the peace conference with the Turks at Focsani (in present-day Rumania) in 1772. Sometime in the early seventies, he was promoted to the ninth class with duties as a gentleman of the bedchamber. His political ideals were altered to accommodate the changing demands of his service career. His "dream" of an ideal ruler who disdained the false glory of military victories gave way to two odes, written during the Turkish War, that praised the exploits of Russian commanders.[36] Since the extended Russian military and naval campaigns were planned by the Orlov brothers, his writings were occasioned by the opportunism of the serviceman, not the principles of the student.

Paul Fonvizin followed a similar course. After the university he transferred to the Light Guards of the Semenovskii regiment. He also was in Orlov's company at Focsani. There is, however, little evidence of what he wrote after 1764 or which ranks he earned during the 1760s.[37] Aleksei Rzhevskii and Aleksei Naryshkin were quite similar cases. Naryshkin continued to publish—selections from articles in *l'Encyclopédie* were translated in 1767—and receive promotions in the service. He was awarded the rank of major, eighth class on the Table of Ranks, in the same year he wrote his translations. Naryshkin was consistent in his literary and bureaucratic interests but inconsistent in relating one to the other. The translations were made at the behest of and in the company of Grigorii Orlov during the famous imperial voyage down the Volga.[38] Naryshkin, the advocate of regularity in politics during his student years, tried only a few years later to ingratiate himself with a man whom he could only regard as a recipient of imperial favor, not a beneficiary of bureaucratic regularity. Rzhevskii also contributed translated articles from *l'Encyclopédie* in 1767, was promoted in the same year to the status of a gentleman of the bedchamber, and won the attention of the Orlovs.[39]

The simultaneous interest in literature and politics is not what differentiates Rzhevskii, Naryshkin, Domashnev, and Paul Fonvizin from Denis Fonvizin, Bogdanovich, and Novikov. The use of literary skills to enhance one's political standing was a common practice among eighteenth-century Russian writers. Fonvizin, for example, published several translations[40] to certify his linguistic skills before Golitsyn offered him his first appointment; he translated *Alzire* in 1763 and, within a year, was rewarded with a promotion in rank; and his career was furthered by *Brigadier,* written by 1769 when he was again promoted. The same timing of literary work and bureaucratic promotion was evident in Bogdanovich's career. There was, nonetheless, not the same correspondence between literary and political interests in the group's works as in those of Rzhevskii, Naryshkin, Domashnev, and Paul Fonvizin. These four men used their literary abilities to improve their political fortunes. Their goal was to find sinecures that facilitated their literary endeavors which, in turn, won them additional notice and promotion. Rather than follow this common sequence the Fonvizin group used its literary talents to publicize political values consistent with the ideals of its university years and careers with Panin.

The Fonvizin group did not take the route of the opportunist but of the idealist. Its members reconciled principle and position in a manner that was quite distinct from Lomonosov's impartiality toward politics and Sumarokov's lack of interest in aligning career and conviction. The members of the Fonvizin group were neither impartial observers of political events nor simply participants in the politics of their day. At the onset of their careers they were advocates of the political plans of the Panin party.

— 4 —

How were the young public servants to promote the advantages of some type of council and discredit the role of favorites? The task surely gave them pause. As students they wrote on the lofty question of the utopian ruler, not the specific issue of a council. In their university days they had no reason to trouble themselves with any concern about a council. When they became members of Panin's clientele network and wanted to describe the purposes of a council, they had few guidelines to follow. Council projects had received only sporadic mention in Russian literature of the first half of the eighteenth century. Existing descriptions, like those in Pososhkov's *Book on Poverty and Wealth* (1724) or in Sumarokov's "Dream of a Happy Society," tended to emphasize the moral character of the councilors, rather than the institutional status of the council as a specific part of the bureaucracy.[41] These precedents could not serve the Fonvizin group well in the formulation of its own plans.

For that assistance Fonvizin and his peers turned to the useful references to a council project in the works of Wolff and Pufendorf. The group invoked a council plan that was consistent with their own ideas of an ideal ruler and capable of providing the legal precision and detail to become part of an integrated conception of an ideal state. As bureaucrats in the mid-sixties no less than as students in the early sixties, the Fonvizin group sought a theoretical basis for its literary and service interests without incurring any serious difficulty in reconciling one with the other.

The Fonvizin group could draw on the idea of a council in the works of German natural law theorists without needing to adapt that model to contemporary Russian politics. German jurists of the seventeenth and eighteenth centuries did not describe the advantages of a council as systematically as they had those of the ideal ruler. A council was not assumed to be a primary part of the organization of a government. It was not to represent an estate in the form of the social and political corporations of medieval Europe. Nor was it to become so independent of the estates, the member entities of society, that it would function as a component of a state apparatus that dominated those constituents. In the writings of natural law theorists, a council was desirable in that it acted to defend the ruled from the potential abuse of the ruler, but it was potentially dangerous in that it improved the monarch's ability to implement his policies, no matter how abusive. Pufendorf and Wolff were reluctant to define the legal status of a council with the juridical precision that characterized their descriptions of a ruler. Rather than discuss the legal functions of a council both men dwelt on the moral qualities of an ideal councilor.

A council would possess no sovereign power but would assist a monarch in the proper exercise of the powers assigned his office. The ruler was expected to tolerate the imposition of a council, organized formally or informally, as a necessary and desirable means of improving his performance of his duties. A monarch's duties were so onerous, according to Wolff, that *"he must avail himself of the counsel of wise and knowledgeable men and draw on each in his particular field of expertise."* [42] These councilors, assembled as a senate or council, were entrusted with "the affairs of state. They should tend to those matters that must be handled as part of the routine business of administration and to those particulars that require immediate action. They should implement the sovereign's decisions and, at his request, provide him with advice on current questions of public policy." [43] The ruler was to rely only on those councilors who met the same standards of rationality and virtue expected of the sovereign himself. The ideal councilors were, in Pufendorf's words, ones who "should turn the eye of their mind to every part of it [i.e., the state]; whatever shall seem to the interests of the state, they must declare with skill and fidelity, without bias or unworthy motives; in all their counsels they must have the welfare of the state as their aim, not their own wealth and power: they are not to humor the evil inclinations of princes by flattery." [44] The image of the flatterer was contraposed to that of the diligent, impartial *homme d'état*.[45] The council, as described by Wolff and Pufendorf, provided the Fonvizin group with a way of revising and expanding their own political ideas. Their attention to an ideal ruler was refocused to include their recognition of the need for a crown council as an administrative guarantee that the monarch observed his proper functions.

The council model in the works of Pufendorf and Wolff provided the Fonvizin group with the theoretical basis for their support of Panin's plans and political values. Catherine was not interested in the proposed Imperial Council after mid-February 1763, but the ideal of a council remained the rallying point for Panin's followers. To some extent the Fonvizin group had a vested interest in a council project. In the 1760s the men were ambitious and wanted to advance in rank and duties. Their professional careers gave them some reason to ingratiate themselves with their superiors by publicizing the advantages of Nikita Panin's political schemes. Yet the inverse was more significant. The three men's experience in the bureaucracy schooled them in the means and forms necessary to adapt the political ideals of their German progenitors to the realities of Russian administrative routine. Their considerations about a council served as the impelling, theoretical force that set in motion the process of elaborating the characteristics of an ideal state, one whose legitimacy was initially ratified by its correlation with the practices of the imperial bureaucracy but later caused the group to lose its enthusiasm for that government.

— 5 —

Fonvizin, Bogdanovich, and Novikov could not publicly comment in direct and detailed terms on Panin's council, for to do so was unwise after 1763. They referred to it in literary rather than political works, and they removed their literary works from Catherinian Russia and commented on council projects in pre-eighteenth-century Russia. Bogdanovich's support for some type of council was evident, though inferentially, in his *Historical Depiction of Russia*,[46] meant as an informal companion to Shcherbatov's *Russian History from Ancient Times*.[47] Bogdanovich's theme was the taming of the unrestrained, warlike chieftains around Kiev by the reasonableness, prudence, and bravery of the Kievan princes. The culmination of the centralizing, enlightening role of these rulers was, in Bogdanovich's opinion, the reign of Vladimir the Wise. Vladimir was allotted the predictable measure of positive moral and political qualities, but one of his policies was singled out for emphasis and praise. The prince strengthened his rule by governing with the advice of a council of elders.[48] This body was mentioned with reference only to Vladimir's reign, suggesting, however indirectly, that a sharing in the exercise of political power was the sign of a mature government. The differences between the traditional council of elders and Panin's plan are obvious, but they are less significant than Bogdanovich's general emphasis on the advantages of some type of council. Bogdanovich admitted that he wrote his sketch "to draw good examples, useful rules, and necessary information from history."[49] His attention to the advantages of some type of council was probably due to his association with Nikita Panin.

Fonvizin adopted the council idea before his service with Panin. While a student, he accepted the idea that a government was bettered by consultation between the ruler and a body of advisers. In a petition to Catherine in October 1762, Fonvizin cited as proof of his knowledge of Latin a translation of Cicero's speech in behalf of Marcus Claudius Marcellus.[50] It should be noted that Fonvizin was not commissioned to translate this oration but chose to do it.[51] The speech was a defense of the deliberative powers of the Roman Senate as a potential brake on the despotic rule of Julius Caesar. Marcellus was exiled to the island of Lesbos for his staunch advocacy of the rights of the Senate. Cicero was one of many calling for the pardon and recall of Marcellus. The oration was not simply a comment on the affair between Marcellus and Caesar. Cicero's implied argument was that the Senate must maintain its independence so that its members could discuss issues and aid the ruler. Fonvizin's choice of this particular speech suggests that, while still a student, he was persuaded of the advantages of some type of political body auxiliary to the sovereign. He definitely did not favor any scheme to limit the ruler's power. He did not translate those parts of the same speech in which Cicero called upon Caesar to issue a constitution. Fonvizin thought that some type of consultative body improved the operation of the government's administration, though he was equally convinced that the sovereign's authority should not be restricted by any division of power.

Political loyalties to Panin and the court party of dignitaries were also demonstrated in several articles praising "honorable men" (*chestnye liudi*), the code words for Panin's party, as capable of countering the influence of the favorites. Novikov composed two articles in 1770, one for the *Babbler* and one for the *Drone*,[52] which described the admirable personal and political attributes of the ideal statesman and compared him with his alleged opposite, the favorite. To be circumspect, Novikov referred to a Chinese rather than a Russian court, a frequent practice among eighteenth-century men of letters.[53] The fictitious Chinese emperor was advised to avoid reliance on favorites whom the people treat "like modish goods." He was to depend on "honorable men" who should be delegated complete power in any affair.[54] If the ruler was himself virtuous, these "chosen men" (*izbrannye liudi*) improved his administration and his popularity with the people.[55] If the monarch was less than morally praiseworthy, his advisers served as a possible check against the sovereign's uncurbed passions.[56] The article in the *Babbler* spelled out the same points. Novikov acted as a client of Panin in advocating the same political values implicit in Fonvizin's and Bogdanovich's support for a council plan.

However indirect the literary evidence in favor of Panin's plans, criticism of his rivals, the favorites, was quite direct. Favorites rose quickly to positions of power through the whim of the ruler rather than their own merit and experience. Their example represented flagrant violations of the group's norms and elicited many literary attacks. Novikov wrote the classic caricature of a court grandee for the pages of the *Drone*: "He dresses according to the mode, bows low, speaks affectionately and decently; often smiles, makes promises to everyone, rarely fulfills [them], praises anyone to [his] face, but abuses [him] behind [his] back, spends more than he receives, and envies everyone in society."[57] Novikov dismissed a career for himself as a favorite since "it is necessary to know the science of pretense better than an actor should know it."[58] This sarcasm was prompted by the favorites' failure to meet the standards Novikov expected of men in power. "There are only a few of those who keep to the truth, love virtue, remember that they are the same as those poorer than themselves, and do not forget that they are raised to [positions of] esteem only so as to be better able to benefit mankind, help the poor, and defend the oppressed."[59] "Do good for them [the poor and oppressed] by duties to everyone without exception or partiality, and look after their well-being before your own."[60] The favorites were no more to be excused than were rulers who deviated from these standards. By contrast, Novikov matched "honorable men" who provided impartial counsel to the ruler with monarchs who abided by the principle of rationality in their conduct as individuals and sovereigns.

The opinions of favorites and honorable men were combined in two remarkable examples of eighteenth-century political biography, Novikov's *History of the Unjust Imprisonment of the Confidant, Boiar Artemon Sergeevich Matveev,* and Fonvizin's *Life of Count Nikita Ivanovich Panin.* Artemon (Artamon) Sergeevich Matveev (1625–1682), suspect among some contempora-

ries because of his interest in European customs, was an adviser to Tsar Aleksei (1645–1676) and a tutor of the future Peter the Great in the 1670s. The
actual Matveev was very much immersed in the court politics of his day. His
unsuccessful maneuvers to have the young Peter succeed Aleksei instead of
the tsar's eldest son, Fedor, led to Matveev's exile. He was recalled to Moscow in 1682 only to fall victim to the *strel'tsy,* the janissaries of Muscovy,
during the palace revolt of May 1682. Novikov's Matveev was a man of in-
corruptible, virtuous character, loyal to his rulers, devoted to the people, and
disdainful of luxury.[61] His exile was not the consequence of political failure
but an example of the arbitrariness of the throne.[62] Matveev was the victim
of slander by the favorites at Aleksei's court. "The one reason for his
exile . . . was the arbitrariness [*proizvol*] . . . of malicious and highly
placed *boiars.*" [63] Novikov interpreted Matveev's trials in political terms contemporary to the author, not the subject. Novikov reordered an episode in
the court history of the 1670s to accord with his own version of the court
politics of the 1770s.

Fonvizin referred to Panin, whom he genuinely held in high regard, in the
same terms that Novikov had used. He described Panin in 1771 as "a man of
true reason and honor [*chestnost'*], an individual embodying the highest
standards of morality of this century!" [64] Why were his merits not appreciated by the empress? His activities were, Fonvizin contended in 1772, kept
from Catherine by the intrigues of court favorites.[65] This reading of court
politics, drawn from Fonvizin's writings and letters, was advanced in its most
elaborate form in his biographical sketch of Panin, written at the time of the
minister's death in 1783.[66]

In the opening pages of the essay Fonvizin reviewed rather quickly the
basic facts of Panin's career. He mentioned Panin's posts in the diplomatic
service and the honors conferred on him by Catherine. Then Fonvizin advised the reader that a narration of Panin's career was not his purpose. He
wanted to describe his subject's principles and "the greatness of his soul." [67]
Panin was removed from the turmoil of contemporary politics and portrayed
as a man of inestimable integrity, unstinting in his concern for the welfare of
the state. Consider this version of Panin's conduct of official business:

Nothing so distressed him as any action that might impede or even threaten
the proper functioning of the apparatus of state. [It could be no more than] a
case of someone bothering the empress with a petition before the facts of the
case were reviewed in detail by the Senate, an example of some type of incon-

sistency in the administration of justice, or instances in which individuals were willing to debase themselves by doing no more than obey when they should have stood up for the truth—even at the price of their lives. In a word, [every time] anyone did something for personal gain, degraded himself by showing prejudice, lied so as to keep the truth from the view of the sovereign and society, or acted in a base manner—each occurrence deeply troubled his virtuous soul.[68]

A model of impartiality and personal humility, Panin was careful to imbue his charge, Grand Duke Paul, with the proper sense of moral self-worth. Fonvizin quoted from Panin's own statement of principles regarding Paul's education and upbringing. "It is incumbent on the mentor to foster virtue by every appropriate means so that [Paul] will be disposed to what is good and honorable and repelled by what is evil and incompatible with decent conduct." [69] The threat to Paul's soundness of character was quite explicitly pointed out. "During the Grand Prince's upbringing it is imperative that he be kept apart from the luxury, splendor, and all else that is likely to corrupt a youth. Let decency and purity be the only adornments to his quarters. He will be, at any age, vulnerable to the influence of flatterers." [70]

Panin's integrity and service were recognized by his contemporaries as the mark of an honorable man ready to "console the unfortunate, defend the oppressed, and counsel the needy." [71] Fonvizin described his subject not as the advocate of a council or any other specific political reform, but as the guardian of the morally good. Panin was transformed from the leading diplomat of Catherinian Russia into the timeless figure of the virtuous adviser to the ruler. Fonvizin's portrayal of Panin was not just a literary creation of a symbolic figure made to represent the values Fonvizin held as his own and expected to find in Panin, but an idealized version of his superior's actual character and career.

The biographical essays by Fonvizin and Novikov are examples of a type of political biography that had many practitioners in eighteenth-century Russia. Obviously Panin could not be expected to meet the ideal standards lent his name by Fonvizin. As one of the dominant figures at Catherine's court, he was as subject to the unrestrained paeans of partisans as he was vulnerable to the biased criticism of opponents. When the extraordinary range of his duties led to inevitable delays in the dispatch of business, what was discounted by admirers because of the variety and importance of his responsibilities was seized on by his detractors as evidence of his limited abilities and his indolence. The English envoy Lord Buckingham wrote his court on September 8, 1764, that "he [Panin] has considerable experience in affairs of state, but he is lazy and always slow to reach a final decision on any matter. He is a man of weak character and indulges himself in a dissolute style of life." [72] Buckingham, whose government was not in league with Russia, distrusted Panin and feared that the Russian minister was "completely in the hands of the French (!) and represents in his person nothing other than an agent of their ministers." [73] In contrast Lord Cathcart, the English ambassador in 1769, filed this assessment of Grigorii Orlov in a dispatch of March 17, 1769: Orlov "is an agreeable man, quite urbane, humane and approachable. In his relations with the sovereign he conducts himself with the utmost respect for her. He compensates for his poor education with remarkable innate faculties, free of the least pretensions. . . . During the last few years he has gone to some length to educate himself and has met with some success, . . . I believe that it would be fair to say that he is a man of honor." [74] Cathcart's evaluation should be discounted somewhat as he was occasionally ready to accept any remarks by any individual about any other person. In this case the general tenor of his comments conveyed his purpose: he spoke well of Orlov to put him in favorable contrast to Panin.[75] These particulars aside, the descriptions of eighteenth-century Russian political figures by foreign diplomats, usually based on relatively short stays in Russia, were often influenced by the visitor's reading of how well the Russian subject served the interest of the diplomat's government. The Fonvizin group wrote with the same degree of partiality. They were quite ready to use their literary portrayals of favorites and honorable men to serve their own theoretical interests.

The political biographies of the 1770s and 1780s were primarily written as statements of political principle and summary judgments on the subjects' engagement with the cause of the Panin party. Support for a council plan signified a common and consistent development in the scope and sophistication of the three men's political convictions. The ideals of the utopian ruler in the student journals became identified with Panin's political values during the 1760s and 1770s. The three men differed, however, in the way they made the association between a general abstract ideal and a specific political proposal. Fonvizin was quite direct in his first comments on a council but later wrote in terms of men of moral integrity contending with the pernicious influence of flatterers. Bogdanovich was quite removed in his remarks. Novikov commented on the values inherent in Panin's proposed council rather than on the body itself. In publicizing Panin's cause the three men did not dutifully echo their superior's opinions in the manner of literary or political hacks. Rather, they carefully fashioned their own versions of his plans and standards.

Within this variety of views the Fonvizin group was increasingly ready over the course of the sixties and seventies to identify the ideal of regularity less with a formally constituted council than with the example of honorable men whose attributes were, above all else, ethical and whose duties were not precisely defined legal obligations. The more the men referred to this contrast of court characters, the more they seemed to share the patterns of thought typical of early eighteenth-century writers. The Fonvizin group referred to a council of morally worthy men in terms similar to those employed by Pososhkov and Sumarokov. In point of fact, Fonvizin, Bogdanovich, and Novikov were neither the first nor the last political commentators to prefer the moral integrity of honorable men to the formal, legal structure of a council. Rather than simply subscribing to an indigenous political convention, however, the Fonvizin group was distinctive in its readiness to draw on notions derived from German natural law. When the three men shied away from describing the legal specifics of a council and wrote about the moral requisites of a councilor, they did no more than rely on the same contrast between honorable men and flatterers that Pufendorf and Wolff allowed themselves. The Fonvizin group did not forsake natural law politics but integrated a longstanding political issue with the principles of German natural law and gave that tradition new theoretical assumptions, implications, and significance.

—— 6 ——

The Fonvizin group used the stereotyped characters of the honorable man and flatterers for reasons quite different from those of Pufendorf and Wolff. The Russian officials were certainly not prepared to understand the significance of a council at the same level of sophistication as the German jurists. The German thinkers were apprehensive about a council's potential role as an administrative agency of a Leviathan, whereas the three Russians were not well versed in the grand questions about a modern state. The group was composed of young men serving in the bureaucracy, not political scientists writing in the university; the group's writings on the council and honorable men were certainly not works of political theory. What accounts for their qualified endorsement of a council plan? Why did the ideal of a council in natural law theory take the form it did in the writings of the three men?

Politics intervened to reveal to the Fonvizin group what their adulation of Panin obscured. They discovered that his interest in a council plan was quite different from their own. Panin changed his mind about the advantages of a council. After Catherine discarded the proposal for an Imperial Council in 1763, he remained an advocate of its advantages for five years, a period during which he was able to maintain his own position and check the power of the Orlovs. In November 1768, however, the empress reversed her opinion about a council. She considered establishing one to direct the war effort against the Turks (and put her plan into effect on January 17, 1769). Catherine's willingness to establish a council in 1768 encountered the opposition of none other than Nikita Panin.[76] He understood the plan as one that would undermine his own power as Catherine's chief adviser by forcing him to make decisions in concert. He would have to contend with Grigorii Orlov's presence on the council. When Panin was out of power, as in 1762, he had favored the council for the same reason he opposed it in 1768 when he was in power. The proposal for an Imperial Council may have been intended to ensure a measure of regularity in the handling of affairs of state, but as Panin's actions in 1768 made clear, the administrative routine was to be under his control. To those members of the bureaucracy who had supported Panin's original proposal as a point of principle, it was surely apparent that his council plan was a matter of bureaucratic design, not theoretical conviction. The Fonvizin group learned in rather direct fashion that they were mistaken in identifying their own ideals with those that informed Panin's political designs.

Panin's turnabout did not reverse his subordinates' opinions on the advantages of a council and the disadvantages of relying on favorites. This theoretical constancy was particularly impressive in individuals who by 1768 had gained a measure of experience in the government service and harbored, at least during the sixties, expectations for advancement in the bureaucratic hierarchy. Their stand on principle and tenacity of purpose were witness to the fact that their support for a council and its political values did not depend on Panin's plans for such a body between 1762 and 1768 or Catherine's preference for one after 1768.

Their disillusionment with Panin had an immediate effect on their literature. As men who were initially schooled in the service by Panin, their view of the issues and personalities of Catherinian politics was brought to a focus through his eyes. When this referent was lost in 1768, the Fonvizin group did not abandon its vantage point but refocused and extended its gaze. Notice when the group deferred direct comment on a council for the sake of emphasizing the contrast between dignitaries and favorites. Novikov's descriptions of favorites were written for the *Drone* and the *Babbler* in 1770; his edited work on Matveev was published in 1776, and Fonvizin's short biography of Panin was printed in 1784. The group's reference to a council after 1768 could be seen as support for an agency only recently created by imperial edict; their change in emphasis from the institution to the personnel a signal of their disengagement from politics. Their experience with Panin in the 1760s led them to draw back from political involvements in the 1770s and 1780s. Though this was less true of Fonvizin than of Bogdanovich and Novikov, they each became wary of enlisting in other political causes. They had reason by the 1770s to be circumspect about supporting particular policies and "reform" proposals. They would even have occasion to be apprehensive about the benefits to the commonweal of any policies of the government.

As the group's interest in politics slackened after 1768, its political horizons receded. The men involved themselves in political affairs only as a way of finding confirmation of their moral values. When they were unable to find this confirmation in the politics of Catherinian Russia, they withdrew from contemporary political contests and maintained their political ideals apart from current rivalries. They were to seek in the 1770s verification of their political values in an idealized conception of the state. The validity of this utopian state could be questioned only by denying the moral duty that had compelled them to fashion and act on political ideals in the early sixties and to recognize political allegiances in 1762 and immediately thereafter, that is, only by denying themselves. In their unwavering belief in their own moral convictions, they became for late-eighteenth-century writers examples of individuals whose political judgments were independent of the ruler's reading of the best interest of the Russian polity and were based instead on their own moral concern for the welfare of the state.

— **V** —

The Just Society

— 1 —

The Fonvizin group's initial interest, gradual involvement, and eventual withdrawal from the politics of the 1760s was a pattern it repeated in its attention to specific social issues. In their work Fonvizin and his peers became familiar with the key social questions under discussion in court and bureaucratic circles. When those in Panin's clique required assistants to draft proposals, circulate information, or simply do the bureaucratic legwork of discovering and recording precedents to a given policy, the Panins employed their trusted and talented aides in the Fonvizin group. These assignments, in turn, brought to the young men's attention particular social problems that had not interested them as students and gave them reason to recognize an additional dimension to their general moral commitment to others. The group's interest in social and economic questions in the mid and late sixties led to unforeseen consequences. Their writing enhanced their status in the eyes of their superiors in the Panin party. Their works also attracted Catherine's attention, but unexpectedly and unfortunately their social interests gradually incurred the displeasure of the monarch.

— 2 —

The Fonvizin group's interest in society was initially quite limited. In the early 1760s the men were concerned with the grand questions of morality to the virtual exclusion of any social or economic issues. They referred to society in the very same terms as those used by many literati of the first half of the eighteenth century. The young men were as ready as Sumarokov to rehearse the familiar litany of social evils. They criticized the foolishness of French fops and the boorishness of ignorant provincial nobles as examples of conduct that was morally deficient rather than socially delinquent.

Fonvizin spoke in the language typical of the group's social comments in his *Moral Fables* (1761),[1] a translation of the work of the Danish enlightener

128

Baron Ludvig Holberg (1684–1754). Each fable was a separate tale with its appropriate moral maxim. Holberg described a society composed of members, both human and animal, whose moral inadequacy he made no attempt to disguise. A French dandy was so consumed with himself that, while walking along a street, he collided with a pig and was knocked down. The coxcomb was angry because he had gotten dung on his clothes; the pig's answer to this was: "The devil take this madcap . . . my bristle is covered with your powder." [2] A mouse spied a large piece of cheese and immersed itself—literally—in the cheese. Because of these excesses the mouse was found by a cat and eaten, despite the mouse's protestations that it was not eating but renouncing the world around it. Holberg admonished his readers that "there are many people in society like the mouse who are willing to withdraw from the world only so as to wallow in luxuries." [3] To the goat who, wandering the streets of a city, noticed that everyone followed the latest fashion by shaving off his beard, except for one man who stubbornly clung to the style of letting his beard grow, Holberg remarked that "he who is the first to accept the latest mode is no less and no more a fool than he who resists any change in the old ways." [4] Society should be purged of these characters by reforming itself according to the standards of moderation and virtue. [5]

The ideal society was described by a fable about the animal kingdom. [6] Several types of small weak animals complained to their god Pan about the dominance of the strong animals and appealed to him to reorder the hierarchy of prestige in their realm. Pan complied by issuing a statute that gave privilege "not according to birth but to one's inner worth, virtue, and industry, for these are the means for one to be of true usefulness to others." [7] Pan's distribution of status favored the small animals whom he found to be productive and useful to the disadvantage of the large, all but parasitical beasts. The old order was inverted; one dominant group did not simply replace another, but came to prominence as proof of the moral justness of the social hierarchy. [8]

Fonvizin did little more than satirize targets of social criticism that were standard in the repertoire of many eighteenth-century commentators, Russian and European alike. Many articles in the student journals, similar in tone and message to Holberg's *Moral Fables,* were witness to their authors' familiarity with contemporary Russian and European literature, rather than a criticism particular to Russian society. [9]

The condemnation or approbation of specific social stereotypes carried, potentially, the means of leading the group to a sophisticated understanding of Russian society. The fable about Pan and the animal kingdom gave a clue to this potential when the god Pan considered all the particulars of civil behavior according to a single set of moral standards, specifically, "one's inner worth, virtue, and industry," and reordered society by these criteria. Similarly, the Fonvizin group's writings of the mid and late sixties were to prove that its members came to apply their personal moral values to an increasingly wide range of social issues. They generalized a personal ethic into a vision of a reformed Russian society. As an individual's fidelity to these values enabled one to honor one's personal responsibilities to others, so the same moral norms regulated all associations of individuals—particularly social classes—in the performance of their obligations to the entity representative of the collective self, society. The Fonvizin group referred to its personal ethical standards as a means of strengthening the existing social hierarchy by a restatement and reaffirmation of the moral conduct expected of each class.[10] The men's writings about society and politics had an integrity sustained by their continued affirmation of the ethical values they had made their own during the early sixties. As this continuity would suggest, what they sought was not a major alteration in the social structure, still less a major upheaval, but rather the moral regeneration of Russian society.

3

The Fonvizin group's moral perspective on social issues became less abstract and more particular during the members' early years in government service. This conversion from the theoretical and general to the specific and immediate was made in the context of the men's links to the Panin party and the consequences of this association for their opinions of Catherine the Great. It would be well at this point to review the social policies sponsored by the empress during the initial years of her reign and to identify the role played by the Panins in these programs.

Catherine made known her general principles regarding social reform in the weeks immediately after June 28, 1762. The overall direction of her plans was to define in consistent fashion the relation between the nobility and the serfs and to reaffirm the corporate status of each. Serfs were reprimanded for fleeing the estates and forgetting their duty to their lords.[11] Nobles were cautioned that their right to own serfs was not a license to use excessive violence.[12] Her general goal was stated as early as July 5, 1762. She recognized "as our first duty always to have an unflagging motherly respect and labor for the prosperity and tranquility of all the holy Russian fatherland, restoring all the people . . . to the highest degree of prosperity." [13]

While Catherine's statements struck an idealistic note, they nonetheless reflected current political issues. Her notions of an ideal social order could be implemented only by opposing vested class interests. What the empress considered a social responsibility of her government was to the Russian nobles an extension of state power into domains they considered in their jurisdiction. To the gentry, Catherine's statement that she intended to curb the abusive treatment of the serfs carried with it a threat that their control of the peasants would be regulated and thereby represented an intrusion of the state into an area they considered inviolate. More generally, the empress staked out her claim to arrange the activities and interests of all social groups under the aegis of a well-regulated state, concerned and responsible for the general welfare.[14] She hoped to benefit from favorable comparison to similar policies of Peter the Great, as well as draw on the political tradition, dating from the times of the Muscovite princes, of relying on state initiative in political, economic, and cultural matters.[15] Nonetheless, the political principles spelled out in her first edicts could quite easily be taken by the nobles, allowing for varying degrees of knowledge and comprehension, as ominous signs of their status with the new empress. They were on notice that she intended to continue the policies that had troubled their relations with Elizabeth and Peter III.

Elizabeth had taken steps in the 1750s to reexamine the service role of the first estate. The Petrine military official's usefulness to the state needed reconsideration by mid-century. The empress convened a Legislative Commission in 1754 and charged Peter Shuvalov with the task of redefining the nobility's functions to include duties on its estates and some unspecified degree of service in local administrative offices.[16] When its meetings were undermined by what Shuvalov called "internal difficulties provoked by the [Seven Years'] war," [17] the empress established another Legislative Commission in 1758, which quickly came under the influence of Roman Vorontsov, the chancellor's brother.[18] To the question of the proper role of the nobility, Vorontsov's commission responded with a draft proposal that gave the nobility legal status as a closed estate, freedom from compulsory service, the exclusive right to own serfs, and substantial commercial privileges.[19] What Roman Vorontsov had in mind was the recognition of the rights of the *dvorianstvo* without any definition of that group's duties as a social corporation subservient to the crown. Peter III rejected the proposal. The emperor compounded the problem of trading off statist for class interests when he issued the famous Manifesto on the Liberty of the Nobility on February 18, 1762. The nobles were thereafter free of mandatory service to the state. What was to be the specific nature of their relation to the state? The manifesto provided no exact redefinition of the gentry's functions.

Catherine sought to remedy this situation and complete what Elizabeth had begun. The Legislative Commission was disbanded on February 11, 1763, and the Commission on the Freedom of the Nobility established in its place. Again the members, all prospective members of Panin's Imperial Council, resisted any retreat from the demands made on Peter III for recognition of the corporate rights of the nobility. Catherine had no more reason to make concessions than her late husband.[20] She was not successful in reaching agreement with the nobility on a definition of its duties and privileges; relations between the two were at an impasse. Her initial edicts regarding the nobles and their relations with the serfs were a continuation of her predecessors' administrative attempts, unwarranted in the minds of the nobles, to regulate matters the nobles preferred to consider within their own purview.

The empress tried again to define the legal status of the nobility by putting the problem on the agenda of the Legislative Commission of 1767. Catherine's policies during the first five years of her reign and their statement in 1767 have been interpreted by Makogonenko, Gukovskii, and, though less so, Pigarev as the politics of deception.[21] Their version has it that the empress's tenure was not secure. She countered the perceived threat from the *frondeurs* in the Panin party by biding her time until 1767. Then she was in a position to use the deliberations of the Legislative Commission to reinstitute her predecessors' policy toward the nobility and defeat the Panins' attempts to wrest from the crown those corporate privileges Elizabeth and Peter III refused to allow the nobility.[22] According to Makogonenko, Panin's supporters, including Fonvizin, Novikov, and Bogdanovich, became interested in social issues as advocates of the rights of the nobility over those of the state and as supporters of Catherine. The illusion that she agreed with them was, however, rather abruptly dispelled in 1767.

If Fonvizin and his associates were in league with the Panins to limit Catherine's political power, the group's opinions on social questions must have been formed in the same manner as its views on the political issues of the 1760s, namely through the eyes of the Panins. The problem with this line of reasoning is that, as Jones and Ransel have argued convincingly, the members of the Panin party were not of a single mind on social issues. Moreover they did not demonstrate any intention of using their influence to wring from the throne the corporate privileges demanded by Roman Vorontsov's commission. Their proposal was made to that body on March 5, 1763, by Mikhail Vorontsov, who stressed the nobility's dependence on the state and its need to recognize that privileges should be accorded it as a corporate group only in strict relation to its service to the state.[23] Peter Panin proposed curbs on the nobility's unchecked arbitrariness with the peasantry and argued for the enforcement of rules for regulating the relations between nobles and serfs. Yet his brother, on reading a similar proposal made by Catherine herself in a draft of her *Instruction,* opposed the empress's measure with his well-known quote: "These are principles capable of overthrowing the established order."

If the party was not of one mind in these instances, what was the nature and extent of its influence with Catherine on questions of social policy? Did the Panins so dominate the empress as to compel her to dissemble in the formulation and presentation of her government's social policies? However beguiling this interpretation, it conflicts with the facts. If Catherine deceived her senior minister, how was she able to ignore the recommendations of the Commission on the Freedom of the Nobility? Nikita Panin's interests in 1762 and thereafter were not primarily social but political and bureaucratic. Even then these interests were not of a type that qualify him as, to use Gukovskii's term, a *frondeur.*[24] Although Panin was not present at the sessions of the commission, his absence was not a sign that Catherine harbored any suspicions about him. He was one of the first to read a draft of the famous *Instruction,* the white paper that the empress wrote for the commission's deputies; he was charged with the task of writing the instruction of the Moscow assembly of nobles, and his brother attended the commission as one of the delegates from the Moscow nobility.[25] Panin was absent because the many political responsibilities bestowed on him in previous instances of imperial favor and trust made him too busy to attend.[26] The interests of the Panin party did not dictate to the Fonvizin group a commonly held, opposition-minded set of guidelines for understanding the social issues of the sixties. Unlike its considerations of political questions, the group formed its opinions about Catherine's social policies very much on its own.

—— 4 ——

The Fonvizin group became acutely interested in contemporary social issues at the time of the Great Commission of 1767. Among the many legislative commissions called by eighteenth-century tsars and tsarinas, Catherine's
commission stood out because of its elaborate attempts to bring to Moscow
representatives from many classes and regions.[27] The empress allowed the
election of deputies from the nobility, bourgeoisie, central governmental institutions, and several variously categorized groups (Cossacks, tribesmen,
state peasants, and *odnodvortsy,* free farmers of small plots of land). Noticeable by their absence were serfs owned by nobles. These peasants were to be
protected and represented by their lords. Within each district of a province,
property-holding nobles elected a deputy to be sent to Moscow; within each
town, the bourgeoisie elected a single deputy; and within the central bureaucracy, the Senate selected representatives. The deputies were ordered by
Catherine to come to the commission with detailed reports on conditions in
their home district. These reports, drawn up by a committee of five in each
jurisdiction, were statements of information, not discontent. They brought
to Moscow notice of the social and economic issues of immediate concern to
nobles in the countryside. When the deputies—460 strong—assembled in
Granovitaia Palace in the Kremlin, their meeting was a spectacle. It was the
only instance in Catherinian history when representatives of so many constit-
uencies had the opportunity to articulate their view of society. Each group
lobbied for its own interests and voiced its grievances while directly countering the sentiments of its rivals. The occasion changed dramatically the
Fonvizin group's opinions on social issues and spurred revisions in the range
and sophistication of its ideas about society.

Two members of the group participated in the meetings of the commission and witnessed the speeches and debates of the deputies. They were
among those called to Moscow to fill the need for educated, knowledgeable,
and experienced individuals who could staff the committees and subcommittees (nineteen in all) of the commission, handle the paperwork, write reports
of the transactions, and, in general, carry out efficiently the routine business
of the commission.

Novikov was drafted from his post in the Izmailovskii Guards to act as
protocol officer for the commission. His duties were to record the minutes of
the General Assembly and write abstracts of the deputies' speeches. He then
routed his memoranda to the appropriate subcommittees for further consid-

eration.[28] Each month he compiled a journal that reported in detail the commission's work and was published in the *St. Petersburg News*.[29] When the General Assembly was not in session, Novikov acted as secretary to the subcommittee on the status of the middle class.[30] How his time was distributed is not known. It is certain that he was not simply a witness to events, as was the case in June 1762, but also a participant in the day-to-day proceedings of the plenary sessions and subcommittee meetings.

In the course of the bureaucratic routine, Novikov had reason to work closely with Denis Fonvizin, who had arrived in Moscow from Elagin's offices. It is possible that Fonvizin came to the commission after having traveled on the famous imperial barge that carried the empress down the Volga from Tver' to Simbirsk in May 1767. Fonvizin's immediate supervisor, I. P. Elagin, accompanied Catherine on her trip into "Asia." En route more than six hundred petitions were submitted to her.[31] Elagin was responsible for the dispatch of these petitions and may have passed them along to Fonvizin. Elagin's secretary, Lukin, was in Europe during 1767,[32] and his absence made Elagin quite reliant on the services of his other aide. Again, there is no conclusive proof, either in Fonvizin's letters or in the secondary literature, that he was in fact with Elagin and Catherine in May 1767. Fonvizin was definitely in attendance at the opening of the commission on July 31, 1767. He did not occupy any specific posts in the bureaucratic offices of the commission; his duties were very likely confined to direct service to Elagin.

Bogdanovich was absent from the commission. In 1766 he was appointed as the secretary to Prince A. M. Belosel'skii on the prince's mission to the court of Saxony. Bogdanovich remained in Saxony until recalled in 1768.[33] Because he was not at the commission's sessions and Novikov and Fonvizin were, it is possible to determine the commission's influence on the development of the group's social opinions.

Several former students at Moscow University and friends of the Fonvizin group also attended the commission. Aleksei Rzhevskii was sent as a delegate by the townspeople of Vorotynsk in the province of Moscow and served on the subcommittee on the police. Sergei Domashnev served on the subcommittee on population growth, agriculture, and home building as a representative of the nobility of the province of the Sloboda Ukraine. The Naryshkin brothers were both deputies. Aleksei was first assigned as an aide to Grigorii Orlov on the cruise down the Volga before appearing in Moscow to represent the interests of the nobility of the Staritsa district of the Moscow province. He served on the subcommittee studying state law. Semen attended the commission as a member of the nobility from the Mikhailovskii district of the Moscow province.[34]

The commission was surely a heady and informative experience for the young public servants. Whether as participants in the debates, reporters of the meetings, or aides to those involved in the proceedings, the young men heard much that was new to them. Until 1767 their service and literary activities were somewhat cloistered; their curiosity confined within the walls of the university, court, colleges, or Guards regiments; their knowledge of society drawn from their reading. Only in 1767 did they have an ideal occasion to reflect on the viewpoint of representatives of provincial noblemen, townspeople, and even some types of peasants. The commission was a revelation to them of several Russias beyond the world of capital society and politics.

The impact of the commission on their writing was significant in some cases, negligible in others. The social commentary of Rzhevskii, Domashnev, and the Naryshkin brothers was not altered one iota in content or understanding. Rather than troubling themselves with the complexities of actual social issues, they contented themselves—in 1767 as in the early sixties—with satirizing literary symbols of exaggerated social ills. In contrast, the debates brought to the social commentaries of Fonvizin, Novikov, and Bogdanovich a sense of immediacy about actual Russian conditions as well as an appreciation of the difficulties involved in improving them. The issues raised in the commission's sessions led the three men to shed their assumptions of the early sixties, dispense with notions of society as little more than a collection of literary stereotypes, and recognize the social issues central to the state and the principal social groups in the mid and late sixties.

The commission forced Novikov and Fonvizin to change the direction and targets of their social commentary. Neither man was in a position to deliver a speech at the commission. They wrote no observations about its meetings. In Fonvizin's case this literary silence is puzzling, for he was usually quite ready to describe his professional activities in his private correspondence with his family. Yet no letters or autobiographical commentary are available.

Rather than reporting on the transactions of the commission, all three men relied on several indirect methods of voicing their expectations in the commission in the months before the first meeting in 1767 and their conclusions about its achievements in the years after the final session in 1768. Fonvizin's opinions were in the reports he prepared for the commission; Bogdanovich's in the timeliness of what he wrote and chose to translate; and Novikov's in his journals.

Novikov edited a well-known series of periodicals during the period 1769–1774.[35] He published the *Drone,* a weekly issued between May 1, 1769, and April 27, 1770, the *Babbler,* a monthly begun in June 1770 and discontinued after its July issue, the *Painter,* another weekly on sale between April 12, 1772, and June 1773, and, finally, the *Purse,* a weekly issued no later than July 8, 1774, and continued for three months. Novikov's journals were quite unlike their predecessors of the early 1760s. The abstract moralism of the student journals gave way to comment on particular conditions of contemporary Russian society. Rather than satirizing man's eternal foibles, the periodicals of 1769–1774 concentrated their literary attack on representations of figures from everyday life in the capitals and provinces. Novikov spread before the readers of his journals a panorama of Russian life. The freshness and intensity of his comments as well as those of Bogdanovich and Fonvizin conveyed the three men's discovery of dimensions and varieties of social intercourse quite foreign to their own worlds of experience.

For all three men the link between their writings and the issues debated at the commission was not a casual association born of chronological coincidence but a causal connection. Every single topic satirized in the journals of 1769–1774 had been the subject of debate at the commission. Not one of them developed on his own an interest in a specific question of social policy. The three men even emphasized what was important to the guiding hand behind the meetings of the commission, namely Catherine's interest in redefining the role of the nobility. When the commission's meetings were recessed sine die, the journals of 1769–1774 began to appear in the capital, but only after the lead was taken by Catherine herself. She sponsored the publication of *Anything and Everything* and used the periodical as a public forum in which to resume her attempts to school the nobles in their proper functions. Novikov's journals, Fonvizin's bureaucratic reports and literary works, and Bogdanovich's writings provided a description of an ideal society, one whose characteristics were not only in clear contrast to the apparent faults of contemporary Russian society but were arranged to exemplify the group's moral values of "worth, virtue, and industry."

—— 5 ——

Many of the Fonvizin group's plays and journals described in detail an extensive campaign to correct the moral standards of the nobility. Two works in particular were classic portrayals of the nobles' life styles. The famous letters to Falalei, which appeared in Novikov's *Painter,* consist of a series of character studies severely critical of provincial nobles.[36] Falalei was a fictitious young nobleman living in St. Petersburg, whose relatives in the provinces suspect he had forgotten traditional mores. In the letters Falalei's father and uncle warn him about his supposed personal failings in terms that unwittingly identified their own moral deficiencies. His father rejected the contention that nobles should not punish their serfs nor act tyrannically. After all, he replied in his own defense, the *Painter* "does not know that in olden times tyrants were those who tortured saints and were not christened . . . but our *muzhiki* are hardly saints: [and so] how can we possibly be tyrants?" [37] What if the serfs were poor? Sacred writings have ordained this condition and sanctioned the masters' right to do whatsoever they pleased.[38] Both Falalei's father and his uncle Ermolai refused to accept any reciprocal understanding of their privileges. Both men had been retired from service for taking bribes, in the uncle's case from Falalei's father.[39] Their only interest was in securing the family's financial position by marrying Falalei to a relative of the local military governor. "What would be better for you than this? Do not chase after honor, . . . honor! It is an ill honor if there is nothing to eat." [40]

Falalei's relatives were obviously not the stock literary characters of Holberg or any other European writer, nor were they noblemen familiar to members of capital society and its institutions. The Falalei series described provincial noblemen whose conduct was by no means motivated by values similar to those of the Fonvizin group.[41] Rationality and virtue, as understood by the Fonvizin group, were alien principles to the typical provincial nobleman. He was quite removed from any appreciation of the regulatory role these values might have on his own personality. He knew of no environment in which the individual accepted these standards as criteria for his conduct in any association, be it with his serfs or with the state. His existence created a dilemma for the group. The three bureaucrats had joined the government service to find confirmation of their personal moral standards. Yet nobles like Falalei's father and uncle had also served the state only to return to their estates and perpetuate the ignorance, exclusiveness, and parochial views of generations of provincial noblemen. Since the service had had such a negligible effect on these men's conduct, did their example force the group to question its personal moral ideals? Were these ideals valid only for nobles in the capital, not provincial nobles? Or was there a more basic challenge to the group's assumption that service, wherever performed, was an arena in which moral values were complemented by professional standards?

Within this context, Fonvizin's *Brigadier,* first presented at the court in 1769, was significant as more than a literary phenomenon. The play reaffirmed the validity of the tie between the group's moral values and commitment to serve the state.[42] Nobles who followed the pattern of going from their homes into service careers of various lengths and then back to their estates in the provinces could be reformed only if their professional values were reinforced by the virtues valued in the Fonvizin group's personal ethic. The lack of this link between service and virtue was clear in Fonvizin's portrayals of two provincial noblemen, the brigadier and the councilor, at home on their estates in the countryside.

The councilor's wife asked the brigadier and her husband if the two men wanted to discuss anything other than ranks. The brigadier implied that he did not.[43] The councilor was "unwilling to talk about any topic that could not be referred to edicts or the law code [of 1649]."[44] Their reliance on rank was the basis of their own friendship since both achieved rank in the fifth class. As the brigadier realized, "a councilor such as you is worthy of being the friend of a brigadier (retired) from the army."[45] Fonvizin's criticism of this attachment to ranks was bitter. Both families' interests consisted in arranging a financially advantageous marriage between the brigadier's son, the foppish Ivanushka,[46] and the councilor's daughter Sofia. To her parents' distress, Sofia was in love with the stalwart Dobroliubov. The marriage of the young lovers was opposed by the councilor. Then Dobroliubov was suddenly enriched, and the councilor reversed his opposition to the marriage. "It seems to me that if someone has two thousand souls, then all his vices can be redeemed. Two thousand souls even without a true landowner's virtues are always two thousand souls, but virtues without them—the hell with [these] virtues."[47]

When the councilor allowed the marriage, he revealed the faults in his moral standards. He could disdain virtue as an expendable quality only at the price of treating his neighbors as "animals"—an opinion they also had of him. When Ivanushka complained to the councilor's wife that his parents were "animals," she replied that she too suffered "from my monster. . . . I have been living with him here in the country for several years and . . . all our neighbors are such ignoramuses, such animals, . . . they think of nothing more than the provisions for the table; [they are] literally swine."[48] These sentiments, typical of those voiced by the other characters about each other,[49] carried Fonvizin's point: rank alone was inadequate to counteract the allegedly corrupt and longstanding traditions of provincial life. Rank had to be matched with virtue if the greed, ignorance, and mutual disrespect among provincial nobles were to be eliminated.

The Fonvizin group made several general proposals in the hope of correcting the moral failings and damaging exclusiveness of the brigadiers and councilors. One suggestion was to broaden the nobles' function in Russian society by improving their relations with the bourgeoisie. This was a particularly difficult task because of the nobility's traditional prejudice against the middle class. The upper class was accustomed to look upon the bourgeoisie as "the innovator of a vulgar, noisy, and loathsome commerce, . . . [and] as a barbaric lover of money, dishonest and devoid of culture." [50] These resentments were apparent in much of the literature of the eighteenth century. Most writers were themselves nobles. A Russian nobleman had few occasions to have direct contact with members of the middle class. What he knew about the bourgeoisie was gleaned from descriptions in books published in Europe; most of these contained disparaging descriptions of supposedly typical bourgeois.[51] From the fictional figures in European literature, Russian nobles—those few who could read—formed their own biased opinions of real-life Russian bourgeois. The Fonvizin group's attempt to counter these opinions was the first signal of its capacity to make judgments independent of social stereotypes and class prejudices.

Fonvizin made the most explicit argument for better relations between the nobility and the bourgeoisie. He translated an essay by the German cameralist Johann Henri Justi (1720–1771) on the merits of the nobility's involvement in commercial matters.[52] Justi's work was itself a translation of two opposing opinions, an article critical of any mingling of noble and bourgeois functions published in 1754 in the Parisian journal *Mercure de France* by the Marquis de Lassay[53] and the rebuttal written by Gabriel-François Coyer[54] in his *La Noblesse Commerçante.* When Fonvizin translated Justi's work, he omitted the Marquis de Lassay's article. Fonvizin's translation was clearly meant to endorse and publicize the advantages of a "trading nobility." [55]

Fonvizin's purpose ran counter to economic realities. He promoted the idea of business enterprise among Russian nobles with arguments proper to the activities of French bourgeois, but the French bourgeoisie was quite different from the Russian. The eighteenth-century French bourgeoisie was economically prosperous and politically powerful. As the engineers and benefactors of the commercial revolution of early modern France, the position of the French bourgeoisie was secure, the infrastructure for its ventures well established, the investment capital available, and the organizational mechanisms in place. The Russian bourgeois were not of the same order. Politically powerless and economically weak, the Russian bourgeoisie was small in numbers, quite poor, and frequently without the requisites for successful commercial endeavors. Quite aside from prejudice, there were sound economic reasons for the nobles' reluctance to become a trading nobility.

Fonvizin overlooked the economic difficulties and argued that the nobles' hesitancy to engage in commerce was based on prejudice, which damaged their own moral character and the best interests of the state. "If my efforts to open the merchantry to the nobility required that I deal with sound reason alone, then all the gates would soon be open. Here, however, we are dealing with prejudices held by society." [56] Some nobles, Fonvizin suggested, were conditioned to fear any exposure to the middle class as a threat to their status in society. They preferred to live in poverty on their estates rather than earn a profit commercially. If these noblemen were willing to engage in some type of business enterprise, they would be better equipped financially to improve the condition of their estates, strengthen their personal security, and have the means to educate their sons.[57] Others led an idle, superficial life and forswore any occupation other than the army, oblivious to the fact that the supply of available officers exceeded the number necessary for military service.[58] Still others believed their personal honor rested in the luxuries and amenities that set the tone of their life style. They refused to enter the commercial world for fear of violating their genteel ways and tainting their sense of honor.[59] "I ask only whether it is better to live in a small village irresponsibly and to harm yourself, your family, and the entire state by your own idleness . . . [or] does honor consist in taking part in the advantages of your fatherland, giving people useful occupations, bringing agriculture into a flourishing condition, putting money in circulation into the government treasury . . . and improving the well-being of the state." [60] Could the nobility, Fonvizin asked his readers implicitly, improve its usefulness to the state by overcoming its reservations about the middle class and engaging in commercial activities?

Confidence was expressed that the nobles would recognize the advantages of better relations with the bourgeois and their own involvement in business affairs.[61] If noblemen who were modish, poor, or unable to serve in the military engaged in commercial dealings, this willingness would eventually be translated into the financial means to improve their estates. When their lands were successfully cultivated, they could support ever larger numbers of people and till ever greater acreage.[62] Estates would then be used at their peak efficiency. The ultimate beneficiary was the government. The full mobilization of the economic potential of the countryside stimulated and increased the population and government revenues, two staples of any state's international prestige.[63] Nobles acted in the best interests of the state by recognizing the value of business enterprises, "the soul of the state." [64]

Fonvizin propagated an essentially Tory-like vision of the Russian countryside in which each estate employed its available resources to the maximum and was economically prosperous. What he did not specify were the mechanics necessary to implement and achieve his goals. In their place was a vague assumption that noblemen who deigned to engage in trade could expect quick profits which could be used for their estates. The profit motive was not acceptable absolutely but condoned as a temporary expedient. Furthermore, the discussion was concerned with a trading nobility, not an ennobled bourgeoisie. There was no mention of mobility into the noble class. Fonvizin appealed to the *dvorianstvo* to overcome its bias against commerce and the middle class in terms that indicated the influence of the same prejudice.

The issues raised in Fonvizin's translation were being discussed frequently in intellectual and political circles in both Russia and Western Europe. Many contemporary thinkers, especially the physiocrats, favored agriculture over commerce, an attitude reinforced in Russia by the traditional beliefs of many poorly educated nobles.[65] Montesquieu criticized the nobility's involvement in commercial affairs in *L'Esprit des Lois,* while Vauban, the famous military adviser to Louis XIV, and Rousseau supported the idea.[66] At first Catherine agreed with Montesquieu. In her *Instruction* to the commission, she censured those who "imagine, that it would be expedient to have Laws, which should encourage the Nobility to engage in Commerce. This would be the Means of ruining the Nobility, without the least advantage to Commerce. . . . The Custom allowed to the Nobility, in some Countries, of engaging in Trade, is one of the Means, which contributed most to weaken the Monarchical Government." [67] The empress's opinion was anything but fixed.[68] In the Charter of the Nobility, published on April 21, 1785, she approved the involvement of the nobles in trading ventures,[69] then reversed herself only to change her mind several more times. Catherine made what was to be her final decision in 1790: she returned to her policy of 1767 and forbade nobles to participate in trade.[70]

Thus Fonvizin's translation dealt with a topic currently under review within the government. The translation was published the year before the opening session of the commission. It might well have been intended for use in those proceedings, possibly to bolster the arguments of an unknown supporter of the nobility's involvement in commercial matters, possibly to furnish Elagin with ready opinions for his own use, or possibly to provide a position paper for those commission deputies soon to meet as the subcommittee on the middle class. What Fonvizin clearly did was prove himself ready to put his duties to the state above the claims of the nobility. He did not, however, simply record the empress's opinions. His translation was published at a time when Catherine was opposed to a trading nobility. It is not that Fonvizin took a firm stand on principle and heroically opposed the empress. Rather, he successfully extended his personal moral code to define the proper functions of a class. In following the guidelines set by the group's general principles and logically extrapolating from overall ideal to particular case, Fonvizin was led to an opinion that was more detailed and definite than Catherine's on the same topic. As her repeated reversals of opinion suggest, her views were formed with an eye to administrative advantage. Fonvizin amplified in scope and complexity standards that were, above all, moral, but at this time the strictures of moral consistency were still consistent with his expectations about government policy.

Concern for the proper functions of the nobility prompted Fonvizin and Novikov to make separate proposals for reforms in the education of young noblemen. Correct moral and intellectual schooling was paramount; Fonvizin's Dobroliubov noted that "upbringing [*vospitanie*] determines all." [71] Improper upbringing was considered to be the key factor incapacitating many young noblemen. It left them forever at the prey of their passions, unable to appreciate the value of virtuous conduct. Men who grew up unprepared by inclination or ability to fulfill their service obligations were bound to end up dissolute. [72] What these men lacked was knowledge and moral rectitude. Their learning was facetiously described in the *Industrious Bee*: "to know as nobles do is to know as much as is becoming to a well-born person, that is very little and not well grounded." [73] As the memoirist G. S. Vinskii (1752–1818?) concisely noted, "the nobility considers ignorance [its] right." [74] Fonvizin and Novikov used their literary talents to portray examples of the dire consequences of poor education and upbringing as well as to suggest the means to correct these noblemen. A young *dvorianin* was to acquire a respect for himself, which would prevent his treating others, whether serfs or peers, as "animals" and would equip him morally for a satisfactory service career. [75]

The primary responsibility for arranging an adolescent's proper moral and intellectual training was allotted to parents.[76] Those who neglected their duties to their children were as blameworthy as those who were so attentive that they retarded a child's maturation. "Those who have bad children should blame themselves since they were either lax in educating them or spoiled them out of a blind love for the children." [77] Nobles who committed either mistake were characterized as "irrational" [*"bezrazsudnyi"*] and were contrasted with "reasonable" [*blagorazumnyi*] parents who attended properly to the upbringing of their children.[78] Parents had the obligation to demonstrate a reasoned, dispassionate concern for the education of their children. When they did less, they behaved toward their offspring other than they were obliged to act toward themselves.

These reprimands to delinquent parents were clearly consistent with the group's personal values. However, the more the group sought to account for the faulty education of the young, the more its members shifted the direction and emphasis of their censure from the parents to the teachers. The journals of 1769–1774 were much more explicit than their predecessors of 1760–1764 in singling out tutors as the agents responsible for the flawed upbringing of many adolescents. Immigrants with exalted notions of their status were numerous in mid-eighteenth-century Russia, and many of them were French-born. Their presence moved La Messelière,[79] the French diplomat stationed in Russia from 1757–1759, to comment that "we have been inundated . . . by a veritable horde of Frenchmen who have descended on us here. They are a varied lot. Most of them had some dealings with the Parisian police before coming to haunt the northern regions. It is cause for astonishment and distress to find ensconced in the homes of many magnates not only deserters, embezzlers, and libertines but also many women of the same repute." [80] Immigrants who had a Russian patron usually entered the government service, others became hairdressers, and the remainder, if all else failed, taught young nobles.[81] Many Frenchmen earned their income by teaching.[82] During the course of the eighteenth century, particularly after 1756, the Gallomania fashionable in high society in the capitals[83] encouraged a steady influx of immigrants, many of whom became tutors.

The problem was that the pretensions of these men far exceeded their capabilities. A few from France, like Paul Aleksandrovich (Popo) Stroganov's tutor Romme, were bona fide instructors, but the teacher La Messelière described was more typical.[84] Novikov's *Painter* carried a classic description of a tutor. "Many of them had great difficulties with the Parisian police. They were so despised by the police that, when apprehended, they were made an offer that was not at all to their liking: leave Paris immediately or dine, take supper, and spend the night in the Bastile." [85] Rather than go to jail they emigrated to St. Petersburg to teach young nobles.[86] Satirical attacks on the vagrant who would be teacher were frequent in the literature of Catherinian Russia. What was said of tutors was less significant than the importance allotted their role in the education of young nobles.

The poor quality of French tutors and commentary on them were not novel to the 1760s or to Russia. Gallomania was no less prevalent in Central and Eastern European societies. Fonvizin's translation of the *Moral Fables* included Holberg's satire of the French tutors' influence on young Danish nobles.[87] In Russia, Elizabeth's government instituted compulsory written examinations for tutors, which improved their caliber by the 1760s and eliminated many poorly qualified ones.[88] When members of the Fonvizin group satirized French tutors, they were attacking a longstanding, superficial social abuse that had already been recognized by the government.

The typical tutor obviously violated the group's personal moral code on many counts. But although it cited the wrongs committed by tutors, the group did not offer an acceptable alternative or come up with any specific proposals for improving the quality of education. Removing every single French tutor would surely not have improved the level of education available to young nobles since the need for the teachers was a result of poor education, not its cause. The criticism of the tutor demonstrated a lack of progress in the group's abilities to broaden the scope of its personal values and apply them to particular situations. These satires were no more than a ready reference of their standards to a well-known social stereotype. The group maintained the consistency of its personal values by restricting the moral jurisdiction of those values; that is, by not expanding them to encompass the actual circumstances of contemporary Russian society.

The same detachment was also present in the group's comments on the essentials of a sound education. In the student journals the working principle had been that the provincial nobles' tradition of ignorance had to be broken if their children were to be equipped to fulfill their service obligations. The means of accomplishing these goals were clear-cut: virtuous conduct and an enlightened mind would purge the child of the damaging effects of traditional mores and prepare him for a successful career.[89] By the late 1760s, however, the Fonvizin group had become quite skeptical of the worth of an enlightened education and was reconsidering the value of a traditional, religiously oriented upbringing. Novikov satirized students who went to Central Europe to study philosophy. Such "foolishness" produced only scholarly imbeciles who differed from typical fools in that "scholarly fools do a great deal more harm to the state." [90] In the same spirit the character Dobronrav in an article in the *Babbler* condemned those who "study French or German so as to be able to chatter in foreign languages with idle Frenchmen or Germans [while] withdrawn from their own fatherland or perhaps only so that they will be held in contempt for their disorderly and dissolute life by honorable and reasonable men." [91] Dobronrav taught his son foreign languages but only for their utility. He put greater value on a knowledge of "Christian law and true reverence." [92] Novikov said much the same in an article for the *Painter* which stressed that a child's upbringing should include "respect for one's parents and courtesy to one's seniors." [93]

The group's redefinition of a proper upbringing did not represent any progression in its views. Generations of ignorance among many noble families could not be corrected by depending, in part, on the environmental effect of that milieu. The Fonvizin group cared for moral, not intellectual, consistency. When its members revised their general statements of the early sixties on the advantages of an enlightened education and came out with their specific comments of the late sixties on the need for traditional elements in the education of Russian noblemen, they did not at the same time reconsider their personal moral values. However inadequate they may have found an enlightened education, Novikov and Bogdanovich did not waver in their assumption that their ethical values were shared by all "honorable and reasonable men." Only the "disorderly and dissolute" would question or deny these standards. These two members of the group extended their personal values to the subject of a proper education so as to find confirmation of those standards. When their confidence in one definition flagged, they reassigned their moral values to a more acceptable definition. Here, as in their comments on tutors, they only skirted the "reality" they wanted to enclose within the jurisdiction of their moral principles.

The results of poor upbringing, unqualified tutors, and parental abdication of educational responsibilities were summarized in the symbolic figure of the French fop. Novikov provided the most famous caricature of French dandies in a notice in the *Drone*. "A young Russian suckling pig who has traveled through foreign lands for the enlightenment of his mind and practical training has returned an absolute pig. Those who want to witness this can see him free of charge along many of the streets of this city." [94] These "suckling pigs" were considered "animals" since they failed to appreciate the gift of reason. Given the fops' pretensions to knowledge and rational behavior, it was necessary, Novikov suggested facetiously, to revise the proverb "live for a lifetime and study for a lifetime" to "study for a week and live for a lifetime." [95] Instead of thinking, fops had an incurable propensity for babbling.[96] Their superficial learning and chatter were characteristics of those unable to control their passions. Fops were creatures of whim rather than individuals guided by reason and reflection.[97] These flaws of character were important because they impaired an individual's ability to carry out his service obligations. Fops were inclined "to laugh over the fulfillment of their duty and consider as base conduct working in a calling entrusted to them. . . . Only those [people] . . . fall into this error . . . who imagine that all merit and honors were created for them even though they did not deserve them." [98]

Fonvizin's Ivanushka, the young dandy in *Brigadier,* epitomized the foolish actions and utterances of the French fop. Ivanushka was careful to remember his gentry status.[99] Yet his character was so flawed as to call to mind Sumarokov's reference to individuals whose forefathers were nobles but who were themselves not noble. Ivanushka's adolescence was marred by the influence of his French tutor, a coachman turned teacher,[100] and a careless upbringing by ignorant parents oblivious of their educational duties. Instead of controlling his conduct rationally, Ivanushka was dominated by his passions, which was evident from his narcissistic regard for his appearance. These personal faults rendered him useless. He disregarded the value of bureaucratic rank and understood merit only in terms of good conversation and social acceptance.[101] Ivanushka's most prominent characteristic was, of course, his Francophilia.[102] He parried his father's abusive comments with witless remarks in debased French. He tried to declaim in French only to return to Russian, sometimes at appropriate points, sometimes at quite awkward ones. When reminded by his father that he was, in fact, a Russian, he replied, "My body was born in Russia, I admit, but my soul belongs to the king of France." [103]

Ivanushka's remarks throughout the play were a catalogue of violations of the group's values. Fonvizin succeeded in associating these comments with foreign influences. French and foreign were interchanged quite casually. The presence of French fops came to be understood by the group as a consequence of the prestige of all things French, rather than personality flaws in the dandies. Novikov summarized this opinion in a letter that blamed "the

French" for the appearance of modish, young Russian noblemen: "That is the type of corruption the French have made among us! To make a provincial fool into a modish fop in three months, an impossibility for a man but the French do [so]. What kind of gratitude do we owe the French: they enlighten us and show us their services even when we do not demand them." [104]

The group's repeated attacks on the example of French coxcombs were directed at a minor abuse in Russian society. Few Russian nobles were Francophiles. Those who could afford the trappings of French cultural fashion were likely to be found only in the capitals. Even then, all Francophiles were obviously not irresponsible, babbling dandies. Those few nobles whose behavior corresponded to that of the figures satirized in the journals were objects of contempt and ridicule by a much more representative number of the nobility.[105] Reference to the harmful effect of French influences relieved the group of the need to propose substantive, meaningful solutions to the social problems that plagued the nobility. From the empress's point of view, their unwillingness to offer and stand by potentially controversial proposals regarding the education of minors made them politically innocuous. On this particular count, she could be amused, not alarmed.

The Fonvizin group's interest in the education of noblemen became associated with a growing concern among many Russian writers about the dire influence the foreigner and his customs had on Russian society.[106] This reaction was a European-wide phenomenon, part of an incipient movement of Francophobic, cultural nationalism which arose during the eighteenth century. The challenge to the worth of all things French was reinforced and refined in the case of the Fonvizin group. The three men had to satisfy their self-imposed demands for moral consistency between their personal values and the specific social phenomena that were to serve as confirmation of those values. Only Fonvizin in his proposal for a trading nobility attempted to write about nobles in terms that were both morally rigorous and, he hoped, relevant to contemporary Russian society. Yet his remarks were quite removed from the actual circumstances of Russian society and appropriate for a French trading nobility, not a Russian one. On other issues—such as the habits of provincial noblemen—he more directly and clearly joined Novikov and Bogdanovich in drawing back from social conditions that did not validate his personal values and instead seeking a way out by describing a morally acceptable version of those conditions.

The Fonvizin group's writings about fops, tutors, and education contained the lineaments of a separate realm in which moral standards were reaffirmed against the exaggerated challenges of would-be opponents. Given the common hostility to French influences this realm attracted Russian national sentiments. The particular characteristics of this domain were still to be defined. In the late sixties and early seventies the three men did not pit the world of their moral certitudes against real-life conditions nor did they assume that the two worlds were to coexist without rivalry. The Fonvizin group found a way to reduce its need to comprehend and accept "reality" without yet choosing to rely on a "reality" born of configurations of moral fictions.

—— 6 ——

When the Fonvizin group turned its attention to the serfs, the three men were able to expand the dimensions of their social interests to include the peasants without becoming involved in any moral realm apart from the world around them. Improving the serfs' position was commonly assumed to be a moral, not an economic problem. The serfs were not considered primarily as possessions of the nobles, but creatures of God and the moral equal of any individual of any class. What was sought was a renewed moral order in which the serf lived "without fear, . . . a man was obedient to another without slavery, and by this means, the interdependence of their services was strengthened." [107]

A model for this type of moral order was provided by Fonvizin in his *Korion* (1764).[108] In this play the moral qualities of Andrei, Korion's servant, were favorably contrasted to those of his master. The serf disclaimed vices and idleness and represented a positive example of behavior. Andrei was quick to brand useless, ignorant provincial noblemen as "animals." They disdained reason, the means by which they could distinguish themselves from the beasts they were.[109] Fonvizin stressed Andrei's recognition of his duties. When he was rebuked at one point by Korion, he responded: "I know that I must always be a servant, . . . I could not live without him [i.e., Korion]: I am accustomed to serving him diligently. Masters are fortunate with zealous servants, and servants are happy with good masters." [110]

Content with his position in the social order and convinced of the mutual dependence of lords and serfs, he was insistent that this arrangement required both parties to fulfill their obligations. At one point Korion chose to abandon capital society and withdraw to the countryside. Andrei rebuked him for his decision. When Korion refused to get in touch with any of his former associates, even when he received word of his promotion to the rank of colonel, Andrei did not hesitate to criticize him. This would-be Onegin figure was repeatedly warned by his servant that his service duties should not be neglected. Andrei equated this conduct with going mad; rational activity was inseparably linked in his mind with service obligations.[111] Andrei even had to save his master from attempted suicide before Korion was willing to reenter military service. *Korion* was the most explicit attempt at designating the rights and duties of the serf within the Fonvizin group's moral order. The serf's social position was justified on moral grounds; by serving he honored his duties to others in a virtuous manner. Fonvizin attributed to the fictional Andrei the same qualities the group esteemed as its own personal, moral standards. He did not provide an idealized version of a serf as much as prove once again that he considered his own values valid for every social group.

All three members of the Fonvizin group assumed that as an incentive to moral behavior, serfs should be given some means of eventually achieving freedom. They did not endorse any scheme for immediate emancipation of the peasants; the possibility of political and economic freedom was the point.

Bogdanovich was quite careful in setting limits to his ideas about improving the status of the peasants. His comments came as part of the public debate on serfdom called by the Free Economic Society in 1765. The society sought responses to the question: "What is more useful to society, that a peasant have landed property or only movable property and how extensive should his right to either one or the other property be?"[112] Among the 162 answers received from all parts of Europe, the response of Jean François Marmontel (1723–1799) attracted Bogdanovich's attention. Marmontel argued the case for emancipating the serfs and letting them buy land. They were to buy their plots from the lords for a mutually agreed fee in cash or labor. Legislation was not the means to bring about this change. Rather, the peasants' recognition of the necessity of freedom was, Marmontel suggested, sufficient impetus to the process of emancipation. Once liberated a serf's standing with his lord was to be that of a "tributary."[113] Bogdanovich published a poem in honor of Marmontel's proposal.[114] The young Russian refrained from explicit agreement with the *philosophe*. He confined his remarks to vague comments on the general benefits of freedom to the people and emphasized moral advantages ("an abundance of good") rather than economic ones. By his willingness to be publicly associated with Marmontel's solution, Bogdanovich revealed that his thoughts on the serf question, however imprecise in nature and detail, included consideration of promising the peasants some type of eventual betterment of their status.

Novikov proved to be more interested than Bogdanovich in the plight of the peasants. He extended a general concern for the welfare of the serfs to a particular regard for the economic conditions that buttressed and safeguarded their moral well-being. In the pages of the *Painter* Novikov described a peasant whose merits as an artist were not appreciated by his lord. A second nobleman purchased the serf's freedom, for it was inappropriate, he remarked, for one so talented not to be free.[115] "There is an example," Novikov wrote, "of a lord who is worthy of esteem for he is a reasonable and distinguished individual with a concern for what is advantageous to society."[116]

Fonvizin succeeded in refining a moral and economic interest in the serfs into specific legal arrangements relevant to the politics of the 1760s. His ideas were expressed in a memorandum, a *Précis Concerning the Freedom of the French Nobility and the Function of the Third Estate*.[117] The *Précis* was, as Griffiths has recently pointed out, a translation of a work by an unknown writer, a M. de Boulard.[118] Fonvizin lent his name to a proposal that emphasized the role of the peasantry as the surrogate for the all-but-absent Russian bourgeoisie.

The proposal was for a legal arrangement that encouraged serfs to conduct themselves virtuously and usefully by giving them a chance of attaining freedom. "What can arouse one more to good deeds than the ever-conscious hope of receiving one's freedom and finding one's happiness?"[119] According to the plan, individuals with professional skills were organized into guilds according to their trade. A guild was obliged to test the qualifications of each of its members. Successful candidates were given their freedom in return for the guild's payment of an unspecified amount to the state treasury.[120] When implemented, this plan would motivate men to act in a positive manner and benefit the state.[121] How quickly should this proposal be enacted into law and executed? In the final sentence of the article Fonvizin qualified what was quite direct in the body of the text. "The people [*narod*] who are currently engaged in farming should not become free but have only the hope of becoming free. They must first prove that their skills as tillers or artists can bring the fields and mills of their masters to the optimum level of production."[122]

Fonvizin chose to associate himself with a proposal that was logically consistent with his personal moral standards and considerably advanced beyond the opinions of Novikov and Bogdanovich in its reference to contemporary social issues. Yet Fonvizin then drew back. In his translation of de Boulard's essay and in his own writings, he did not support immediate emancipation. To do so would have violated his own rationale for the serf's performance of his duties. As Andrei's conduct toward Korion demonstrated, a serf acted virtuously and obediently not to merit freedom but to fulfill his own moral obligations.

The Fonvizin group was unanimous and unsparing in its condemnation of anything that hindered the serf's execution of his proper functions. Nobles who treated their peasants cruelly were denounced for abusing seigneurial rights as well as impeding the serfs' fulfillment of their own duties. The basis of this criticism was twofold. Both parties were obliged to conduct themselves according to the group's personal ethical values. The lord who was ever ready to beat his serfs was not master of himself. He lost control of his passions and, in doing so, put his peasants in a position that could only arouse their passions, not encourage them to act virtuously and usefully.

Novikov described nobles who tortured their serfs "as wild animals." [123] One Zlorad, the malicious one, personified this abuse of power. He was "rough, terrifying and proud in front of those subordinate to him. . . . He breathes evil into everything and calls those landowners animals who do not consider their own servants and serfs as animals. . . . I call these [individuals] animals whom Zlorad calls human beings: for there is greater similarity between them and animals than between serfs and animals. According to him, both animals and serfs are equally created for the satisfaction of our passions." [124] Novikov advised nobles "to be loved by your subordinates. . . . Arrange . . . [your] actions and conduct so that they consider you [their] defenders and providers, not their tyrants." [125]

Novikov was not alone in voicing these sentiments. *Anything and Everything,* the journal published under Catherine's supervision, carried an unsigned article that stressed the same qualities by referring to the essential equality of all men. The author praised a nobleman who did not mistreat his serfs since "it is not enough that I do not whip a single man among them when they are at fault, . . . for I know that they are from Adam's breed as much as I . . . ; on all occasions I act with them not so much as a master but as a friend. . . . I always try to be sure [they] are . . . nourished, clothed, happy, and tranquil." [126] Whippings and beatings were a violation of the proper relationship between the nobility and the peasants. Masters should act like "fathers," not tyrants.[127] Each estate was to be an example in microcosm of the Russian state as a whole. Serfs were not to be maltreated by the arbitrary fury of the lord's whip any more than citizens ought to be subjected to administrative arbitrariness.

This moral argument for curtailing the authority of an abusive noble was supplemented by an economic rationale. An unsigned article in the *Drone* described a village where the lord was harsh with his peasants and immoderate in his demands on them. The results were depicted in dismal terms, a village devastated by the master's greed and lack of foresight.[128] Novikov did not explicitly draw the final and obvious conclusion; his readers could easily and accurately infer from the description the dire consequences of a noble's brutality toward his serfs. Short-term economic advantage was attained at the cost of giving reason for a peasant rebellion, one whose wrath would avenge the cruelty of the landlords.[129] Poverty in the villages resulted in tax arrears and robbed the serfs of that minimal wherewithal that was the backbone of the government itself.[130] The economic and moral arguments were complementary. A reaffirmation of the group's moral values sufficed, Novikov as well as Fonvizin and Bogdanovich seemed to imply, to eliminate abuses such as the nobles' maltreatment of their peasants and bring about the conditions necessary for a prosperous Russian economy.

Yet the three men gave themselves no reason to expect that the provincial nobles could, in fact, be reformed. The Fonvizin group's hopes for harmonious and productive relations between the nobles and serfs on every estate came after the gradual extension of its personal values to the peasants. The peasants appeared in the group's writings neither as stereotypes taken from European literature nor as idealized targets of cultural phobia. The serfs, virtually absent from the student journals of the early sixties, commanded the group's interest by the mid-sixties. The figure of the peasant in Fonvizin's *Korion* and Bogdanovich's verse on Marmontel was a moral personality, one not harmed by economic circumstances. By the late sixties and early seventies, consideration of the serf's moral welfare was joined to concern for his economic status, the economic element a potential threat to the integrity of the moral. It was probably not coincidental that this danger was singled out for emphasis by Novikov, who had recorded the speeches of the provincial nobles at the commission and become familiar with conditions on estates in the hinterlands. The group's extension of its values to encompass the peasants progressed steadily during the 1760s and led the group to form exact and decided opinions on the actual conditions of the serfs. The group's perception of these circumstances caused them to stop thinking in terms of the peasants' moral and economic status and start concerning themselves with the proper relations between nobles and serfs. At this point, after extending the personal moral values of its university years to a detailed consideration of reforming every estate according to those standards, the group shied away from the consequences of this extension.

If the nobles' control over their serfs had to be regulated, who was to be the regulator? The issue was one of corporate self-management versus government intervention. Novikov described the ideal landowners as "defenders" and "providers," beloved by their serfs, but omitted any explanation of how this ideal could be attained save by force of moral admonition. Fonvizin made the classic case for the intercession of the state between serfs and aberrant nobles. The *Minor,* published in 1783, presented a cast of characters similar to those in the *Brigadier.*[131] The young fop Mitrofan, his parents the Prostakovs, and his uncle Skotinin were readily comparable to the families of the brigadier and councilor. Prostakov's wife stood out from her crude and ignorant relatives by the magnitude of her barbaric practices. She beat the serfs regularly, curbed only by the limits of her physical stamina.[132] Fonvizin contrasted this familiar portrayal of the provincial noble with the figure of the virtuous Pravdin. A nobleman and a "member of the local provincial government," Pravdin was on a mission to "investigate the environs" for the viceroy (*namestnik*). "My conscience does not allow me to countenance those malicious, ignorant persons who use their absolute power over their serfs for evil and inhumane purposes."[133] Pravdin was empowered by the viceroy to deprive abusive landlords of their authority. When he confronted Prostakov's wife, she was unrepentant, defending herself with the claim that her power over her serfs could not be restricted. "No, madam," Pravdin warned, "nobody has the right to act in such tyrannical fashion."[134] Then Pravdin turned to Prostakov and delivered his famous condemnation of both Prostakovs: "In the name of the government I order you to assemble all your serfs within the hour so that they may be informed that the inhumanity of your wife and your own utter stupidity compel me to act for the government and put your home and villages under the control of the state."[135] Pravdin warned all Prostakovs and Skotinins that they would suffer a similar fate.

Was an ideal estate—such as one under Pravdin's supervision—to be a model in miniature of a well-ordered state where the individual nobleman emulated the example of a virtuous, rational ruler? Fonvizin allowed Pravdin to hint at the character of an ideal order in the countryside. The noble's conduct toward his serfs should be guided, Pravdin urged, by his "compassion" for them.[136] Fonvizin, the advocate of government intervention, did not expect nobles to be rational administrators of their estates. He and Novikov conceived the ideal nobleman in moral rather than legal terms.

This retreat from the demands of moral and logical consistency was similar to the group's acceptance in politics of virtuous, "honorable men" instead of the symbol of political regularity, the council. In political and social concerns, the group came to recognize in the 1770s limits to the validity of its ideals. The Fonvizin group maintained its moral values while commenting on the education of the nobility only by resorting to national fantasies; it described the nobles' control over the serfs only by abandoning any hope that its moral expectations would be met.

The Fonvizin group's comments on the serf question were more advanced than those of the empress. In the *Instruction* she ruled out, of course, any idea of emancipation but proposed that peasants be allowed to own movable property.[137] She supported the Free Economic Society's debate about the potential benefits of the serfs' ownership of landed and movable property and was in favor of carefully defining the lord-peasant relationship. "Of whatever Kind Subjection may be, the civil Laws ought to guard, on the one Hand, against the *Abuse* of Slavery, and, on the other, against the *Dangers* which may arise from it." [138] Catherine was reluctant to specify the peasants' rights and duties and gave no sign of interest in the group's notion of encouraging the serfs to act properly by offering them the hope of freedom.

This disagreement on the particulars of the serf issue had important consequences. The group's willingness to apply its personal values to the status of the serfs led it to make known in print opinions that the empress probably preferred to discuss in private and ponder in the abstract. The group's moral rigor and consistent advocacy of these opinions created the bases for a potential split between its interests and those of the empress. The group's opinions on the peasants were hardly detrimental to Catherine, yet she reacted as if the three public servants were a social menace and their writing seditious. Ironically, the danger Catherine detected in these writings about the serfs and noble-serf relations was not only exaggerated but probably nonexistent. The group had already extended its personal values as far as it could without calling into question the validity of those moral criteria. The men could not have gone any further without incurring the risk of ultimate self-denial.

The Fonvizin group's comments on each social class were descriptions, consistently related, of an ideal social order, one reformed to accord with its personal values. The men's detailed descriptions of an ideal nobleman and an ideal serf provided models to show how individuals, be they nobles or peasants, should fulfill their proper role in society. Neither the group's moral approach to social issues nor its endorsement of particular social purposes was contrary to the interests of the empress. After all, many controversial issues were not mentioned while inordinate concern was shown for what were only symbols of superficial social problems. The group's social commentary seemingly represented a less than lethal threat to the stability of the throne.

Yet Catherine reacted sharply. On the pages of *Anything and Everything* she criticized the group in the tone of a scolding patroness, angry if not embittered by the wayward concerns of her literary wards. She likened them to the pathologically ill: "The individual begins to fall under the spell of the boredom and melancholy that are born of inactivity and reading books. He proceeds to complain about everything around him and eventually about the order of the universe itself. . . . The patient becomes enamored with the idea of building castles in the air. . . . Even the government itself, no matter how zealous its efforts, becomes completely unacceptable to him. In the end he will offer his advice and work for the general good only according to the dictates of his own ideas." [139] The empress concentrated her attack on Novikov. His writings represented nothing more than the arrogance of one criticizing the failure to achieve the impossible, the literary mutterings of an idle, superficial man, and the pretentiousness of an intellectual unwilling to lead a useful life.[140] Novikov and his colleagues failed to understand society as it was.[141] They were, Catherine charged, quixotic figures whose suggestions for the moral reform of society were to be dismissed as the well-meaning but ineffectual activities of superficial men.

Catherine acted quite perceptively and prudently in attacking the Fonvizin group's moral idealism rather than its specific policies. She passed over particulars so as to satirize the totality of the group's social opinions and dismissed as "dreams" their vision of a morally reformed society. Catherine discredited with a single sweep what the three men carefully fashioned over the course of the 1760s into an image of a utopian society. In the early sixties the group's social concerns were quite limited; only the glimmerings of their ideal social order appeared in the fable about the god Pan. During the mid-sixties the group expanded the periphery of its social interests into several areas then under debate within the government or at the Legislative Commission. The progression was steady, as the men applied their moral values to an increasing range of social issues. When the group's interest in a particular social problem could not be reconciled with its personal values, the men maintained their moral standards in unrevised and unqualified form by detaching them from the troublesome problem.

The image of society was not meant to be a comprehensive model, available as a point of comparison to contemporary society. Rather, the image required a moral integrity that was acceptable and personally satisfying to each member of the group. The moral dynamism that both caused and limited the group's comprehension of "society" was the force behind the creation of an ideal social order, one laced with national sympathies and contempt for the blind imitation of cosmopolitan fashions. The members of this ideal society were not only morally consistent parts, but elements that could be arranged to form a corporate image of society. The Fonvizin group was on the brink of conceiving a mental image of what Lomonosov visualized as his "pyramid" and Sumarokov described in his "Dream of a Happy Society" and other works. The group's utopian society anticipated a unitary social order whose functions and purposes were conceived and advocated according to the dictates of moral conviction rather than political policy.

From Catherine's vantage point, the Fonvizin group's social writings were omens of the ability of individuals, moved by demands of conscience, to elaborate an image of society whose validity did not require ratification by the state. Though many of the features of this utopian society did not differ from those sought by Catherine's own policies, the similarities were matters of coincidence. Her aims were no less idealistic in their particulars than those of the group; the totality of her social views was similar in many respects to that of Fonvizin, Novikov, and Bogdanovich. To the empress the danger was that they had worked out their own version of "the general good" and, in so doing, made government policies toward social problems vulnerable to criticism on moral rather than statist grounds. In that eventuality, "even the government itself, no matter how zealous its efforts, becomes completely unacceptable to" them. The members of the Fonvizin group were not starry-eyed idealists any more than Catherine was herself one. She had to shunt their version of social "reality" into the realm of "dreams" to prevent theirs from interfering with her own.

The split between the interests of the throne and those of the group was irrevocable. The empress discouraged the publication of journals after 1769. Novikov continued to publish, but the periodicals of 1770–1774 were feeble successors to the *Drone*. Without this means of publicizing their moral reforms, Novikov and his associates were left with no single, effective medium for making their ideas known. Their literary activity during the 1770s relied on a variety of genres, particularly poetry and historical works. They recognized that, after almost a decade of support for Catherine, they had to reconcile themselves to the fact that their enthusiasm for the empress could never be restored. After 1769 each side was separated by its consistent adherence to its own convictions. Fonvizin, Bogdanovich, and Novikov learned that the accord between demands of their moral convictions and interests of state policy was fortuitous and coincidental. Without this harmony the three men had to find the means of maintaining their personal values without referring to the political and social policies of the state. Should they fail in this quest, they would have no alternatives but to renounce the primacy of their moral values or founder in national fantasies.

Custodians of the National Idea
in the 1770s and 1780s

——— 1 ———

The parting of the ways between Catherine and the Fonvizin group presented the three men with an unwelcome dilemma. They assumed the personal moral values they had cherished for a decade were inseparable from
their obligation to serve the state. Fonvizin and his peers did not merely
labor in bureaucratic offices but did so to accomplish ethical and universalist
goals. These moral aims were, the group assumed in 1762, articulated by the
person and policies of the empress. Impelled by a moral dynamism and
confident of the mediating role of the state, the group overcame the utopian
character of its early remarks on the ruler and society. During the mid-sixties
the three men acquired knowledge and opinions on the key political and
societal questions under discussion within the government. Their comprehension of these matters was limited by self-imposed restrictions. Their interest in particular political or social issues only extended to those that could be
integrated into a harmonious moral order. The more the group succeeded in
enlarging the jurisdiction of its personal values, the more the three men enhanced the moral stature of the state in their own minds. Where were they
to turn in the early 1770s when Catherine seemingly disowned this moral
heritage? If they abandoned their engagement with political and social issues,
they would deny themselves. The dilemma was never resolved, but avoided.
They could not bring themselves to renounce either their moral convictions
or their obligation to serve the state. In the early 1770s Fonvizin, Novikov,
and Bogdanovich sought to find a way out of their difficulties by discovering
a unifying principle that maintained the moral integrity and coherence of
their ideals.

The group's writings of the sixties foretold what was to be the new representative of moral order. Whenever the men did not find confirmation of
personal values in political and social circumstances, they were ready to refashion these particulars into their own image of reality. Their advocacy of a

council was transformed after 1768 into support for the timeless image of a government administered by the sovereign's virtuous advisers. When the Fonvizin group commented on the education of young noblemen, the men avoided substantive opinions and only criticized quite innocuous topics. Apparently, when they became interested in a particular matter, they committed themselves to finding in it characteristics corresponding to personal values; when that proved impossible, they withdrew to the point at which consistency could be achieved. Their creation of an ideal polity superseded efforts to understand the real one.

The pattern served the group well when Catherine forsook the moral import of her policies. The three men retreated from a world of politics that they no longer perceived as a hospitable arena for the display of their moral talents. They dwelt in a realm apart—one that was detached from the affairs of Catherine's government and confirmed their political ideals and moral values. Without a central principle and the capacity to reorder "reality," this moral kingdom would have been no more than a flight of fancy. A hint of their new ordering principle was provided by the men's comments on the nobles' education. In criticizing the French tutor and his foppish Russian offspring, the Fonvizin group referred to anticosmopolitan sentiments. These remarks of the late sixties were the prelude to the group's interest in the principle of nationality in the seventies and thereafter. Were this principle to be substantively and commonly defined, the group would have a new reference and rationale for its convictions and services. They could restore a harmonious relationship between their personal values and political convictions. There was one major pitfall to be avoided before this accord could be reestablished. The three men risked becoming what Catherine labeled them in 1769, namely, dreamers whose schemes were so removed from contemporary circumstances as to be irrelevant. They might well attain moral integrity and consistency in an order that was no more than the creation of patriotic reveries.

—— 2 ——

The Fonvizin group first attempted to define the specific characteristics of the national principle in some halting remarks on imperial foreign policy made in the late 1760s and early 1770s. Catherine revised the diplomatic policies of the first six years of her reign and embarked on a course of war and expansion. This major redirection of policy tested the capacities of Nikita

Panin to maintain his position as her chief adviser on foreign affairs. What was to Catherine a reorientation of policy was to Panin a challenge to his own diplomatic principles, the same ones she had made her own in 1762.

In the months following the coup of 1762, Panin recommended to the empress his Northern Accord, the informal grouping of Prussia, Denmark, Sweden, Saxony, Poland, and Russia. In accepting Panin's system, Catherine was maintaining the diplomatic status quo. Her official endorsement of his policy in October 1763 gave a clear signal to all European governments that her foreign policy would continue to be nonaggressive. Panin's program was given a trial again in October 1763, when the Polish King Augustus III died. His death gave the states on Poland's borders an opportunity to take direct control of Polish affairs. The interested parties, Russia, Prussia, and Austria, could either intervene directly and partition Poland or manipulate Polish politics indirectly by rigging the election of Augustus's successor and leaving the borders formally intact. When the empress chose election over partition, Panin's policy of nonaggression was ratified.[1] Panin was accurate in his assessment of Catherine's goals: "The empress has adopted as a constant maxim no desire for aggrandizement of her state."[2]

Catherine's decision against intervention was not, however, a triumph of Panin's diplomacy. Catherine had decided on the new king, Stanislas Poniatowski, as early as August 2, 1762.[3] She carried on direct correspondence with the Prussian King Frederick II early in 1763 and herself made the arrangements for the Russo-Prussian treaty of March 31, 1764. The empress's Polish policy vindicated Panin, enhanced his status with his supporters, and benefited him in his rivalry with the Orlovs. But Catherine initiated the policy and did so more than a year before she approved Panin's Northern Accord. The empress was not dependent on Panin and his party nor on any other single court faction but relied on all of them.[4] She enlisted their services by different strategies; in Panin's case she stressed their mutual preference for a foreign policy of restraint. Panin's tenure as her senior adviser depended on this similarity of opinion.

In the late 1760s this common purpose was lost. When in 1769 partitioning Poland again became a distinct possibility, Panin was steadfast in his opposition. In October of the following year Prince Henry, the younger brother of Frederick of Prussia, got in touch with Grigorii Orlov about a partition plan.[5] The prince reported to his brother that Orlov was amenable to the proposal but could not hope to overcome Panin's refusal to recommend the Prussian plan to the empress. In January 1771 circumstances changed when partitioning was urged on Prince Henry by none other than Catherine herself.[6] The empress's decision was not readily accepted by Panin. As Prince Henry reported to his king on January 11, 1771: "All those who support aggrandizement wish that everyone else would take something so that Russia might profit at the same time, whereas Count Panin is for tranquility and peace." [7] When Panin finally approved the partition of Poland, it was belatedly done—according to some reports, not more than a month before the very fact.[8] Panin acted with consistency to principle when the empress was ready to seize an opportunity at the expense of principle.

Russia's policy toward Poland was inseparably linked to its relations with the Ottoman Empire. The events leading to the Turkish War of 1768 are well known. The Turks viewed with extreme apprehension the chaotic state of Polish politics in the 1760s; potential Russian intervention in Poland to restore order was considered a lethal threat to the territorial integrity of the Ottoman state. When a detachment of Cossack irregulars violated Turkish borders in September 1768 and sacked the town of Balta,[9] the Turks seized on the incident as proof of their charges against the Russians. In October the Ottoman Empire declared war on Russia.

The Russian provocation and the Turkish response set the terms for the war itself. In formal diplomatic terms Catherine was not the aggressor since the declaration of war was issued by the Turks, not the Russians. Yet Russia was hardly fighting for defensive purposes. The hostilities were a means for Russian expansion. Russian victories on land and sea aroused Catherine's interest in a solution to the "Eastern Question." She became acutely interested in expansion into the Turkish territories of Moldavia and Wallachia as well as the Crimea. If she were to carry out these designs, Catherine would have to dispense with the Northern Accord. No ally rallied to her side during the war. For the empress to fulfill her dreams of territorial aggrandizement at the expense of the Ottoman Empire, she required peaceful relations with Austria, not Prussia.

Catherine gave several signals of her interest in expansionary plans during the 1770s. When the empress agreed to a preliminary peace conference with the Porte at Focsani in late July 1772, she appointed none other than Grigorii Orlov as her envoy. The choice was significant for, by late 1768, Orlov had plans of his own for partitioning the Ottoman Empire. To Panin, these schemes were "the thoughts of a madman." [10] When the treaty of peace with the Turks was signed on July 10, 1774, at Kuchuk Kainardji the imperial state increased its power dramatically in the region of the Black Sea, particularly in Moldavia and Wallachia. Catherine's diplomatic purposes can be clearly seen, not in the treaty itself but in her revision of its key clauses.[11] She did not expect to win so much from the Turks at the conference table,[12] yet she was quick to make the most of Turkish concessions. Two clauses in the final text, the seventh and the fourteenth, recognized Russia's right to build in Constantinople an Orthodox church for Russian diplomats, pilgrims, and merchants, as well as to make representations to the Porte in behalf of this church.[13] Catherine reinterpreted the meaning of these two clauses. In an imperial manifesto of March 17, 1775, she claimed, though only implicitly, that the treaty recognized Russia's right to defend all Orthodox churches and believers throughout the Ottoman Empire.[14] Two minor points in the treaty of 1774 were altered to suit the diplomatic realities of 1775. The message was clear: the empress intended to discard the policies of the 1760s and pursue expansionary plans. If Panin was to retain his office and his influence with her, he would have to abandon his Northern Accord and accommodate himself to a fundamental reorientation in Russian foreign policy.

He did not. In the late 1770s he began an effort to win the empress's endorsement of a pact with Russia, Prussia, and the Ottoman Empire.[15] He acted as if unaware that the empress was dismantling his Northern Accord. She was then playing the role of neutral mediator in the dispute between Prussia and Austria over the Bavarian succession. Her policy of Armed Neutrality of 1780 was directed against England and its war effort against the American rebels.[16] Her designs on Turkish territory were displayed quite explicitly in 1779 on the occasion of the birth of her grandson. The infant was christened Constantine, at once a symbol of a political lineage that extended back to the last Byzantine emperor and a claim to a new empire in Constantinople. The empress arranged for an alliance with Austria, to be signed in 1782, that allowed her to renew belligerencies against the Porte, while her minister advised her to act in league with Prussia and the Ottoman Empire. As Griffiths has succinctly stated: "The Empress told a Polish countess that the Foreign Minister served as a mask behind which she could carry out her own policies without alarming other courts, and especially her Greek Project, 'my greatest, dearest and most glorious plan . . . to chase the Turks out of Europe and to enthrone myself in Byzantium.'"[17] Panin's position was untenable; he was relieved of his duties in the fall of 1781.

Panin proved himself to be consistent in his ideas on Russian foreign policy. He built his professional reputation on his services in Copenhagen and Stockholm and on his advocacy of the Northern Accord. After working for nearly two decades to maintain close relations between Russia and the Northern powers, he had a stake in a system which he did not choose to abandon. Panin was hardly in a position to impose his diplomatic preferences on the empress. Her authority was never challenged—nor did Panin ever contemplate such a challenge. He could only try to persuade Catherine that her interest in expansionary policies was ill-conceived. When these efforts were unsuccessful, Panin lost favor with the empress and forfeited his post.

The lesson was not lost on the Fonvizin group. The men's opposition to war and expansion had been on record since the early 1760s. They could be expected to criticize Catherine's military policies on principle alone. Circumstances, however, had changed. When they first debated the merits of a non-aggressive foreign policy, the government's involvement in the Seven Years' War was quite unpopular. In the late sixties and early seventies a pacific stand ran counter to the widespread support for the Turkish War. It was far easier for the group to win the enthusiasm of the journals' readers in 1760–1762 than in 1769–1774. More important, the men had first publicized their support for a diplomatic policy of restraint while students at Moscow University. During the Turkish War Fonvizin and Bogdanovich were stationed in the offices of the College of Foreign Affairs, and Novikov's support for Panin, the senior member of the college, has been noted. Public criticism of the war was no longer a matter of the abstract moral declarations typical of the student journals but commentary by members of Panin's clique. All three men viewed the war through Panin's eyes. When they criticized the war, they were moved by considerations of its detrimental effects on Panin's power and status in the bureaucracy as well as by its violations of their principles.

Panin endowed his diplomatic system with a hallowed quality. By the prestige of his person, he lent the Northern Accord a legitimacy in the minds of his clients that did not accurately correspond to its standing with the empress. When imperial policies became increasingly expansionary after 1768, the Fonvizin group was slow to comprehend the change, their apprehensions allayed for a time by their confidence in Panin and his control of diplomatic affairs. Once Catherine's redirection of Russian foreign policy was clearly perceived and its significance appreciated, the Fonvizin group wrote to publicize an idealized version of Panin's policies. In the men's comments on the Turkish War they were explicit about what they had only suggested in their works on the council project. Once Panin's preferences in policy had been rejected by the empress, they began to associate them with the principle of nationality.

— 3 —

The Fonvizin group's criticisms of the Turkish War were initially quite mild, gradually more explicit and forceful, and finally quite clearly censorious of Catherine's plans. Novikov dedicated the first issue of the *Babbler* in June 1770 to an unidentified military leader who "fights with the enemies of our fatherland, [and] . . . will share in those glorious laurels which justly crown the bravest of Russian warriors." [18] The dedication was probably an attempt to take advantage of the popularity of the war as well as win the attention of an important individual whose influence was useful to Novikov in his constant battles with the censors. He added in a separate article an almost messianic opinion of the purposes of the Turkish War. "The Turks are in the exactly same disastrous situation with the Russians as the Greeks have been for several hundred years with the Turks." [19] Novikov seemingly had little trouble in reconciling principle with the war: he was simply quick to sacrifice his ideals.

He wrote in 1771, however, one poem that he did not include in his journals, did not sign, and allowed to be published only as an addendum to the last issue of the periodical the *Scrupulous Parnassian*. Novikov had reason to be circumspect. He had modified his support for the Turkish War. Novikov translated Voltaire's "Sur La Guerre Des Russes Contre Les Turcs en 1768," rewriting the forty-eight-line poem as a short essay.[20] He retained Voltaire's principal argument: however detestable were wars and bellicose rulers, war against the Turks was an exception to the rule because the Ottoman rulers were "tyrants," ignorant and disdainful of their subjects. This argument allowed him to support the Turkish War without relinquishing his opposition to all other wars.[21]

He then, however, added comments of his own, thereby substantially altering the political significance of the ode. In what Novikov referred to as the opinion of "one citizen," he again struck the messianic note he had sounded in the *Babbler*. "The fatherland of Themistocles . . . is breaking its fetters from afar looking at the Eagle of Catherine; but it cannot yet destroy them. . . . There is no one in Europe . . . who dared follow the course shown to us by that triumphant eagle." [22]

Novikov clearly foundered in his attempts to balance principle and politics. The Voltairean defense of the war was substantially buttressed by comments that catered to the popularity of the Turkish War among his journals' subscribers. By making accommodations with popular enthusiam and aligning his opinions with the policies of the government, Novikov posed the problem that was left to Fonvizin and Bogdanovich to resolve. Novikov could retain his unqualified support for his convictions only if he demonstrated some degree of independence from the decisions of the throne; Bogdanovich and Fonvizin recognized that their principles and political loyalties could not, ultimately, be reconciled.

Bogdanovich's initial remarks on the Turkish War were similar to those of Novikov. He referred to Voltaire, translating in 1771 the ode "A l'Imperatrice de Russie Catherine II, à l'occasion de la prise de choczim par les Russes, en 1769." [23] By lending his name to this translation, Bogdanovich endorsed Voltaire's argument that Russian military victories were the lesser evil in comparison to the rule of the Ottoman Turks. After this poem, Bogdanovich ceased comment on the Turkish War. He wrote nothing specifically directed at the increasingly aggressive military policies the government promoted during the 1770s. He returned to commenting on contemporary events in the 1780s. Bogdanovich praised the empress's annexation of the Crimea in 1783, the capture of Ochakov in 1788, and the treaty of peace concluded with the Turks in 1792.[24] These odes surely suggest that Bogdanovich abandoned his opposition to expansionary military policies. Bogdanovich seemingly chose the path all but taken by Novikov and, it must be remembered, followed by Sumarokov.

Bogdanovich's literary silence in the 1770s did not indicate that he had come to believe his principles did not apply to Catherine's military and political schemes, but, rather, that he was looking for ways of retaining his convictions despite these policies. His search continued for some ten years and was evident in several of his works. In the same year the Voltaire ode appeared, Bogdanovich also translated Rousseau's *Extrait Du Projet de Paix Perpétuelle de Monsieur l'Abbé de Saint-Pierre*. Written in 1713 after the disastrous wars in seventeenth-century France and England, the book was an investigation of the general problem of wars, their causes, and prevention. St. Pierre proposed to limit each European state's absolute claims to national sovereignty. The plan, which Rousseau thought was "a well-argued and wise course of action," [25] proposed the creation of "the Republic of Europe." [26] It was "necessarily a coercive agency with the power to direct and coordinate the policies of its members. In this way their common interests and mutual endeavors were given a strength of purpose which would otherwise not be the case." [27] This European confederation was particularly necessary as a control on any potentially aggressive rulers. "Conquests must not be tolerated.

The conqueror must be made to assume that his aggression, once initiated, will be opposed and defeated by greater forces than he can himself muster." [28] The coercive powers of the confederation were to compel monarchs to renounce military ambitions so that they would be more attentive to the needs of their people. "The prince, however considerable his wealth, is in a position to encourage [the growth of] commerce, agriculture, and the arts. He can see to the founding of institutions of such benefit to the public good that they increase the material prosperity of his people as well as bring even more wealth to his own treasury. His actions can bring his state the security that it cannot derive from the power of its armies." [29]

Bogdanovich's translation was by its timing and content an endorsement of St. Pierre's position. Though Catherine changed her policies after 1768, Bogdanovich did not abandon his opposition to aggressive military sovereigns. As he witnessed with dismay Russian expansion in the 1770s and 1780s, he began to consider possible remedies in terms of a vision of an ideal political order, transcending the one he found repugnant and reordering the relations between the constituent members.

Bogdanovich sought in Russia's past an ideal polity, a fictional version of the political and moral order violated by Catherine after 1768. He turned to the study of Russian history and the writing of his *Historical Depiction of Russia*. To his disappointment his research yielded precedents to the empress's actions. He described the Kievan princes Igor and Sviatoslav as examples of rulers whose activities were almost exclusively military. However successful Sviatoslav was as a warrior, he failed as a ruler because he did not consolidate his victories on the battlefield by arranging a lasting peace.[30] Igor's policies were also proof of the hollowness of military efforts. "War, often harmful to the state, is always beneficial to military rulers bent on serving their own interests in the destruction of humanity." [31]

Bogdanovich's discovery was hardly unusual. It was a historiographical commonplace in his sources, the chronicles, to recount the military feats of the Kievan rulers. What he added were moral judgments and political commentaries on Kievan princes similar to those he had made in the early 1760s. Bogdanovich also introduced an additional criticism of military rulers. He condemned them for satisfying their individual desires at the expense of the commonweal. The distinction was based not on their violations of his expectations in the sovereigns and their governments, which were his standards in the early 1760s, but on their failure to abide by the traditions of "the Slavs." The latter were presumed to share a marked dislike of wars and rulers of

Igor's variety. "The Slavs" demonstrated a common respect for an order that was disturbed, never strengthened, by military ventures. They had in their cultural heritage a moral domain that was distinct from the realm of the warrior-prince. Bogdanovich disassociated the interests of the commonweal from those of the ruler and state.

He made this distinction again, this time with the detail of definition that gave it clarity and significance, in the *Slavs*, a play written in 1787. In this play Bogdanovich described the love affair between Alexander the Great and Dobroslava, "a Slavic woman" captured and held hostage by the Greeks. The choice of Alexander was obviously significant given the many references to him in the student journals. Bogdanovich's Alexander recognized the limited benefits of military campaigns and victories. "I realize . . . that war is not a beneficial profession and can be justified only by absolute necessity." [32] "I [will be] satisfied only when I do not find it necessary to subject people to my commands; that is when people realize and fulfill their duties on their own [initiative]." [33] Admitting his rule was one of coercion at home and military expansion abroad, Alexander claimed he had discovered in the Slavs a people who carried out their duties without any prodding by their government.[34] Bogdanovich suggested a subtle comparison between a government run by a militarily ambitious monarch and a people at peace and free of coercive intervention by any political administration.[35] His belief in a nonexpansionary foreign policy was preserved by removing foreign policy from the ruler's control to a fictional realm apart from the throne.

Bogdanovich was able to retain his principles by refraining from using them to judge Catherine's politics. In this way he was able to write several odes in praise of the empress's military successes of the 1780s and 1790s without having any qualms of conscience. He could curry imperial favor while harboring the mental image of a fictional world that preserved and confirmed his convictions. Bogdanovich maintained a harmony between his personal values and political principles, but only by removing his inner, moral self from involvement with the disharmonies that surrounded him.

This tactic did not serve Bogdanovich well. The link between his personal self and social self was the key assumption supporting his moral and political activities. Without this dynamic element, his remarks on wars and the Alexanders of the 1780s remained quite similar to those of the early 1760s. His opinions did not grow in sophistication of argument or definition of detail. He had followed just such a sequence when he had transferred his political expectations from the monarch to the council. He was capable of refining and extending ideals dating from his university years but chose not to. Because the impelling force of personal moral ideals was lacking, he did not refer in his comments on wars and military rulers to the theoretical guide to his political opinions, namely the dictums of German natural law theories. Once Catherine's Turkish policies invalidated Bogdanovich's rationale for service to the government, the preservation of the tranquility of his inner self took precedence over combatting a ruler whose policies violated the canons of natural law philosophy. For this reason Bogdanovich did not invoke Pufendorf or Wolff on the nature of a just war.

Bogdanovich's opinions on the Turkish War were confined to those he borrowed from Voltaire. If his works of the 1770s and 1780s were to document convictions held independently of the throne, he needed to define the specific characteristics of the ideal order that was to replace that spoiled by the empress and to place it not in the Russia of Igor or Sviatoslav but in that of Catherine. He had to add precision to the generalities in his history and the *Slavs*, lest his fictional order be little more than the fantasies of one who was in moral disarray.

Fonvizin made the first attempt at identifying a morally reformed version of Catherinian Russia, a configuration of political fictions that lent validity to his personal convictions and emphasized the political imperfections of the imperial government. When Catherine embarked on her expansionary course, Fonvizin withheld comment until the time of the first partitioning of Poland. Rather surprisingly he approved of this initiative, though as reluctantly and belatedly as did Nikita Panin. In a letter of April 17, 1772, to Peter Panin, Fonvizin agreed that a tripartite division of Poland was necessary. "[*We acq*]*uire for this price* the elimination of a large major war which is exhausting us, we *ach*[*ieve the elimination*] of the Polish rebels who distract our attention from other matters and cause us excessive troubles and interminable care. Above all, our participation in the partitioning of Poland assures us a satisfactory share *from it* for ourselves. It would be extremely regrettable if new disputes or, God forbid, even a new war were to begin for the sake of some portion of partitioned Polish land." [36] To prevent a larger war, Fonvizin could countenance the partitioning. When Catherine selected a representative for the peace conference with the Turks at Focsani in July 1772, Fonvizin was disappointed by the choice of Grigorii Orlov as Russian envoy. "It is true that it is wise to compare the character necessary for an ambassador with the character of the one who is appointed: is it possible that God is so unkind to his own creation that human blood is shed on account of one vacuous head?" [37]

Fonvizin's despair over Catherine's war policies led him to make the same type of comparison as had Bogdanovich. In a letter to Peter Panin, Fonvizin commented that "your [that is, P. Panin] patriotic [*patrioticheskie*] discussions about peace, dear sir, do not of course find any opposition from any true citizens." [38] The association of nonaggressive policies with "patriotic citizens" was not a casual one. The word "patriotic" was not used with any specific connotation in the 1760s when Fonvizin was working for the reform of the administration. The term "patriotic" took on significance after aggressive policies became the official plans of the government. Panin was complimented for being "patriotic" to the fatherland or nation rather than to the government.

Fonvizin's remarks were significant in two respects. He did not invoke the standard of patriotism as a fallback to national sentiments he had hitherto ignored. The appeal was one there had been no need to make before the 1770s. National interests were, Fonvizin could assume in the 1760s, identical to those of the state. When Catherine's diplomatic policies changed, Fonvizin was given reason to distinguish between the two objects of his loyalties. The principle of nationality made it possible for Fonvizin to maintain harmony between his personal convictions and his political loyalties. His praise for Panin's patriotism was the first reference to the role that the national standard played in the writings of all three members of the group. Each man arrived at his own definition of the national idea, but the idea enabled them all to bridge the gap between personal convictions and political loyalties.

As the three men began the process of interpreting, even if only to themselves, the meaning of the principle of nationality, the common assumption was that they no longer had a primary interest in committing themselves to particular political and social issues through the good offices of the ruler and her regime. They considered their personal well-being to be distinct from that of the government. The individual's moral impulse toward self-perfection was still inseparable from service and concern for the common welfare. The latter, however, was served through the agency of the national principle.

—— 4 ——

The Fonvizin group identified the national idea in its commentary on the events leading to Grand Duke Paul's majority on September 22, 1772. The importance of the occasion and the group's comments have been exaggerated by historians, particularly two recent Soviet historians. According to Makogonenko and, though less so, Pigarev, Paul's majority caused a political crisis that threatened Catherine's tenure as sovereign. The empress was confronted by Panin and his associates and clients, who urged her to do in 1772 what they expected her to do in 1762, namely step aside and allow her son to rule. When Fonvizin and his peers celebrated Paul's majority, they were moved, according to Makogonenko and Pigarev, by their disillusionment with Catherine's tactics between 1762 and 1767, their "unmasking" of the despotic nature of her reign, and their intention of replacing her despotism with the rule of a sovereign who allowed constitutional restrictions on his exercise of power. Panin's followers rallied around the banner of patriotism as a sign of their opposition to Catherine and support for Paul.

These arguments depend, among other things, on the group having maintained a consistency of political purpose. The remedy for a despotic ruler was a new and reformed monarch. Yet Fonvizin's writings on the Turkish War did not exhibit this consistency. The comments of Bogdanovich and Novikov show no steadfastness of political purpose. In Bogdanovich's case it is particularly clear that the war dispelled his interest in the government rather than provoked a reassertion of his political convictions. The strength of Makogonenko's and Pigarev's interpretation rests on the claim that loyalty to the government was discredited and replaced by allegiance to the "fatherland." Did the Fonvizin group define this term, politically or otherwise, as a signal of their dissent from Catherine's policies and their intention to combat them? [39]

The Fonvizin group was acutely aware of the importance of the grand duke's majority. The three men were closely associated with Paul. They had received permission to attend Paul's court, no doubt because of their connections with Nikita Panin, the grand duke's tutor, and they made frequent use of this privilege. As the day of Paul's majority drew near, the Fonvizin group used the occasion to make the comparison between the government, one that neither honored its commitments nor justified expectations in its policies, and the "fatherland," the word that was to serve as the symbolic term for the national principle. The group's first references to the fatherland in the early seventies were not made with any precision of definition, but simply showed their attachment to the national principle and their intention to associate Grand Duke Paul with the "fatherland."

When Novikov published in 1772 his *Historical Dictionary of Russian Writers*, he dedicated the book to "the Crown Prince and Grand Duke, Paul Petrovich, heir to the throne of all the Russias." [40] These seemingly innocuous terms were laden with political significance. Unlike his mother, Paul, who was officially recognized as the crown prince by Peter III, had legitimate claims to the throne. Novikov's dedication, like Sumarokov's dedication of the *Industrious Bee* to Catherine, was a timely and bold reminder of Paul's status. Unlike Sumarokov in 1759, Novikov did not have any confidence in the beneficial effects of a change of monarchs. Rather, Novikov's purpose was "to be of service to my fatherland." [41] He publicized not his disloyalty toward Catherine and the government but his disaffection with her regime.

Bogdanovich made the same point in his writings about the grand duke and the twin issues of succession and legitimacy. He wrote two odes, one on each of Paul's marriages in 1773 and 1776. In both odes he was no more than dutifully adulatory. [42] Bogdanovich refrained from direct, explicit statement on Paul's political status as heir and addressed himself only to the general problem of succession. In a brief essay, "Remarks Concerning the Rights of the Germans," he outlined the history of the Holy Roman Empire from the time of the Reformation to the Treaty of Westphalia. His thesis was that the decline of the empire was to be attributed to the lack of a clearly stated and commonly accepted law of succession. [43] What was necessary was a legally ordered succession on the model of the Golden Bull of 1356. [44] Bogdanovich surely did not intend to endorse the particulars of the Bull, namely its listing of electoral princes, their immunity from the jurisdiction of the emperor, and the like. He saw merit in it as a legislative act formally codifying the rules for the selection of a new emperor. When the rule of law did not apply on this issue, Bogdanovich argued, the rule of force prevailed. The consequences for the Holy Roman Empire were the same as those anticipated in St. Pierre's book: strife within the royal family and political disarray within the government. The German princes were willing to witness the decline of the empire rather than turn to the standard of legality. In doing so, they abdicated their political responsibilities to the government and "the people." [45]

Bogdanovich's point was the same one he had made in his history: aberrant rulers threatened the well-being of their subjects. Beyond that generality, his lack of clarity of terms veiled his confusion of principles. On one hand, he argued for a legal process to resolve the problem of succession; on the other, laws were a potential infringement on the "rights of the Germans" and an intrusion into a world ordered by their customs and traditions. Laws ceased to be rational guides to the conduct of persons and governments and came to be emotional and psychological means of describing Bogdanovich's reading of the traditions of the "people," whether the Germans in this case or the Russians in his history.

Bogdanovich's thoughts on the issue of succession were expanded in a short poem, "The Bliss of Peoples," published the year after Paul reached his majority.[46] He appealed to Paul to revive the tranquility of bygone years and promulgate laws to protect the weak from destruction by the powerful.[47] Though the terms were still less than lucid, his purpose was to sketch only the outline of a comparison between the contemporary rule of force, both at home and in foreign affairs, and the presumed existence of secure domestic and foreign conditions in the past. Bogdanovich employed the same terms that Novikov had used in 1772, but added specific references to Russia's history as a means of distinguishing the attributes of the national idea from those of the state. Bogdanovich rephrased and reformed the same line of thinking that had shaped his comments on the Turkish War. His distinctions remained nebulous until Fonvizin provided the first detailed definition of the fatherland. In giving the fatherland an identity he gave it political significance.

Fonvizin was probably better known to the grand duke than the other members of the group. Nikita Panin arranged a reading of *Brigadier* at Paul's dinner table, giving Fonvizin the opportunity to be formally introduced to Paul. Fonvizin was particularly talented at reading from his own comedies, and his efforts on this occasion were received with "a great deal of laughter."[48] He very much appreciated the grand duke's favorable opinion of *Brigadier*. "For his part, His Highness was pleased to make some very flattering compliments to me for my reading."[49] As a gesture of approval Paul gave Fonvizin permission to dine at his table. This informal association was enhanced by Fonvizin's appointment as the intermediary for Peter Panin's correspondence with Paul. At the time of the grand duke's majority, Fonvizin was closely attached to the grand duke.

Fonvizin's interest in Paul was publicly expressed in the summer of 1771. The grand duke became seriously ill with what Catherine called "a catarrhal ague which lasted approximately five weeks."[50] A catarrhal ague is a type of influenza that can be fatal. When Paul's health was completely restored by the fall of 1771,[51] Fonvizin celebrated the grand duke's recovery in a short essay.[52] Novikov considered the essay so important that he published it in its entirety in the *Painter*. What Fonvizin wrote was a clear statement of the group's increasing detachment from Catherine and the government.

He described the empress and the grand duke in mutually exclusive terms. She was praised for her concern and care for her son. She was "the source of our fame and bliss." [53] "Guided by her wisdom, successes follow her actions, her victories are crowned with laurels, and Russia becomes famous from her fame." [54] The praise was, however, limited to these remarks about Catherine's maternal compassion and military prowess. Paul was described in an entirely different manner. He was "the hope of the fatherland," the man who was brought up aware of "those sacred bonds that united him with the fate of millions of people and by which millions of people are united with him." [55] When the grand duke became ill, "Paul's sickness, though still in its initial stages, caused rumors to spread instantly from one home to another like the flame of a wild fire. All at once everyone felt sincere sadness." [56] The spiritual bonds uniting ruler and ruled made the people bewail the threat to Paul's life for his death would signify "the ruin of our fatherland." [57] Similarly, his recovery was "the hope of our future happiness." [58] For Fonvizin the empress was a successful military ruler while the grand duke was the embodiment of the fatherland.

Paul's qualities were so defined as to have certain similarities to the mythical imagery of the father-tsar, one who enjoyed a spiritual communion with his people while remaining apart from any administrative involvement. Fonvizin's image of the sovereign had undergone considerable revision. The legal ruler of the early 1760s was transformed into the all-but-mythical monarch of the early 1770s. The change was fraught with dangers and threatened Fonvizin's attempts to salvage something of the ethical spirit that so fired and diversified his interests in the 1760s. Once he vested in the "fatherland" the responsibility for maintaining some type of harmony between personal and political obligations he could not let his understanding of the national principle slip into the language of myth.

Fonvizin spoke for the group in withholding his support from the regime and preferring the fatherland. The group's writings in the early seventies were clear evidence of their difficulty in defining that detachment and newfound enthusiasm. Even the very code word for the national idea, the "fatherland," came to have different meanings to each of the three. In the sixties, the "government" was commonly understood to represent standards readily reconciled with their personal values. Yet the fatherland could be variously defined because its relation to each man's personal norms was becoming a matter of emotional, not logical, coherence. The term itself connotes a range of possible meanings. The Russian word for fatherland—*otechestvo*—is semantically derived from *otets*, the word for father. As Leonard Krieger pointed out in referring to *patria* and *pater*, the "fatherland" is an expression that alludes to the care and protection the father provides his dependents as well as their expectation of these benefits.[59] The "fatherland" had in its psychological roots an understanding of its responsibilities that was similar to the legal conception of the functions of the state, as interpreted by German natural law theorists and the Fonvizin group. What was meant by the German jurists to reinforce the moral tone of the subjects' lawful obligations to the state was for the Fonvizin group the means to remove and shelter their own sense of personal moral integrity. Loyalty to the state was no longer to have a moral dimension but was strictly a legal duty, willingly observed by Fonvizin, Novikov, and Bogdanovich. Patriotism was parallel, not opposed to statism.

This withdrawal, as much psychological as theoretical, left the group to resolve all the difficulties and ambiguities inherent in the nature of the term "fatherland." As the writings on Paul's succession demonstrated, the three men grappled with this problem but foundered in the process. For Novikov, who offered his moral services to the fatherland, the principle clearly played a mediating role, although the concept still lacked a clear definition. Bogdanovich lent the fiction of the fatherland an anthropological character. The more consistently he did so, the more he needed to revise his personal values to align them with his version of reality. He was less interested in reordering the politics and society of Catherinian Russia in imitation of his personal ideals than in allowing his reading of the world around him to intrude and mark the realm of his inner moral self. Fonvizin's reference to the fatherland could potentially serve as the fiction reuniting his moral criteria and political commitments and do so on bases that did not violate the norms he had held so dearly since his student days. The three men sought to reestablish the links between their inner moral selves and the worlds external to them via the symbolic term for the national principle. They began anew the venture that had started in the early sixties and was sustained until the late sixties. The group sought in the fatherland a better guide to the discovery of an ideal, morally reformed Russia than they had found in the state.

—— 5 ——

Novikov wanted to replace the moral and political order discredited by Catherine by referring to previous orders. He sought in Russia's past evidence of a consensus violated by the empress. Russia's history, not its ruler, was to serve as the agent leading him to his own understanding of the fatherland and thereby certifying his personal ideals and political convictions. Clearly the risk was that his investigations would lead to the idealization of early Russian history. Novikov was aware of this danger. In the first issue of the *Painter* he criticized those who deceived themselves by allowing their imagination rather than their rational faculties to be their guide in unfamiliar territory.[60] He looked for episodes and individuals in Russia's past that could demonstrate the presence of his own ideals of rationality and virtue.

This ambitious task was the reason he began to edit the *Old Russian Library* in 1773.[61] In the preface, Novikov stated his purpose: "It is useful to know the morals, customs, and rites of ancient, foreign peoples; but it is much more useful to know about one's own forefathers. It is praiseworthy to admire and do justice to the merits of foreigners, but it is shameful to disdain one's own countrymen and all the more to loathe them." [62] The *Old Russian Library* carried descriptions of many events of varied importance in pre-eighteenth-century history, such as notices on the marriage of Tsar Michael Romanov (1613–1645), the construction of the first vessel in Russia, the order of succession of Muscovite grand princes, and many reports of Russian ambassadors abroad. While the *Old Russian Library* served to disseminate information about pre-Petrine Russia, its editor found no documentation to prove that his personal ideals were present in pre-eighteenth-century Russia.

Novikov admitted this himself in an article in the *Purse* in 1774. He wrote a sharply critical letter to the editor and then debated with himself the results of his investigations in the *Old Russian Library*. Novikov the editor allowed the debate to be carried by Novikov the critic. The latter ridiculed the editor's optimistic assumptions about Russia's history.[63] The customs typical of Kievan and Muscovite Russia were, as any man of an enlightened age must admit, the traditions of a barbarous people at a primitive stage of development.[64] Russian civilization had nothing of its own worthy of mention. Whatever level of culture it achieved was due solely to the beneficent influence of French civilization. The critic characterized both the editor's loyalty to Russia's past and his love for the fatherland as madness.[65] The editor did not refute any of the criticism. The only rebuttal came from the critic himself, who made remarks damaging to his own case. He undermined the significance of his comments on the alleged dependence of Russian culture by describing French influence only in superficial terms of dress, manners, and speech. The main point was that Novikov allowed to stand his critic's suggestion that he separate his interest in Russia's past from his loyalty to the fatherland. The fatherland was to be defined without reference to pre-Petrine history. The national principle was not a means of finding in a utopian past confirmation of an order denied in a repellent present. Novikov's refusal to qualify his standards of rationality and virtue compelled him to reconsider the Russia of Catherine. To avoid becoming solipsistic in his attachment to his personal values, he had to devise a means of recasting an existent political order that he abhorred into one that was morally acceptable and fulfilling.

His solution was to give the "fatherland" the particular connotation of an evolutionary understanding of Russian history. In so doing he avoided comment on the incongruities between his values and the characteristics of contemporary state and society. He stood by his convictions without needing to denounce the failings of Russia in the eighteenth century and without threatening the validity of his principles. Novikov made his point in an article published in 1773 in the *Painter*. In a letter to the editor from a "Russian" (*rossiianin*), he sketched his image of the evolutionary process.

Novikov understood the essence of this evolution to be not historical and philosophical in nature but ethical, reducible in the first instance to questions of personal morality. The individual was to seek self-perfection by extending the inner moral self into the realities around him. "It is necessary," Novikov wrote at the very beginning of the article, "that we make our concern and affection for those near us the primary basis for all our actions." [66] The obligation to commit oneself to others was to be weighed against the consequences of involving oneself in a corrupt society, one that threatened one's moral integrity. Novikov restated the general ethical questions that were so typical of the student journals. In the early sixties, the students overcame their apprehensions about participating in a morally contaminated world and succumbed to the urge to reform it; in 1773 Novikov felt no such ethically compelling force. His response was to advise his editor, that is, himself, to go abroad and take note of the moral decadence common to European states and societies. Russia's moral debility was neither peculiar to its own history nor any worse than that of France. The key to understanding Russia's present condition was chronology. "Every people has been truly happy if it emerged from the shadows of ignorance and cruelty by accepting at first the virtues and eventually the sciences, arts, and enterprises of that people from whom its own enlightenment was borrowed. But it should be said that nothing can be perfect in the beginning. The grievous vices are already being eliminated everywhere while the minor ones will go out of style [*iz mody*] with time." [67] This organic approach to Russia's history relieved Novikov of the need to idealize the past or condone the present. He could afford to be optimistic about Russia's ultimate fortunes for, whatever its present moral state, time guaranteed its ultimate redemption.

Novikov assumed that Russia's future would witness its independence from foreign examples and its eventual improvement on them. He made his point clearly, if indirectly, in the *Purse*. The reader was allowed to overhear a conversation between two émigrés, a Frenchman and a German. Each man bewailed his own fate and commiserated with the other. The fates had been unkind to them. Each had forsaken a career at home—though the reader was later told that each had had little to abandon—and the privileges of the well-born—again it eventually was clear that they were men of quite humble origins—to become tutors of young Russian nobles. Given these backgrounds, it was striking when one of the tutors said that "the difference between a Frenchman and a Russian in the appreciation of the sciences consists entirely in the fact that one undertook the sciences a great deal later than the other." [68] The tutor continued by noting, as if stating a known certitude, that Russia was changing at a faster rate than her predecessors. He predicted that Russia would eventually become the center of Europe's attention. With this assumption in mind, the tutors thought about each other's pupils and expressed only disdain for them. For what did they do, the two admitted, but substitute pretensions for knowledge and then deceive their gullible students. The Russians readily deferred to them and aped their manners and speech. "In a word it can be said that the conduct of a Russian with a Frenchman can be likened to a man enslaved by vices." [69] The minors failed to recognize that the influence of French culture was like the legendary philosopher's stone; instead of turning base metals into gold, it changed Russian virtues into vices and French vices into virtues. [70]

Novikov spoke through his characters in associating the uncritical adoption of foreign customs with the lack of rationally restrained, virtuous conduct. His opposition to foreign influences was qualified. In the Matveev volume, published two years after the article in the *Purse*, he praised his subject's knowledge of the arts and sciences of Western Europe as well as his interest in the work of foreign scholars.[71] Novikov assumed that it was his duty as a "son of the fatherland" (*syn otechestva*) to publicize Matveev's use of this knowledge to better his service to the fatherland.[72] Both Novikov's esteem for the critical acceptance of Western influences and his disdain for the minors' blind adoption of all things French had been apparent in the pages of the *Drone*. Yet there was a significant revision in his ideas. In 1769 the presence of ignorant French tutors and foppish minors was blamed on the influence of French culture. Now, in 1774, the culpable agent had changed. The dominance of French mores was not itself pernicious but characteristic of one stage in Russia's development. The same process that created the temporary need for certain elements of French culture would gradually reduce Russia's dependence on France and ultimately eliminate it. The folly of those Russians who would be Frenchmen lay not only in their conduct but also in their failure to appreciate the direction and significance of Russia's evolution. Russia itself was absolved of responsibility for the phenomena of foppish minors and French tutors. The relation between the two was temporal, not causal. The young Russians were themselves responsible for their bondage to their passions and, as a consequence, their vices.

Novikov returned in the two articles in the *Purse* and the *Painter* to the questions of the moral responsibilities of the individual that were common to the student journals of a decade past. He reviewed and reconsidered the nature and scope of his values after the tumultuous events of the late 1760s. As a student and then as a public servant his goal was to perfect the personal self by commitments to the social self. His moral quest was not violated by his loyalty to Catherine's government. In serving Catherine, he sought to attain universal ethical goals that transcended the Russian government. Service was given a compelling moral force by its association with cosmopolitan ethical ideals.

After the late sixties this moral dimension to service was removed. Novikov redirected his moral values and loyalties toward the fatherland, which all but forced him to sacrifice universal ideals for ones that were national and particular. The fatherland as an evolutionary understanding of Russian history was but one step short of recognition of Russia's particularity and independence. Novikov never took this next step. The term never acquired in his writings the philosophical or historicist connotation that could give it the capacity to dominate rather than serve his moral purpose. After the mid-seventies the "fatherland" remained what it had been in the *Painter* and the *Purse*, the symbol of the moral realm within which Novikov reestablished the links between his inner self and those arenas of social commitment that fulfilled and ratified his personal values.

This consistency of purpose is useful to remember in evaluating Novikov's priorities after 1774. He left clues in the *Painter* of what was to come later in his life. He hinted that he might enter the publishing business, sell books, and edit works on Russian history. In point of fact Novikov formed the first Russian publishing society in St. Petersburg in 1773; in 1779 he leased the press at Moscow University from his friend Mikhail Kheraskov, then curator of the university, and began a vigorous program of publication; in 1784 he made his first plans for a private printing company and, most significantly, in 1787 he organized a system of famine relief. Novikov's enterprises of the 1770s and 1780s were so successful that they provided a catalogue of precedents to the social activities of many nineteenth-century writers.

Many of Novikov's biographers were quick to recognize these activities as signals of his interest in Masonry, which dated from his first visit to a lodge in 1775. He was frequently with the Masons in St. Petersburg after 1779. Longinov, Vernadskii, and, though less so, Bogoliubov cited this association as evidence that Novikov became "disillusioned" with the ideal of rationality by 1774 and thereafter stressed the importance of ethics.[73] Vernadskii was most emphatic: Masonry represented a retreat to the company of morally stalwart individuals to compensate for a society proven corrupt and impervious to Novikov's efforts to reform it.

The difficulty with these arguments is that, as Makogonenko pointed out, Novikov's interest in publishing and editing books in the 1770s and 1780s was hardly evidence of his renunciation of the standard of reason. It must be added that the opposition of reason to morals is in Novikov's case a false one. Reason and ethics were intertwined for Novikov at every point in his career. The question is not one of the balance between the rational and the moral— the latter emphasized by Longinov, Bogoliubov, and Vernadskii, the former by Makogonenko—for analyses based on the relative priority of one or the other risk becoming no more than exercises in disputatiousness. Novikov's biographers have been too quick to divide his life into stages. The change in his thinking did not represent a reassessment of the relative importance of the rational and the moral but a recalculation of the immediacy of the rational to the ethical. Novikov explained this distinction by referring to the evolutionary character of the fatherland. In the article, quoted above, in the *Purse*, he exclaimed: "Alas, when will it be within the powers of man to continue the process of enlightening Russians while also recovering their customs of bygone years, now debased. Then—and only then—will it be possible to recognize in them again the image of a human being." [74] The point was not that rationality threatened to defile the moral integrity of the Russians. Rather, the sciences could be neither appreciated nor advanced without a revived ethical background. The moral element was to be accentuated until the course of Russian history reached the point at which the Russians were adequately prepared. Again, it was only a question of time.

Novikov maintained his moral values intact after 1774, but his success had a price, one that involved the nature of his political ideas and loyalties to Catherine the Great. After 1774 he was not as intensely interested in the fortunes of the Panin clique as he once had been, nor did the struggle between favorites and honorable men retain his acute attention. As his interests and enthusiasms diverged from the current policies of the government, his reference to the fatherland signaled not only his disappointment with Catherine's policies but also his adoption of an alternative conception of change. Political commentary of the 1760s readily assumed that the only means of bringing about reforms of any type was through the initiative of the state. Strictly speaking, the ruler, as distinct from the government, was the only effective agent for change. Now, in the 1770s, Novikov put these assumptions to the side. Change was an inevitable consequence of Russia's organic development. The mediation of the monarch was no more than evidence of this process. Novikov could allow himself to believe that his political convictions and his enthusiasm for the empress in the 1760s were not discredited by Catherine's policies of the 1770s, but misplaced. No disloyalty to the empress was present. Nonetheless, Novikov sustained his ethical values and political convictions by removing himself from the politics of Catherinian Russia. The state that was originally expected to be the means of bringing about a morally reformed Russia was left unattended by one whose interest in the fatherland provided a fictional representation of such a utopian order.

Novikov overcame his predecessors' fascination with the monarch only to arouse an enthusiasm for the fatherland that was misdirected or, at the same time, too widely directed. His definition of the national principle was so broad and vague it undermined the very function it was to serve. It gave Novikov's ideals and activites only a loose cohesion, not the rigorous order provided by his reference to the state. The national idea ratified his convictions but on terms that were derived by association, not logic. Novikov devalued the very unity to his ideals and career that he strove to maintain. Moreover, his version of the national idea was not informed by theory.[75] He dispensed with the unqualified endorsement of state initiatives but did not define substantively an alternative to the state as the moving force in historical change. It was not a failing in his writings as much as a characteristic of one who wrote before the age of Romanticism in Russia. Novikov referred to the fatherland on bases that diminished both the significance of his conception of change and the value of the totality of his interests. His thinking progressed no further after 1774. His references to the fatherland in the journals of the early seventies served Novikov's primary interest, the maintenance of his own moral ideals.

—— 6 ——

Bogdanovich was less deliberate than Novikov in his formulation of the national idea and even less interested in deriving its attributes from the ideals of rationality and virtue. This was to be expected. After 1768 his writings were witness to hopes abandoned and principles undermined by Catherine's changes in policy. Even before the time of Paul's majority Bogdanovich was ready to disavow publicly his expectations in the state and succumb to an ideal version of what was denied in reality. His translation in 1771 of St. Pierre's plan for European unity was a telltale sign.

Bogdanovich had little trouble in referring this utopian order to Russian history. In "The Bliss of Peoples," written two years after the St. Pierre translation, he presented an idealized picture of ancient Russian history. He sketched a poetic image of a people at a primitive stage of development. Bogdanovich presumed that individuals in the earliest stages of a society's evolution were free of the vices that corrupted all advanced civilizations. Man in early Russian history—Bogdanovich did not bother with any specific chronology—lived the life of the natural savage. "The feelings served only to satisfy him: he did not know then how to use them for evil. The passions did not corrupt his innocence: he did not extend his desires beyond his needs; he desired only what was within his power, and consequently he had everything he wanted."[76] During this period men were untainted by "scorn, hatred, insinuation, deceit, lies, pride, slander, pretense, and hypocrisy."[77] "Innocence, truth, love, and virtue were preserved happily everywhere on the earth."[78]

This paean to Russia's lost innocence was repeated in the *Historical Depiction of Russia*. Bogdanovich presented an idealized account of Kievan Russian history. He characterized Kievan Russians as innocents in a Rousseauian state of bliss. In his history, he was also prepared to do what he did not do in "The Bliss of Peoples." He explicitly and repeatedly referred to his version of Russia during the Kievan period as the "fatherland." [79] Bogdanovich relinquished his confidence in the ordering powers of reason for the sake of embracing the illusion of a fictional world of virtue. Rationality was no longer the necessary complementary value to the cultivation of virtue, which was removed from the world of Catherinian Russia and secured in a distant past. From this perspective on Russian history, he created a vantage point from which to complain of the corruption of his own era and mourn the lost innocence of earlier times.

Bogdanovich waived the demands of logical rigor in matters of moral self-perfection and social commitment. In return he assured himself an inner moral sanctuary, protected from contemporary circumstances by its remoteness from them. Within this reserve he could keep safe his personal moral tranquility. He no longer engaged himself with specific policies and personalities of the imperial government, but he did nothing that prevented him from carrying out diligently and loyally his duties in the bureaucracy. After the 1770s, Bogdanovich, unlike Novikov, did not try to make the politics and society of his day fit his personal ethical values. However much emotional and psychological satisfaction Bogdanovich drew from his notions of the fatherland, he remained morally listless.

Bogdanovich added to his understanding of the national idea the same evolutionary understanding of the principle as had Novikov. Bogdanovich's conception of this evolution was quite rudimentary, denoting only an unfolding, historical process toward increasingly complex stages. Again, in "The Bliss of Peoples," man's initial innocence was corrupted when he was unable to satisfy his passions. Thereafter vices became more dominant than virtues: "Then the most happy of all was he who was the most powerful; friend rises up against friend, and the sword is drawn for revenge. One sees profits, the other vain glory, another forestalling his own fears. . . . The fate of the people was in the hands of the powerful. . . . Man heeded neither duty nor honor, whose voices were then silent, and deceit reigned." [80] The period of lost innocence was replaced by the times of passion, vice, and force. Bogdanovich did not date this basic change, yet his concluding appeal to Paul provided a fairly accurate measure. The grand duke was implored to shield the innocent from destruction by establishing protective laws and restoring the tranquility of former centuries.[81]

No matter how vague his use of terms and how bland his definition of the evolutionary character of Russian history, Bogdanovich's writings conveyed significant themes. He contrasted Catherine's policies of the 1770s, particularly the diplomatic designs and the rule of favorites, with earlier periods of Russian history in which the individual enjoyed security from force. Bogdanovich also described his apprehensions about the modern state, apart from the specific plans of any one monarch at any one time or place. His fears certainly arose from his experiences with the Panin party during the 1760s. For it was then that he became familiar with the capacities of the state and the futility of any faction's effort to control its apparatus. These particular circumstances led Bogdanovich to conclude that the state was not an appropriate repository for the trust of virtuous citizens but a threat to their moral well-being.

He followed Novikov in disassociating himself from the government. Their renunciation of contemporary politics was exclusively an ethical one. Their attachment to the fatherland represented their appropriation of the national principle as a surrogate for their moral interests. Both men appointed themselves custodians of the national idea. While they retained their political loyalty to the imperial government, they subordinated that allegiance to their duty to act as guardians of an ethical order whose integrity vouchsafed each man's personal well-being and the welfare of all. Fonvizin took the next step: he called attention to the danger of Catherine's policies to the moral commonweal that was the fatherland.

—— 7 ——

Fonvizin's most general comments on the national principle were made in his letters from France in 1777–1778. His remarks were interspersed with notes about cities he visited along his route to Paris, chance meetings with fellow voyagers, and reassurances to his family about his health and safety. In many ways Fonvizin's letters from abroad were the jottings of a tourist, in others the descriptions of heightened expectations on traveling to the new "Jerusalem," and in still others the words of one who anticipated a larger audience for his letters than his friends alone.[82] The random nature of his references to Russia's history belied his purpose, which was to convey his notions about the evolutionary nature of Russian history.

On January 25, 1778, he wrote his close friend Iakov Ivanovich Bulgakov (1743–1809), a classmate at Moscow University and career official in the College of Foreign Affairs, describing his conception of Russia's relationship to Western Europe: "If they began to live here before us, then we who are only beginning, can at least give ourselves the form that we want and escape those disadvantages and troubles that have been engrained here. Nous commençons et ils finissent. I think that one who has just come into the world is more fortunate than one who is leaving it." [83] Fonvizin included in his version of Russia's evolution the same quality given it by Novikov, namely approval for the selective use of Western European influences. Yet Fonvizin went so far as to outline a sequence of chronological cycles that ensured Russia's eventual predominance over European states. What was for Novikov a question of Russia's temporary dependence on Western Europe was for Fonvizin a basis for assuming that Russia's historical progression was to take place in a sphere separate from Europe. In his letters Fonvizin went no further in specifying and refining this organic conception of Russian history.

Fonvizin's ideas on Russia's evolutionary development acquire a particular political significance when contrasted to those of Catherine. The empress spelled out her opinions in her famous "Antidote," a rebuttal to the Abbé Chappe d'Auteroche's *Voyage en Sibérie*. The "Antidote," published initially in Amsterdam in 1770, refuted the Abbé's particular criticisms of Russia's backwardness by enveloping them in a grand schema of historical change. Catherine argued that there were laws of history that regulated the evolution of every civilization. Russia's development was parallel to that of France, England, or any European country. All were participants in the same evolutionary process. The tempo of this change was uniform until the Time of Troubles, the period of cultural disarray and political strife after the death of the last Muscovite ruler (1598–1613), interrupted Russia's steady advance. Nevertheless, the empress was quick to add, the pace was resumed and ensured the eventual elimination of any vestiges of backwardness.[84] Catherine stressed Russia's equality with Europe and the universality of the historical laws governing Russian history. Fonvizin asserted Russia's particularity.

The empress also appealed to national sensibilities. She presumed a long-standing harmony between the state and its subjects and was prepared to extol the virtues, industry, and, above all, honesty of the Russian people. She was even willing to allow that a monarch deficient in "energy" and respect for the national feelings of his subjects was subject to removal by revolution. This circumstance was described by reference to Peter III: "This sovereign surrounded himself with such foolhardy men that they aroused in him a hatred of his own people. This could not be concealed by [Peter]. . . . Everyone recognized that the empire would be rent asunder by a sovereign who ruled without regard for prudence and justice. During his reign the words 'the fatherland' were considered criminal. In these circumstances the state soon had to face a revolution." [85] Catherine repeated in 1770 the interpretation of Peter III's reign that she initially made in the manifesto of July 6, 1762. For this reason the charge that the tsar threatened the sanctity of the fatherland is important only as a clue to her reading of the relationship between state and nationality. However much she made of the virtues of the Russian people Catherine reserved greater praise for the state. The empress wanted to appropriate the national idea to shore up her own government. She wished to encase ruler and ruled in an evolutionary process that pointed up the primacy of the state. The empress subordinated the principle of nationality to the interests of state. Fonvizin recognized no identity between nationality and monarchy.

Upon his return from France Fonvizin added detail and sophistication to what were in his letters only notions about Russia's history. He defined its evolution according to the criteria of rationality and virtue. Moreover, he identified his ideas with the fiction of the fatherland, a term he used with a logical rigor absent in the works of Bogdanovich and Novikov. To Fonvizin the fatherland was neither remote in Russia's past nor apart from the politics of Catherinian Russia. He used his understanding of the national idea as a political standard against which the empress's policies were to be evaluated. In so doing, Fonvizin proved to have more consistency of political and moral conviction than Bogdanovich or Novikov. This mark of Fonvizin's thinking compelled him to answer Catherine's changes of policy by writing an indictment of her for violating the very ethical and political principles that had first aroused the group's interest in her.

His detailed indictment of Catherine appeared in the "Discourse on Immutable State Laws." Unfortunately, it is not clear that Fonvizin wrote this essay. Among recent commentators Makogonenko attributed the work to Fonvizin, dating its composition in the fall of 1778, whereas Ransel considered it the joint effort of Fonvizin and the Panin brothers. [86] The evidence supports Ransel though additional detail on Fonvizin's role is in order. Peter Panin noted in a letter of October 1, 1784, to Grand Duke Paul that his brother Nikita conceived and initiated the proposal for fundamental laws but his death prevented its completion. Nikita Panin also wrote, according to his brother, some type of initial statement for the project which was "preserved" by Fonvizin. Peter Panin admitted that his brother's health was so poor in the years before Nikita's death in 1783 that "this entire discourse was written from the verbal instructions of the recently deceased." [87]

Peter Panin was engaging in obfuscation. He was obviously reluctant to provide precise details, and herein lies a clue to Fonvizin's relation to the "Discourse." Ransel pointed out that the essay should not be considered as an individual document but as one in a series of papers composed by the Panin brothers and Fonvizin in the years before Nikita Panin's death. In addition to the "Discourse" they drafted an outline for a constitution, a statement of the principles that were to guide Paul upon his accession to the throne, and a manifesto to be issued at that time.[88] The "Discourse" is unique among the four papers in its moral tone and references to premises and arguments particular to Fonvizin. Apparently he was entrusted by Peter Panin with the task of setting in print the ideas that Fonvizin had acquired by daily contact and discussion with Nikita Panin over the course of many years' service to him. Peter Panin's statement to the contrary, Nikita was so ill during the last few years of his life that he lost all use of his tongue and memory. He could not have dictated any part of the "Discourse." Fonvizin probably summarized Nikita's ideas without his assistance. It was, however, far more advantageous for Peter Panin to propose the reforms as the political testament of the highly admired and recently deceased Nikita Panin. Fonvizin wrote the "Discourse" in the literal sense, was guided *in spiritu* by Nikita Panin, and adapted the political lessons learned from him to the ethical and political concerns that were his alone.

The "Discourse" was, in many respects, a restatement of Fonvizin's political ideals: "Sovereign power is entrusted to the monarch to enable him to tend to the welfare of his subjects and for no other reason." [89] The ruler was invested in his office by God to serve this purpose. God "rules by eternal truths which he himself cannot change, by which he governs the universe and which he himself cannot transgress without denying himself. By following God's example, a sovereign, the heir on earth of the supreme power, is similarly able to distinguish neither his powers nor personal worth other than by establishing in his state [*gosudarstvo*] immutable rules [*pravila*], based on the general good [*obshchee blago*], which he himself cannot violate without ceasing to be a worthy sovereign." [90] God certified the powers of a monarch because of the nature of his supervision over the universe. If God was the omnipotent, Davidian God and not the deist one, the ruler as earthly trustee did not need to abide by immutable rules. If God was conceived in a deist image but the sovereign did not realize the necessity of imitating the divine model, then the monarch's tenure was unjustifiable. Fonvizin's terms were those of a man of the sixties. The hierarchy of functions representing the affairs of individuals, rulers, and God was still intact.

He again turned to the terminology of the student journals when he identified the parties who discredited his utopian order. What caused monarchs, Fonvizin asked his reader, to ignore the restraints of laws, to subordinate the welfare of all to the promotion of their own reputations, to undo in a moment the accomplishments of their predecessors, and to regard as criminal what had always been considered legal? Arbitrariness [*proizvol*] was the single cause for these aberrations. A monarch who ruled by caprice was no better than the fictional Alexander the Great; both were examples of men who failed to control their own passions. To this explanation Fonvizin added another, taken from his political involvements with the Panins during the 1760s. An arbitrary ruler was one

> enslaved to one of his own unworthy *favorites*. I label him as unworthy because the term *favorite* is not one that I ascribe to any honorable [*dostoinyi*] man who has proven his true merit to the fatherland. He is usually one who has acquired a great deal of power by using his wiles to win the favor of the sovereign. In a state of such depravity the abuse of sovereign powers reaches truly unforeseeable dimensions. The distinction between the ruler and the ruled is lost as is that between the ruler and the favorite. All of the above are the consequences of arbitrariness.[91]

Fonvizin's criticism of the favorite was venomous. The favorite elevated his drunkenness from a personal vice to a social fashion, his poor upbringing from a disadvantage to an admirable trait, and his titles, wealth, and powers from a reward for service to a means of self-aggrandizement at the expense of the government. When the sovereign succumbed to the corrupt influence of the favorite, the symbol of moral order was discredited: "And what then can stop the spread of vice once the sovereign himself has set an example of illegality and dishonor in his very own quarters for all of society to see? What can be done when he becomes so bloated by his own shamelessly hedonistic ways that he is wont to utter publicly profanities against the sacred bonds of kinship, the code of honor, and the service he owes his fellow man? And what is to be done when he, the representative of legality, dares to flout the laws of God and man?"[92] Fonvizin added somewhat coyly that he would "not enter into the details of such a ruinous state of affairs" but did not refrain from offering this warning about arbitrariness: "The moral disease will become widespread. Vices will pervade and infect the court, city, and, ultimately, the state. The young will be contaminated and begin to show unmitigated disdain for everything that ought to be respected by them." [93] *Proizvol* was a malignancy that could undo the proper ties linking the people to the monarch and, in turn, the sovereign to God. The hierarchy of the morally just and dutiful would be destroyed by the denial of their common bonds and the ruler's power unleashed to wreak havoc on his subjects.

Moral and political disarray in the government was not a spectacle Fonvizin viewed as an observer removed from possible moral contamination and secure in his own ethical well-being. The specter of moral disorder was a threat to the serenity of his inner moral self. If an arbitrary ruler could usher in a period of moral chaos, "souls would be left to languish, hearts corrupted, and ideas and assumptions degraded and disdained." [94] How was he to remedy this situation? He did not linger on past hopes that a new ruler might lead his state and subjects away from the moral abyss. Although Fonvizin was at the point in his thinking at which Novikov and Bogdanovich had chosen to eschew involvement in contemporary politics and seek consolation in the national principle, Fonvizin maintained his interest in the politics of his day and expressed publicly and unequivocably his discontent with the course of action the empress had followed since the late sixties.

Two remedies were considered, a popular revolt and the enactment of immutable laws. Fonvizin invoked the horrors of a revolution against the state. An arbitrary ruler eventually provoked "all particular interests, crushed by the essence of a despotic government, to unite . . . at one point. Suddenly all strive to destroy the bonds of an unbearable enslavement. And then what is the state? A colossus held together by chains. The chains are broken, the colossus collapses and is destroyed. Despotism, born usually from anarchy, very rarely does not return to it again." [95] These remarks were reemphasized in an article written in 1779, "Ta Hsüeh or the Great Learning Which Comprises Higher Chinese Philosophy." This essay, a collection of Chinese sayings translated from the French edition of Abbé Pierre Marial Cibot (1727–1780), was published in the May issue of the *St. Petersburg Messenger.*[96] The dominant theme of "Ta Hsüeh" was the problem of controlling a ruler who was delinquent in his observation of his proper duties. A monarch who did not honor his obligations forfeited the right to expect obedience from his subjects. He eventually discovered that his misconduct "imparted in them [i.e., his subjects] his own ferocity and degraded them with his vices. A sovereign forbids in vain that which he allows himself; [for then] no one will obey him." [97] The consequences were clear. The ruler's "throne will fall under the burden of arrogance, and its ruins will be your grave." [98]

Fonvizin surely looked upon an actual revolution in the countryside with abhorrence. A social revolution was, aside from other considerations, a denial of the moral hierarchy described in the opening sentences of the "Discourse." In more immediate terms Fonvizin was both a privileged member of the social order endangered by a revolution and a public servant of the state threatened by a revolt. Though he decried the morally corrupting influence of an arbitrary ruler, he did not wish to avert one nightmare by calling forth another, one with even more capacity for wanton ruin. Fonvizin probably mentioned a revolution so that he could play on the then recent memories of the Pugachev revolt. He used the haunting image of a popular revolt to impart to his warnings about Catherine a sense of urgency and to point up the value of his recommendations for "immutable state laws."

To stave off these worst possible consequences, Fonvizin reminded the ruler of his responsibilities, returning in the eighties to what he had first stated in the early sixties and reiterated throughout the sixties: a monarch was answerable to God. Now, however, he introduced a new element: the ruler was as accountable to the ruled as to God. The monarch was obliged to observe the rights of what Fonvizin designated as the "fatherland" or the "nation." He used these terms to connote every social group led by the upper class. His association of the nation with the Russian nobility was made in the same way the supporters of the Third Estate in prerevolutionary France linked its interests with those of the bourgeoisie. The *dvorianstvo* was "the most respected of all classes, obligated to defend the fatherland with the sovereign and, led by honor alone, to represent the nation by its own estate." [99] The nation or fatherland was the repository of the subjects' "natural freedom," a moral and political heritage which was entrusted to the ruler by the ruled. The very essence of this fictional contract was its voluntary and reciprocal character. The nation did not renounce any part of its own freedom but allotted it temporarily to the monarch. Should the latter be delinquent in the performance of his proper duties, the nation or fatherland could and must recall its pledges to him and revert to its original status. "All human societies are based on mutual, voluntary obligations which are destroyed as soon as they are no longer observed. The obligations between the sovereign and subjects are similarly voluntary for there has never been . . . a nation that forcefully compelled someone to become its sovereign. If it can exist without a monarch, he cannot exist without it. Obviously the original power was in its hands. The accession of a sovereign means nothing other than that he is entitled by the nation and with whatever power it invests in him." [100]

In these sections of the "Discourse" it is tempting to see Fonvizin as a propagator of the ideal of popular sovereignty, an opponent of Catherine, and a "constitutionalist." [101] His version of a social contract was in some respects similar to the rationales for popular sovereignty current in eighteenth-century Europe, but comparisons between Fonvizin and political commentators in Western Europe should not be pushed too far. It is also doubtful that Fonvizin drew on German natural law theorists. German natural law did not allow for popular sovereignty as a potential check on the policies of the monarch, and in any case by the 1780s the link between the Germans' works and Fonvizin's writings was very tenuous. There is no evidence in the content or tone of the "Discourse" that Fonvizin returned to particular points in the works of Pufendorf and Wolff to bolster his own arguments about the rights of the nation or fatherland.

The "Discourse" is best understood not by its links to particular intellectual forebears, German or otherwise, but by reference to the moral bases of Fonvizin's political ideas. He always assumed that the functions and jurisdiction of the state were coextensive with the proper operation of society. In turn, the welfare of the polity was considered an extension of his moral concerns. The immediacy of ethics to Fonvizin's politics limits the value of a technical, legalistic reading of the "Discourse." When Fonvizin spoke of the mutual character of the compact between the monarch and his people, he restated in legal terms his longstanding ethical belief in a transcendent moral order that enclosed the affairs of the governor and the governed and provided the framework for the precise formulation of the legal relations among the constituents.

The moral relationship between sovereign and subjects was emphasized by the voluntary quality of the nation's submission to the ruler. "In reviewing the relations between the sovereign and his subjects, the first question that comes to mind is what exactly is meant by the word 'sovereign'?" [102] He was, Fonvizin was quick to add, "the soul of the political body," the one whose duty was to represent and lead his subjects along the road from barbarism to enlightenment. Fonvizin warned of the pitfalls awaiting the ruler along the way and held out an eventual reward to one who stayed the course.

"His heart will be pure, his soul unblemished, and his mind serene." [103] A monarch's character, once purged of all moral imperfections, gave him the capacity to resist the influence of the favorites and act only as the first servant of the state. As a model of moral purity and impartial service, the ruler imparted to his nation the very qualities he perfected in his own personality.

Steadfast at his post as guardian of public morality, a virtuous monarch shunned any resort to "despotism," the misuse of the moral and political powers vested in the ruler. A morally sound ruler recognized that the "law of the despot is the rule of force" and that law and compulsion can never be reconciled. If a monarch ordered his subjects to obey a law that was contrary to "sound reason," did they, no matter how helpless their position, have a moral obligation to comply? "A true law is one that reason judges to be beneficial to our interest. Consequently it arouses a certain inner impulse that compels us to obey it willingly. In any other circumstance our compliance is not based on obligation but compulsion. Where there is no obligation there can be no law." [104] Laws that derived their power from force rather than obligation should be resisted. Fonvizin was quite chary on this point. He referred not to arbitrary rulers but to God. If the latter compelled his faithful to act in a manner contrary to their nature and ruinous to their well-being, "we would yield out of necessity to his almighty power, but there would thereafter be nothing more than a physical relationship between God and us." [105]

Authority without a moral dimension was inappropriate for creatures endowed with a rational nature. Without the voluntary submission of the subjects to the ruler, the latter was deprived of his rights as sovereign. "Force and law are completely different in essence as in reality. Law demands merit, talents, and virtues. Force requires prisons, chains, and axes. It is quite superfluous to investigate where a sovereign is absolute and where he is limited. A tyrant, wherever he may be, is a tyrant, and the right of the people to protect its own existence is eternally and universally immutable." [106] When the monarch dispenses with this moral element and rules by arbitrary methods, "the fundamental tie [between ruler and ruled] cannot exist. There a state exists but not a fatherland. There are subjects but not citizens, not the political body whose members are united by the tie of mutual rights and duties." [107]

In these paragraphs of the "Discourse" Fonvizin succeeded in affirming the political ideals of his university years by associating them with the national principle. He reaffirmed the validity of the moral order he had first described in the "Just Jupiter." In the 1780s, however, he took refuge from the arbitrariness he criticized as a student and feared as a public servant in the security offered not by the state but by the national idea. He preserved his convictions of the sixties by linking them to a version of the fatherland that neither denied his personal values nor required his abstention from contemporary politics.

Fonvizin had no doubts as to the type of government that best served the fatherland. He went through archetypal political systems, ruling out despotic states for their lack of security for their subjects, oligarchies as "a callous form of government in which the apparatus of state was moved only by the arbitrariness of the sovereign power," and democracies as inappropriate for an unenlightened people. He preferred in the early 1780s what he had in the early 1760s, namely a monarch regulated by laws. The laws were not a means of lending routine and rationality to the functioning of the ruler and government—his assumption of the sixties—but the legal formulas of the contractual relationship between the monarch and the fatherland.

What was the nature of these "fundamental laws"? How were they defined so as to serve the purpose he assigned them? Fonvizin provided only a few guidelines. After considering the four classic forms of government, he concluded by admitting that "the truth is that the art of politics consists, ultimately, in the capacity to make people live under a good government." [108] Laws were without influence unless the moral disposition of the people was in order. "Sound reason and the experiences of the past demonstrate that the sound moral sense of a people is formed by—and only by— the integrity and conduct of its sovereign. In his hands is the power to lead the people along the way of the virtuous or put them on the path of the vice-ridden." [109] The virtuous ruler "will come to be recognized by his nation and so become its model. The respect he shows for merit and experience will stand as the sternest possible prohibition against any form of brazen disregard for others. The sovereign as good man, good father, [and] good master will not need to resort to the mildest command to succeed in bringing to every home an internal tranquility." [110] The monarch did not serve his subjects by complying with legalities; Fonvizin explicitly dispensed with "all subtle distinctions and distribution of political rights." [111] Rather the ruler stood as an ideal moral example. His character served as an emotional and psychological center, steadying the moral equilibrium within each home in his realm and, ultimately, within each of his subjects. The image of the ruler was one of moral benefactor, caring for his people's welfare and standing before them as the symbol of moral rectitude.

This figure of a monarch was seemingly inconsistent with one who was expected to govern according to "fundamental laws." Yet Fonvizin did not deny the worth of these particular laws nor abandon his opinions about the legal order of a deist God, legal ruler, and law-abiding subjects. As the opening paragraphs of the "Discourse" attest, these principles remained in his thinking but lost their immediacy. Fonvizin now gave first priority to the moral hierarchy of God, moral ruler, and ethically sound subjects. In defining the relations between the ruler and the ruled, Fonvizin's criteria were more ethical than legal. By identifying the ideal ruler—"good man, good father, [and] good master"—as the image to be admired and emulated by the nation, Fonvizin placed his vision of a moral order under the jurisdiction of the national principle. He denied the state any sovereignty in the moral realm and reduced its claims to rule its subjects to a question of its power to control them. Though the people "would yield out of necessity . . . there would be nothing more than a physical relationship" between the state and its subjects.

Fonvizin wrote a devastating bill of particulars against the politics of Catherinian Russia. Disappointed with the empress's policies after 1768, Fonvizin characterized the "nation" or "fatherland" as the symbol of that voluntary reciprocity he sought but did not find in Catherine's regime. He was quite apprehensive about the role of the state and its reliance on force as a justification for its policies, and he questioned the state's willingness to improve the general good. Fonvizin's indictment was qualified and, to a certain extent, vitiated by his redefinition of its terms. In the 1780s his image of the sovereign was no longer that of a ruler clearly distinct from the state. He abandoned what had previously been an increasingly sophisticated understanding of the ruler and the state and all but identified the two. In the "Discourse" he showed less interest in the sovereign as the agent of legality and described the monarch as primarily a moral personality. The ruler provided for the spiritual welfare of his subjects and enjoyed a communion with them that was the essence of "the political freedom of the nation." The public good was allowed to depend on the benevolence of the sovereign. In so assuming Fonvizin served notice that his appeal to the "fatherland" was ultimately a limited one. He wanted to design the political symbolism of the fatherland so that it stood as witness to the aberrant characteristics of the state. He was also ready to spell out the lessons to be gained from this contrast. Yet Fonvizin was not prepared to act on these conclusions at the price of jeopardizing his personal moral tranquility. However acute his interest in protecting the fatherland against encroachments by the state, he was firm in his decision to shun politics. In this way he could retain the psychological security and emotional stability afforded his ethical self by a confident sense of personal moral order. In Fonvizin's last major political essay, he chose, as did Novikov and Bogdanovich, to impose limits on his political interests.

—— 8 ——

The fictional realm of the fatherland and the actual realm of imperial Russia were autonomous worlds, distinct in characteristics and purposes. The ideal moral order, which was originally conceived on the pages of the student journals and was then used to reinforce the political authority of Catherine the Great, was quite apart from the actual world of the 1780s. The state was recognized as an entity separate from the revised version of the moral utopia, the ideal polity that was the fatherland. This theoretical construct was to furnish the members of the Fonvizin group with what they could no longer trust the state to provide, namely an agency to give order to their personal values and act as a reliable intermediary between them and the worlds of politics and society. Yet the national principle was not well suited to accomplish this task. Novikov sustained his own appreciation of the national idea only by putting its political import into the future and reformulating its immediate significance in cultural terms. Bogdanovich dispensed with contemporary politics and culture to seek in an idealized past proof of the existence of the order he vainly sought in Catherinian Russia. Fonvizin's "Discourse" was the most explicit attempt to associate the ideas and values of the sixties with a vision of a politically and morally reformed Russian state in the eighties. Yet even this effort buckled under the threat posed to the moral self. The more Novikov, Bogdanovich, and Fonvizin were interested in the fatherland and reconsidered their personal values and perspectives on contemporary politics, the more they were led by diverse paths to positions that discredited their original purpose in referring to the national principle.

This impasse could not be overcome. As students and as public servants they advocated the values of rationality and virtue, ideals that applied equally to all men. The Fonvizin group was confident that its steadfastness of principle was, to employ the language of the group, one instance of the progression of humanity toward the attainment of these ideals. When the three men wrote of the perfectibility of man in the student journals, they assumed a teleological progression toward the perfection of their fellowman. Once the Fonvizin group adopted the national principle, its members seemed to be undermining the validity of a priori ethical values. Were they to be rigorous in their reference to the fatherland, they would oblige themselves to understand the ideal of human perfectibiliy according to standards relative to their fatherland. This requirement was strengthened when the three men designated as the key characteristic of the fatherland the evolutionary nature of its history. Their understanding of the national principle was too unsophisticated and narrow to attain a universalist dimension. The three men left themselves no recourse but to recognize that the universal ideals dating from their student years and the national principle, by definition particular and relativistic, were irreconcilable.

The Fonvizin group's thinking progressed no further nor did it need to do so. While the characteristics attributed to the fatherland were indeed irreconcilable with those associated with the state, the differences did not require reconciliation. The group found in the national principle the means of achieving what had been its primary goal since the early 1760s. Its aim had always been to maintain a harmony between the personal and social selves so as to preserve the autonomy of the inner self. By a variety of theoretical strategies the three men withstood challenges to their sense of inner moral order and tranquility. Given that purpose, their reference to the national principle need not be considered as anything more than an attempt to resolve their personal moral concerns of the 1770s and 1780s. It was for later political commentators to elaborate the full political significance of the contrast between the state and the fatherland.

VII

State and Nationality in Late-Eighteenth-Century Russian Thought

The Fonvizin group's fate is one that besets moral idealists of all times and places. The lives of these three men testified to the appearance in eighteenth-century Russia of opposition to Catherine the Great's regime. Theirs was a moral confrontation with political policies and personalities that they found repellent. Once they made so bold as to speak truth to the ruler and were rejected, they took consolation in a renewed appreciation of their sense of ethical self-esteem. Fonvizin recognized this inescapable conclusion to the group's moral endeavors. In 1786 he made the famous story of Callisthenes serve as a Socratic apology for the political ideals of those who dared dissent from the politics of Russian absolutism.

"Callisthenes: A Tale from Ancient Greece" told the story of a virtuous man who was an adviser to Alexander the Great. Callisthenes was asked by Aristotle to go to Alexander's court on a "mission in the service of mankind." "You want to send me to the court of so powerful a monarch? What could I hope to accomplish there? I refuse to extol the vicious and depraved actions of the sovereign and his favorites. You taught me to honor virtue in word and deed." [1] When Aristotle rebuked him for shirking his moral responsibilities, Callisthenes was taken aback. "You know that I never hesitate to carry out zealously my duty to serve. I am prepared to die for the truth!" [2]

Callisthenes was received by Alexander with respect and accorded the place of honor immediately next to the ruler at the meetings of his council. Callisthenes was given the opportunity to reverse several "barbaric" decisions of Alexander's councilors. These successes aroused the enmity of Leonnatus, the favorite of the ruler. Leonnatus was "a creature of his passions, utterly possessed by a high—and mistaken—regard for himself and obsessed by an unrestrained desire for riches. He respected no man and was, in turn, not respected by anyone. This was to be expected: one who esteems only himself is not worthy of the regard of others." [3] Callisthenes' moral authority was a threat to Leonnatus' influence with Alexander. The mentor and the favorite joined in contest for the favor of the monarch. The rivalry was decided by Alexander himself. He withdrew to the temple of Jupiter where Callisthenes' enemies had "sufficient opportunity to employ their dastardly skills as flatterers so as to cast a spell over Alexander." [4] The ruler, once a disciple of Aristotle, now considered himself the son of Jupiter. Callisthenes condemned the new man-god for his moral wantonness. Angered by Callisthenes' denunciation, Alexander ordered him fettered and imprisoned. There Callisthenes wrote a confession of faith. "I am perishing in the dungeon. I am grateful to the gods for giving me the opportunity to suffer for the cause of truth." [5] When the statement was read by Aristotle, he added his own comment. "With a monarch whose inclinations are all but totally depraved, this is all that an honorable man can possibly accomplish." [6]

"Callisthenes" was very much a collective biography of the Fonvizin group, a description of the men's lives and moral purposes written in the 1780s that encompassed their political involvements and defeats in the 1760s and 1770s. Their fate was symbolically similar to that of Callisthenes. Although the Fonvizin group had no confidence in the government, the men could not appeal to "society" instead. They made no claim to represent the voice of society in opposition to the throne. Indeed, the group forfeited that right when its members gave pride of place in their utopian society to the integrity of the moral order rather than the complexities of the actual social realities. The Fonvizin group could not speak to society or the government. Its opposition to Catherine's regime was that of individuals, not representatives of political or social movements. Its cry was that of the morally outraged and politically alienated.

The members of the Fonvizin group were not literally martyrs on the model of Callisthenes. They did not require of themselves anything more than a moral retreat from the politics of Catherinian Russia. Fonvizin and Bogdanovich abandoned neither their service posts nor their moral idealism. They continued to work in the bureaucratic offices of a government whose policies they abhorred. Both men attained relatively high ranks. Bogdanovich became a collegial councilor, sixth class on the Table of Ranks. He retired in 1795 and died in 1803. Fonvizin retired in 1782 at the rank of state councilor, fifth class, and died ten years later. [7]

Novikov was the exception. He resigned from the Izmailovskii regiment in 1768 at the rank of lieutenant, tenth class. The only member of the group able to operate outside the bureaucratic system of ranks and offices, Novikov, with his book-publishing and humanitarian ventures of the 1780s, endeavored to serve society directly. His initiatives were inseparably linked to his consistency of moral purpose. As Kliuchevskii noted, the importance of these enterprises lay as much in the number of books translated, volumes published, and newspapers edited as in the quality of this activity.[8] Novikov took the initial steps in the formation of "public opinion" and did so in ways that prefigured the social action of many Russian writers of the nineteenth century. When his health worsened in 1791, he confined himself to his estate. There he was arrested in April 1792 by an empress suspicious of his Masonic connections. Novikov was released by Tsar Paul and returned again to his estate where he lived in isolation and poverty until his death in 1818.

The legacy of the Fonvizin group to later generations of Russian writers and intellectuals is its contribution to Russian national thought in the late eighteenth century. The group did not follow the example of Elizabethan commentators, particularly Lomonosov and Sumarokov, or, still less, Petrine apologists on the order of Feofan Prokopovich. These men were willing to serve as literary agents for publicizing the primacy and beneficial role of the imperial state. The glories of the state were one with the heroic feats of the rulers. In Prokopovich's odes and Lomonosov's writings this identity served as confirmation of the majesty and purposes of the government. In the late eighteenth and early nineteenth centuries statism was linked by many writers to the cause of nationality. Nicholas Karamzin (1766–1826) wrote the most famous statement of this view in his *History of the Russian State*, published in twelve volumes between 1818 and 1829. Karamzin wrote in the manner of Prokopovich and Lomonosov by honoring the heroism of the rulers and emphasizing the military prowess of Russia's most famous monarchs. Their accomplishments reflected well on the greatness of the state. Yet Karamzin also appealed to national sentiments. His aim was to arouse patriotic zeal and document the instrumental role of the Russian people in the origins, development, and refinement of the autocracy.[9] "Karamzin's emphasis on the continuity of historical evolution and on the interdependence of all classes in Russia was typical of a growing view that a nation state formed a uniform whole, with systematically arranged parts."[10] Nationality remained the servant of the state. Patriotic pride was not distinct from service to the state.

The members of the Fonvizin group were not zealous supporters of state authority, but advocates of the national principle. Their earliest references to the national ideal were in their poems, plays, and essays of the late 1760s and early 1770s. The satires of French fops, ridicule of foreign tutors, and disdain for an enlightened, European education led the group to discover and cherish what was particular to Russia. In so doing they opened the quest for the definition of the Russian national character. By their emphasis on the evolutionary nature of Russian history and by their selective use of European influences, the members of the Fonvizin group fostered the notion that Russia had its own unique history and urged their contemporaries and successors to recognize and fully describe that history. The Fonvizin group could do no more, for its ideas could develop no further. The three men's understanding of Russia's national identity was ahistorical. Without a philosophy of nationality they could not transform particular traits of the Russian fatherland into precisely defined, consistently related characteristics of Russia's historic individuality. The Fonvizin group performed a valuable service in providing the basis and indicating the direction for the further development of Russian national ideals.

The Fonvizin group's version of the national principle acquired its key political significance in the 1770s and 1780s. The group relied on the national ideal to identify its opposition to Catherine's government and the imperial state. By setting nationality apart from statism the three men made it impossible for the monarchy and its apologists to use the principle of nationality. The distinction between state and nationality had grave consequences for Catherine and her dynasty. By taking away from the empress and her successors the prop of nationality, the Fonvizin group deprived them of support they could ill afford to lose. Nationality and the throne were linked, the patriotic reinforcing the statist, in the political philosophy of imperial as well as Muscovite rulers. The grand princes of Muscovy enhanced the influence of their official ideology, a revision of the Byzantine imperial code, with traditional, religious nationalism. The tsars of the imperial state secured the theoretical bases of their political sovereignty by using the secular philosophy of German natural law. Without popular pride in the achievements of the rulers and the accomplishments of the government, without a common vision of an improved social order, the imperial state risked becoming simply an administrative apparatus whose authority was based on force alone. Fonvizin warned Catherine of this ominous possibility in 1783 in the "Discourse." Only six years later Fonvizin's prophecy was confirmed. The French Revolution of 1789 made startlingly clear to the empress and every other head of state that no monarchical government dared neglect the national sentiments of its subjects.[11] Where national enthusiasm was not an agent for political and social cohesion, its potential might well be unleashed against a regime that neglected the common good.

The limited capacity of the imperial state to make its policies intelligible to its subjects hampered its ability to ward off such grave dangers. Because Fonvizin, Novikov, and Bogdanovich had been schooled in German natural law, they accepted its terms for political discourse until the government violated its own code of political conduct. Thereafter they could only voice their disdain for a monarchy ready to act contrary to its own claims to theoretical legitimacy. In their dissent the members of the Fonvizin group opened the way for new formulations of political ideals. For its part the imperial state was left to contend with the vagaries of the future without assurance of the political loyalties of some of its best educated and most idealistic men. As imperial Russia entered the nineteenth century, its rulers spoke a legal language, endorsed a set of political fictions, and addressed political and social issues in terms that were not only not shared by many of its writers and intellectuals but were not even comprehensible to them. The imperial state incurred the risk of operating by theoretical norms that were intelligible only to itself. In this respect, the relationship between the Fonvizin group and Catherine ultimately proved to be fraught with tragic consequences.

Notes

Abbreviations

F.S.S.	D. Fonvizin, *Sobranie sochinenii.*
L.P.S.S.	M. V. Lomonosov, *Polnoe sobranie sochinenii.*
S.B.	I. Bogdanovich, *Sochineniia Bogdanovicha.*
S.P.S.S.	A. P. Sumarokov, *Polnoe sobranie vsekh sochinenii v stikhakh i proze.*

Introduction

1. For a splendid discussion of the role of ideology in Muscovite Russia, see Ihor Ševčenko, "A Neglected Byzantine Source of Muscovite Political Ideology."
2. Robert Lee Wolff, "The Three Romes: The Migration of an Ideology and the Making of an Autocrat," p. 306. The quote refers to Muscovite times but is no less valid for the imperial period.
3. For a useful discussion of the commentators of Peter's time, I. Pososhkov, F. Saltykov, K. Zotov, and A. Kurbatov, *inter alia*, see Margaret Blamberg, "The Publicists of Peter the Great."
4. N. Karamzin, "O Bogdanoviche i ego sochineniiakh."
5. M. N. Longinov, *Novikov i moskovskie martinisty*; E. Shumigorskii, "Gosudaryniapublitsist"; V. Bogoliubov, *N. I. Novikov i ego vremia*; A. Nezelenov, *Nikolai Ivanovich Novikov, izdatel' zhurnalov 1769–1785gg.*
6. K. V. Pigarev, *Tvorchestvo Fonvizina*; G. Makogonenko, *Denis Fonvizin. Tvorcheskii put'*; idem, *Nikolai Novikov i russkoe prosveshchenie XVIII veka*; idem, *Ot Fonvizina do Pushkina*; I. F. Bogdanovich, *Stikhotvoreniia i poemy*; G. Gukovskii, *Ocherki po istorii russkoi literatury XVIII veka. Dvorianskaia fronda v literature 1750-kh-1760-kh godov*; idem, *Russkaia literatura XVIII veka*; P. N. Berkov, *Istoriia russkoi zhurnalistiki XVIII veka*; D. Blagoi, *Istoriia russkoi literatury XVIII veka.*
7. V. I. Lenin, "Ot kakogo nasledstva my otkazyvaemsia?"
8. I. Ia. Shchipanov, *Filosofiia russkogo prosveshcheniia. Vtoraia polovina XVIII veka;* and Z. A. Kamenskii, *Filosofskie idei russkogo prosveshcheniia.*

Chapter I

1. M. V. Lomonosov, "Oda blazhennyia pamiati gosudaryne imperatritse Anne Ioannovne na pobedu nad turkami i tatarami i na vziatie khotina 1739 goda," *L.P.S.S.*, VIII, 16–30.
2. Ibid., p. 27.

3. Ibid., pp. 20–21.

4. M. Raeff, "Staatsdienst, Aussenpolitik, Ideologien (Die Rolle der Institutionen in der geistigen Entwicklung des russischen Adels im 18. Jahrhundert)," p. 162.

5. M. V. Lomonosov, "Oda na den' vosshestviia na prestol velichestva gosudaryni imperatritsy Elisavety Petrovny 1748 goda," *L.P.S.S.*, VIII, 215–25.

6. Ibid., p. 219.

7. Ibid., p. 218.

8. Lomonosov, "Slovo o rozhdenii metallov ot triaceniia zemli," *L.P.S.S.*, V, 346.

9. Ibid.

10. Lomonosov, "Oda eia imperatorskomu velichestvu . . . Elisavete Petrovne, samoderzhitse vserossiiskoi, na torzhestvennyi prazdnik tezoimenitstva eia velichestva sentiabria 5 dnia 1759 goda . . . ," *L.P.S.S.*, VIII, 648–57.

11. Ibid., p. 648.

12. Ibid., pp. 656–57.

13. Lomonosov, "Oda vsepresvetleishei derzhavneishei velikoi gosudaryne imperatritse Elisavete Petrovne . . . na presvetlyi torzhestvennyi prazdnik eia velichestva vosshestviia na vserossiiskii prestol noiabria 25 dnia 1761 goda . . . ," *L.P.S.S.*, VIII, 742–50; idem, "Oda vsepresvetleishemu derzhavneishemu velikomu gosudariu imperatoru Petru Feodorovichu . . . na novyi 1762 god . . . ," *L.P.S.S.*, VIII, 751–60; and idem, "Oda torzhestvennaia eia imperatorskomu velichestvu vsepresvetleishei derzhavneishei velikoi gosudaryne imperatritse Ekaterine Alekseevne . . . na preslavnoe eia vosshestvie na vserossiiskii imperatorskii prestol iiunia 28 dnia 1762 goda," *L.P.S.S.*, VIII, 772–81.

14. Lomonosov, "Oda na den' vosshestviia na vserossiiskii prestol eia velichestva gosudaryni imperatritsy Elisavety Petrovny 1747 goda," *L.P.S.S.*, VIII, 205.

15. Ibid., pp. 203–5.

16. Lomonosov, "Rassuzhdenie o bol'shei tochnosti morskogo puti . . . ," *L.P.S.S.*, IV, 161–62.

17. Lomonosov, "Slovo o pol'ze khimii . . . ," *L.P.S.S.*, II, 349–69; idem, "Nizhaishii doklad i nepredrassuditel'noe mnenie imperatorskomu solianomu komissariatu o solianykh delakh . . . ," *L.P.S.S.*, V, 243–47; idem, "Rassuzhdenie o bol'shei tochnosti morskogo puti . . . ," *L.P.S.S.*, IV, 125; idem, "[O sokhranenii i razmnozhenii rossiiskogo naroda]," *L.P.S.S.*, VI, 381–403.

18. Lomonosov, "Proekt feierverka i illuminatsii k torzhestvennomu dniu tezoimenitstva eia imperatorskogo velichestva sentiabriia k 5 dniu 1753 goda," *L.P.S.S.*, VIII, 529.

19. Lomonosov, "Slovo o pol'ze khimii . . . ," *L.P.S.S.*, II, 362.

20. Lomonosov, *Demofont, L.P.S.S.*, VIII, 484; idem, "Oda na den' rozhdeniia eia velichestva gosudaryni imperatritsy Elisavety Petrovny, samoderzhitsy vserossiiskiia, 1746 goda," *L.P.S.S.*, VIII, 155.

21. Lomonosov, "Slovo pokhval'noe eia velichestvu gosudaryne imperatritse Elisavete Petrovne, samoderzhitse vserossiskoi, govorennoe noiabria 26 dnia 1749 goda," *L.P.S.S.*, VIII, 235–56.

22. Ibid., pp. 249–50.

23. Ibid., pp. 250–51.

24. Lomonosov, *Demofont, L.P.S.S.*, VIII, 411-86.

25. Ibid., p. 442.

26. Ibid., p. 467.

27. See also the travails of the character Mamai in Lomonosov, *Tamira i Selim*, *L.P.S.S.*, VIII, 292–364.

28. The apt use of the word "iconography" is due to Henry Murray in his "Introduction to the Issue: Myth and Mythmaking," *Daedalus* 88 (1959): 211–12.

29. Michael Cherniavsky, "Russia," in Orest Ranum, ed., *National Consciousness, History, and Political Culture in Early Modern Europe*, pp. 136–37.

30. G. Gurvich, *"Pravda voli monarshei" Feofana Prokopovicha i eia zapadnoevropeiskie istochniki*.

31. F. Prokopovich, *Russian Primer*, in R. W. Blackmore, trans., *Doctrines of the Russian Church* (London: Masters, 1845), p. 11. For a recent interpretation of Prokopovich's writings, consult the works of James Cracraft. Prokopovich was, according to Cracraft, an advocate of the tsar as legal and paternal figure, one whose legal status was supplemented on a psychological level by the traditional sense of paternal authority. For a succinct statement of this opinion, see J. Cracraft, "Feofan Prokopovich," in J. Garrard, ed., *The Eighteenth Century in Russia*, pp. 75–105, esp. pp. 98–101.

32. F. Prokopovich, "Slovo pokhval'noe o preslavnoi nad sveiskimi pobede . . . ," in *Sochineniia*, pp. 23–38. When Prokopovich again described the battle, he was writing as Peter's confidant and adviser on matters of ecclesiastical organization. Nonetheless, the image of the tsar in the ode of 1717 was unchanged from that of the poem of 1709.

33. G. Korovin, *Biblioteka Lomonosova*. For the references to Wolff, see pp. 60–63, 64, 68, 136–39, 373–75. Korovin cites a list of books Lomonosov purchased on October 15, 1738. Of the fifty-nine entries, eleven were by Wolff. No other writer was listed as often as Wolff; see pp. 407–11.

34. M. Lomonosov, ["Posviashchenie i pribavleniia ko 2mu izdaniiu volfianskoi eksperimental'noi fiziki 1760 g."], *L.P.S.S.*, III, 432.

35. For a provocative study of the comparative institutional history of the period, see Marc Raeff, "The Well-Ordered Police State and the Development of Modernity in Seventeenth and Eighteenth Century Europe: An Attempt at a Comparative Approach."

36. The discounting of principle was taken to the extreme by Florinsky who thought the odes were only worthy of note as they "saved him more than once from the unhappy consequences of an impetuous temperament stimulated at times by an excessive use of alcohol." See M. Florinsky, *Russia. A History and an Interpretation*, I, 492.

37. N. Novikov, *Opyt istoricheskago slovaria o rossiiskikh pisateliakh*, in P. Efremov, ed., *Materialy dlia istorii russkoi literatury*, p. 66.

38. Ibid., p. 63.

39. P. Pekarskii, *Istoriia imperatorskoi akademii nauk v peterburge*; G. Vasetskii, "Filosofskie vzgliady M. V. Lomonosova"; P. N. Berkov, *Lomonosov i literaturnaia polemika ego vremeni 1750–1765*; Z. Kamenskii, *Filosofskie idei russkogo prosveshcheniia*.

40. A. A. Morozov, "M. V. Lomonosov i teleologiia Kristiana Vol'fa."

41. B. M. Menshutkin, *Russia's Lomonosov*, p. 22.

42. Quoted in B. Grekov, "Lomonosov-istorik," in *Izbrannye trudy*, III, 405.

43. Ibid., p. 421.

44. M. Lomonosov, *Drevnaia rossiiskaia istoriia ot nachala rossiiskogo naroda do konchiny velikogo kniazia Iaroslava pervogo ili do 1054 goda*, *L.P.S.S.*, VI, 171.

45. Lomonosov, [letter to Ivan Shuvalov], dated March 3, 1752, *L.P.S.S.*, X, 472–73.

46. A. Kizevetter, "Moskovskii universitet (istoricheskii ocherk)," p. 18.

47. See, for example, his generalities in praise of Vorontsov's constancy in M. Lomonosov, "[Posviashchenie i pribavleniia ko 2mu izdaniiu volfianskoi eksperimental'noi fiziki 1760 g.]," *L.P.S.S.*, III, 431–33.

48. Lomonosov, [letter to Ivan Shuvalov], dated April 17, 1760, *L.P.S.S.*, X, 539.

49. Pekarskii, *Istoriia imperatorskoi akademii nauk*, II, 484.

50. M. Lomonosov, [letter to Ivan Shuvalov], dated August 15, 1751, *L.P.S.S.*, X, 470–71.

51. Berkov, *Lomonosov*, pp. 148 ff.

52. Pekarskii, *Istoriia imperatorskoi akademii nauk*, II, 560. For the letter, see M. Lomonosov, [letter to Ivan Shuvalov], dated January 3, 1754, *L.P.S.S.*, X, 498.

53. P. Biliarskii, *Materialy dlia biografii Lomonosova*, p. 302.

54. Berkov, *Lomonosov*, pp. 102, 133 ff., 241 ff.

55. Ibid., pp. 241–42.

56. Pekarskii, *Istoriia imperatorskoi akademii nauk*, II, 287–88.

57. Ibid., pp. 455–56; *L.P.S.S.*, X, 809.

58. Lomonosov, [letter to V. Tatishchev], dated January 27, 1749, *L.P.S.S.*, X, 462.

59. Lomonosov, [letter to Ivan Shuvalov], dated January 4, 1753, *L.P.S.S.*, X, 475.

60. Ibid., VI, 573; X, 503.

61. Lomonosov, [letter to Euler], dated February 12, 1754, *L.P.S.S.*, X, 503.

62. Lomonosov, [letter to G. Orlov], dated July 25, 1762, *L.P.S.S.*, X, 560–61.

63. Quoted in Berkov, *Lomonosov*, p. 283.

64. Sumarokov, *Khorev*, *S.P.S.S.*, III, 1–57.

65. Ibid., p. 18.

66. The same contrast of characters as that between Kii and Khorev was also made in *Semira* in the persons of Oleg and Rotislav. See Sumarokov, *Semira*, *S.P.S.S.*, III, 275.

67. Sumarokov, *Artistona*, *S.P.S.S.*, III, 185–254.

68. Ibid., p. 223.

69. For details about the intricacies of the relationships among the key figures at Anna's court, see William Slany, "Russian Central Governmental Institutions 1725–1741," pp. 277 ff., esp. pp. 307–9.

70. Sumarokov, *Sinav i Truvor*, *S.P.S.S.*, III, 121–83.

71. Ibid., p. 140.

72. Sumarokov, "Epistoly," *S.P.S.S.*, I, 323.

73. Ibid., p. 324.

74. Sumarokov, *Opekun*, *S.P.S.S.*, V, 1–54.

75. Ibid., p. 27.

76. Ibid., p. 52.

77. Sumarokov, "O blagorodstve," *S.P.S.S.*, VII, 356–58.

78. Sumarokov, *Pustynnik*, *S.P.S.S.*, IV, 281–302.

79. Ibid., p. 287.

80. Ibid., pp. 290–91.

81. Ibid., p. 295.

82. Ibid., p. 287.

83. Ibid., p. 290.

84. Sumarokov, "O blagorodstve," *S.P.S.S.*, VII, 358.

85. Sumarokov, *Iadobityi*, *S.P.S.S.*, V, 155–96.

86. Ibid., p. 171.

87. G. Gukovskii, *Ocherki po istorii russkoi literatury XVIII veka*; and P. N. Berkov, *Aleksandr Petrovich Sumarokov, 1717–1777*.

88. For one example, see S. M. Solov'ev, *Istoriia rossii s drevneishikh vremen*, XXIII, 283.

89. A. Sumarokov, "Oda gosudaryne imperatritse Elizavete pervoi, na den' eia rozhdeniia 1755 goda, dekabria 18 dnia," *S.P.S.S.*, II, 13–19.

90. Sumarokov, "Oda gosudaryne imperatritse Elisavete pervoi, o prusskoi voine," *S.P.S.S.*, II, 24–28.

91. Berkov, *Sumarokov*, p. 20.

92. Herbert Kaplan, *Russia and the Outbreak of the Seven Years' War*, p. 106.

93. Ibid., pp. 111–12.

94. The best review and analysis of the attempted coup of 1758 is that of Bil'basov. See V. A. Bil'basov, *Istoriia Ekateriny vtoroi*, I, 360–422. Bil'basov's work was seized by tsarist censors in St. Petersburg, and only three volumes, the first, second, and twelfth, were ever published. See also Solov'ev, *Istoriia rossii*, XXIV, 444–61.

95. Solov'ev, *Istoriia rossii*, XXV, 10.

96. Elagin's politics and career are discussed in Chapter IV. For a complete bibliography of his literary works, see G. Gennadi, *Spravochnyi slovar' o russkikh pisateliakh i uchenykh*, I, 341; and M. N. Longinov, "Russkie pisateli XVIII veka," II, 197–200.

97. M. N. Longinov, "Poslednie gody zhizni Aleksandra Petrovicha Sumarokova (1766–1777)," p. 1639.

98. Panin's proposal for an Imperial Council can be only approximately dated. As Ransel has pointed out, Panin probably began working on the project during Peter III's reign. Its first mention by a court observer was in the dispatch of Bérenger to Choiseul, dated July 16, 1762. See Ransel, *Politics of Catherinian Russia*, p. 117, n. 51.

99. For a useful review and sound interpretation of the book-publishing trade and the circulation of books and journals, see Gary Marker, "Publishing and the Formation of a Reading Public in Eighteenth-Century Russia," esp. pp. 161–220.

100. V. V. Kallash, "Ocherki po istorii russkoi zhurnalistiki," p. 13.

101. A[lexander] S[umarokov], "Rastavanie s muzami," *Trudoliubivaia pchela*, December 1759, p. 768.

102. A. Sumarokov, "Posviashchenie," *Trudoliubivaia pchela*, January 1759, p. 3.

103. A[lexander] S[umarokov], "Son, shchastlivoe obshchestvo," *Trudoliubivaia pchela*, December 1759, p. 739.

104. Ibid., pp. 741–43, 745.

105. Ibid., pp. 739–43.

106. Ibid., pp. 745–46.

107. Gukovskii, *Ocherki*, pp. 70, 91 ff., 127–28. See also idem, *Russkaia literatura XVIII veka*, pp. 135–39.

108. A. Sumarokov, "Oda gosudaryne imperatritse Ekaterine vtoroi, na den' eia vosshestviia na prestol, iiunia 28 dnia 1762 goda," *S.P.S.S.*, II, 43.

109. Sumarokov, "Oda gosudaryne imperatritsy Ekaterine vtoroi, na pervyi den' novogo 1763 goda," *S.P.S.S.*, II, 54–58.

110. Sumarokov, "Oda gosudaryne imperatritse Ekaterine vtoroi na den' eia koronovaniia 1766 goda, sentiabria, 22 dnia," *S.P.S.S.*, II, 76–79.

111. Sumarokov, "Oda gosudaryne imperatritse Ekaterine vtoroi, na pervyi den' 1764 goda," *S.P.S.S.*, II, 70.

112. M. Khmyrov, "Ocherk zhizni i literaturnoi deiatel'nosti Sumarokova," in V. Pokrovskii, ed., *Aleksandr Petrovich Sumarokov. Ego zhizn' i sochineniia*, p. 23. In this and all subsequent references to the rank of *deistvitel'nyi statskii sovetnik* the title is translated simply as "state councilor," as the qualifier "*deistvitel'nyi*" cannot be satisfactorily translated. The class is added to distinguish this rank from that of "*statskii sovetnik*," fifth class on the Table of Ranks.

113. Bil'basov, *Istoriia Ekateriny vtoroi*, II, 180.

114. A. Sumarokov, "Khory k bol'shemu maskeradu, byvshemu v moskve v 1763 gode," *S.P.S.S.*, VIII, 354–64.

115. Sumarokov, "Khor ko zlatomu veku," *S.P.S.S.*, VIII, 363.

116. Bil'basov, *Istoriia Ekateriny vtoroi*, II, 84–91.

117. Ibid., p. 85.

118. Ibid., p. 84.

119. Ibid., p. 91.

120. Ibid., p. 99; note to Z. G. Chernyshev.

121. M. Lomonosov, "Oda torzhestvennaia eia imperatorskomu velichestvu vsepresvetleishei derzhavneishei velikoi gosudaryne imperatritse Ekaterine Alekseevne, samoderzhitse vserossiiskoi, na preslavnoi eia vosshestvie na vserossiiskii imperatorskii prestol iiunia 28 dnia 1762 goda . . . ," *L.P.S.S.*, VIII, 772–81; idem, "Oda vsepresvetleishei derzhavneishei velikoi gosudaryne imperatritse Ekaterine Alekseevne, samoderzhitse vserossiiskoi . . . v novyi 1764 god . . . ," *L.P.S.S.*, VIII, 788–99.

122. Longinov, "Poslednie gody Sumarokova," pp. 1642–46.

123. N. Drizen, "Ivan Perfil'evich Elagin (1725–1794)," p. 120.

124. N. Karamzin, *Izbrannye sochineniia*, 2 vols. (Moscow-Leningrad: Izdatel'stvo "khudozhestvennaia literatura," 1964), II, 170.

125. A. Sumarokov, *Dmitrii samozvanets*, *S.P.S.S.*, IV, 61–64.

126. Longinov, "Poslednie gody Sumarokova," p. 1680.

127. A. Sumarokov, "Oda gosudaryne imperatritse Ekaterine vtoroi, na vziatie khotina i pokorenie moldavii," *S.P.S.S.*, II, 106–9. The ode was first published in 1769.

128. Sumarokov, "Oda gosudaryne imperatritse Ekaterine vtoroi, na den' koronovaniia eia sentiabria 22 dnia, 1770 goda," *S.P.S.S.*, II, 113–16.

129. Sumarokov, "Oda gosudaryne imperatritse Ekaterine vtoroi, na zakliuchenie mira s portoiu otomanskoiu, 1774 goda," *S.P.S.S.*, II, 145–47.

130. Sumarokov, "Oda gosudaryne imperatritse Ekaterine vtoroi, na torzhestvo mira s portoiu otomanskoiu 1775 goda," *S.P.S.S.*, II, 148–52.

Chapter II

1. Mitropolit Evgenii, *Slovar' russkikh svetskikh pisatelei*, I, 43.

2. "Liubopytnye documenty iz portfelei Millera," *Moskvitianin*, 1854, p. 8. Letter of Bogdanovich to Müller.

3. A. A. Polovtsov, ed., *Russkii biograficheskii slovar'*, III, 129–30. See also N. Karamzin, "O Bogdanoviche i ego sochineniiakh," p. 4.

4. Polovtsov, *Russkii biograficheskii slovar'*, III, 130.

5. Evgenii, *Slovar'*, I, 43–44; I. F. Bogdanovich, "Avtobiografiia I. F. Bogdanovicha," p. 184.

6. The lineage of the Fonvizin family has been traced in extensive detail by P. Viazemskii. See P. Viazemskii, *Fon-Vizin*, pp. 450–64. See also, N. Novikov, comp., *Rodoslovnaia kniga kniazei i dvorian rossiiskikh i vyezzhikh*, II, 394.

7. Viazemskii, *Fon-Vizin*, p. 23.

8. The exact date of Denis Fonvizin's birth cannot be definitely determined; the evidence is scarce and contradictory. On his tombstone the inscription reads "born on April 3, 1745, died December 1, 1792, lived 48 years, 7 months, and 28 days." The arithmetic is faulty. The lifespan recorded on the stone would put Fonvizin's birth in 1744, not 1745. The case for the 1744 date is supported by indirect references in Fonvizin's autobiographical essay, *Sincere Confession*, and by the historiographical decision of Viazemskii and Tikhonravov. If, however, the lettering on the tombstone is correct as to date of birth and incorrect as to number of years, the date of 1745 can be corroborated, as Moser and Strycek have recently argued, by the records of Fonvizin's home parish. In 1751 the records list Fonvizin as six years old. The 1745 date is more probable, in the views of Moser and Strycek, given the years of birth of Fonvizin's sisters and brothers. Three points challenge this claim for the 1745 date. Paul Fonvizin was probably born in 1745. In any case the sequence of births in the Fonvizin family is not definite enough to set Denis in 1745. Second, the same church records that suggest the 1745 date in 1751 also indicate in 1768 that Fonvizin was twenty-four and so born in 1744. The parish records are not reliable. Third, Moser and Strycek refer to Fonvizin's statement in *Sincere Confession* that he was "no older than fourteen" (*F.S.S.*, II, 92) when he first arrived in St. Petersburg. Moser noted that the trip "apparently took place in 1759" while Strycek refers to the winter of 1759–1760. Both cite the timing of the trip as proof of the validity of the 1745 date. However, Fonvizin's first trip to St. Petersburg was probably made in 1758, though his memoir obscures the exact date by saying only that the journey occurred "during the winter months" (*F.S.S.*, II, 91). Though the evidence is scanty, contradictory, and circumstantial, the 1744 date is more likely than 1745. For a detailed analysis of this question, see K. V. Pigarev, *Tvorchestvo Fonvizina*, pp. 290–91, n. 3; Charles Moser, *Denis Fonvizin*, pp. 12–13; and Alexis Strycek, *Denis Fonvizine*, p. 24, n. 29.

9. D. I. Fonvizin, "Chistoserdechnoe priznanie v delakh moikh i pomyshleniiakh," *F.S.S.*, II, 83.

10. M. I. Demkov, *Istoriia russkoi pedagogii*, 2d ed., II, 201.

11. *F.S.S.*, II, 82.

12. Ibid., p. 83.

13. M. N. Longinov, *Novikov i moskovskie martinisty*, pp. 8–9.

14. M. Confino, *Systèmes Agraires et Progrès Agricole*, p. 257.

15. [N. Novikov], "Avtor k samomu sebe," *Zhivopisets*, 1772, p. 10.

16. Longinov, *Novikov*, p. 9.

17. In 1743 Elizabeth reminded parents explicitly that this was the desired goal.

18. [Novikov], "Vmesto predisloviia," *Koshelek*, 1774, p. 1.

19. M. N. Longinov, "Russkie pisateli XVIII veka," IV, 574–75.

20. Gennadi, *Spravochnyi slovar'*, I, 319–20; Longinov, "Russkie pisateli XVIII veka," III, 205–7; and S. A. Vengerov, *Istochniki slovaria russkikh pisatelei*, II, 292.

21. Longinov, "Russkie pisateli XVIII veka," II, 74–75; and Gennadi, *Spravochnyi slovar'*, II, 117.

22. Sankovskii contributed to several of the journals staffed by the Fonvizin group but was a writer of secondary importance. For *Useful Entertainment* he translated several selections from Ovid's *Book of Sorrows* and an excerpt from Seneca, and wrote a few articles of his own. In 1764 he edited *Good Intention*. He translated for his journal two additional extracts from Ovid's same work and wrote a few minor entries. In 1769 his translation of the first song of the *Aeneid* was advertised in the *Drone*. He published the second song of Virgil's epic in 1772. Sankovskii also was probably the author of a letter to the editor of the *Drone* in the April 1770 issue. After these efforts Sankovskii apparently wrote very little. In the eighties he was the editor of two journals, *The Solitary Wise Man of Gotham* (*Uedinennyi poshekhonets*) and *Monthly Composition* (*Ezhemesiachnoe sochinenie*). The date of his death is not known. For the references to the *Drone*, see [Vasilii Sankovskii?], "Pis'mo," *Truten'*, April 1770, pp. 322–24; and March 1770, p. 284.

23. For an enlightening discussion of the seminaries, see G. Freeze, *The Russian Levites: Parish Clergy in the Eighteenth Century*, pp. 78–106.

24. A. A. Kizevetter, "Moskovskii universitet (istoricheskii ocherk)," p. 40.

25. *F.S.S.*, II, 88.

26. M. V. Sychev-Mikhailov, *Iz istorii russkoi shkoly i pedagogiki XVIII veka*, p. 77; and Kizevetter, "Moskovskii universitet (istoricheskii ocherk)," p. 22.

27. *Biograficheskii slovar' professorov i prepodavatelei imperatorskogo moskovskogo universiteta*, II, 558–74. See also Demkov, *Istoriia russkoi pedagogii*, II, 425–27. Fonvizin, who was one of Schaden's students, described Schaden "as a scholarly man who had an excellent gift for giving lectures and explaining so clearly that our [Denis and Paul Fonvizin's] success was evident." *F.S.S.*, II, 93.

28. Ibid., I, 301–11.

29. Ibid., I, 403–4; II, 340–48, 362–69, 536–37.

30. Marc Raeff, *Imperial Russia 1682–1825*, pp. 140–41.

31. Quoted in Leonard Krieger, *The Politics of Discretion*, p. 97.

32. Ibid.

33. See, for example, Grigorii Kozitskii, "O pol'ze mifologii," *Trudoliubivaia pchela*, January 1759, p. 22.

34. See, for example, "Chelovek est' namereniem i sposobom," *Prazdnoe vremia v pol'zu upotreblennoe*, October 1759, pp. 221–24.

35. V. Priklonskoi, trans., "Velikodushie Bianta filosofa," *Poleznoe uveselenie*, July 1760, pp. 11–14; and Ivan Slotvinskoi, trans., "O Biante grecheskom filozofe," *Dobroe namerenie*, October 1764, pp. 476–79.

36. V. Priklonskoi, trans., "Velikodushie Bianta filosofa," *Poleznoe uveselenie*, July 1760, p. 12.

37. Ibid., pp. 12–13.

38. M. N. Longinov, "Mikhail Matveevich Kheraskov," p. 1454.

39. P. Berkov, " 'Rassuzhdenie o rossiiskom stikhotvorstve' neizvestnaia stat'ia M. M. Kheraskova," p. 289.

40. Polovstov, *Russkii biograficheskii slovar'*, XX, 151.

41. M. Khmyrov, "Ocherk zhizni i literaturnoi deiatel'nosti Sumarokova," in V. Pokrovskii, ed., *Aleksandr Petrovich Sumarokov*, p. 17.

42. A. O. Kruglyi, "I. P. Elagin (biograficheskii ocherk)," IV, 97.

43. P. Berkov, "Neizdannoe ranee stikhotvorenie Kheraskova," p. 194.

44. M. Khmyrov, "Mikhail Matveevich Kheraskov," in S. A. Vengerov, ed., *Russkaia poeziia*, p. 488.

45. D. Fonvizin, "Pravosudnyi iupiter," *Poleznoe uveselenie*, November 1761, pp. 161–78.

46. Semen Naryshkin's more important publications include a comedy, *True Constancy* (*Istinnoe postoianstvo*), which Novikov praised as being "in the style of Diderot," and the translation of the articles from *l'Encyclopédie* on natural law and the economy. See M. N. Longinov, "Russkie pisateli XVIII veka," II, 76–77. For the original articles of his translated pieces from *l'Encyclopédie*, see M. David, "Droit de la nature ou droit Naturel," *Encyclopédie*, V, 131–34; and J. J. Rousseau, "Economie," *Encyclopédie*, V, pp. 337–49. For a bibliographical digest, see Vengerov, *Istochniki*, IV, 495.

47. Longinov, "Russkie pisateli XVIII veka," II, 76–78; and Vengerov, *Istochniki*, IV, 494.

48. Rzhevskii contributed to the *Industrious Bee* and *Useful Entertainment*, wrote more than 250 poems and several odes, translated short pieces from *l'Encyclopédie* and wrote an unpublished tragedy in 1769, *Smerdii i prelesta*. See Longinov, "Russkie pisateli XVIII veka," II, 78–80 and Dmitry Cizevskii, *History of Russian Literature*, pp. 434–35.

49. One other journal was published in Moscow at this time. The *Collection of the Best Compositions for Spreading Knowledge and Bringing Pleasure* was a quarterly published in 1762 under the editorship of Professor Reichel of Moscow University. The periodical had few ties to the student journals. In fact, the scholarly orientation of its articles, all translated from European originals, was akin to Müller's *Monthly Compositions*.

50. F. Andrew Brown, "On Education: John Locke, Christian Wolff, and the 'Moral Weeklies,'" pp. 161–62, 169–70.

51. "Prodolzhenie sbytiia snovideniia soobshchennago v marte mesiatse," *Poleznoe uveselenie*, June 1762, p. 268.

52. "Pis'mo k chitateliu," *Nevinnoe uprazhnenie*, January 1763, p. 4.

53. Ibid., p. 3.

54. Bulich, *Sumarokov*, p. 207.

55. These analyses were parts of Princess Dashkova's translation of an unspecified work of Voltaire. See Evgenii, *Slovar'*, I, 157–59.

56. "Pis'mo k obshchestvu ot izdatelei," *Nevinnoe uprazhnenie*, June 1763, p. 304.

57. Dashkova was under the strain of caring for her dying sister Nastasia, while she was herself in an advanced state of pregnancy. Her health was seriously impaired to the point that her left arm and leg were temporarily paralyzed. See E. Dashkova, *The Memoirs of Princess Dashkova*, p. 100; and D. I. Ilovaiskii, "Ekaterina Romanovna Dashkova," p. 260. According to Diderot this condition was probably the only reason she was not arrested for her complicity in the Khitrovo affair of May 1763 (D. Diderot, "Sur la Princesse Dashkof," XVII, 489). For details of the Khitrovo "crisis," see Bil'basov, *Istoriia Ekateriny vtoroi*, II, 285–96. Khitrovo charged Catherine with usurpation of power. When he carried his accusations into the quarters of the Guards regiments, he was arrested and exiled. Dashkova's role in this affair was, much like her participation in the revolution of

June 28, 1762, exaggerated. In this case it was confined to loose talk with Khitrovo and his allies. See Ilovaiskii, "Ekaterina Romanovna Dashkova," p. 259.

58. See Bulich, *Sumarokov*, pp. 206–7; and Berkov, *Istoriia russkoi zhurnalistiki*, pp. 139–43.

59. The simultaneous publication of *Free Hours* and *Innocent Exercise* led Berkov to note a split between those, like Kheraskov, who supported the revolution of June 28, 1762, and those, like Bogdanovich, who did not. His own evidence reveals the weakness of this opinion. He cites Kheraskov's appointment to arrange and write the poetic commentary to the festival of Minerva in Moscow in 1763, but neglects to mention that Bogdanovich was also appointed and served in this procession. See Berkov, *Istoriia russkoi zhurnalistiki*, p. 140.

60. The evidence that these three were students is that their signatures to articles were prefixed with the letter "S," presumably for "student."

61. Gukovskii, *Ocherki*, p. 204; Bogdanovich, *Stikhotvoreniia*, pp. 6–8; M. Kheraskov, *Izbrannye proizvedeniia*, pp. 15–19; and In-Ho Lee Ryu, "Freemasonry under Catherine the Great: A Reinterpretation," pp. 47–60, esp. pp. 58–59.

62. For a recent analysis of Kheraskov's works, one rich in comparative literary detail, see Michael Green, "Mixail Xeraskov and His Contribution to the Eighteenth Century Russian Theater."

63. M. Kheraskov, "Pis'mo," *Poleznoe uveselenie*, January 1761, pp. 14–15.

64. Kheraskov, "Nichtozhnost'," in *Izbrannye proizvedeniia*, p. 98.

65. Kheraskov, *Bakhariana, ili neizvestnyi . . .* , in *Izbrannye proizvedeniia*, p. 239. Zapadov has made available the introduction to Kheraskov's work. Zapadov's book is more readily accessible to scholars than the original. For the original text, see Kheraskov, *Bakhariana, ili neizvestnyi volshebnaia povest', pocherpnutaia iz russkikh skazok*, pp. 5–12.

66. Kheraskov, "Zlato," *Poleznoe uveselenie*, April 1760, p. 161.

67. Kheraskov, *Drug neshchastnykh*.

68. Ibid., p. 21.

69. Kheraskov, "K evterpe," in *Izbrannye proizvedeniia*, p. 109.

70. Kheraskov, "Pis'mo," *Poleznoe uveselenie*, January 1761, pp. 15–16.

71. Kheraskov, *Bakhariana ili neizvestnyi*, in *Izbrannye proizvedeniia*, pp. 239–40.

72. For example, see M. Kheraskov, "Puteshestvie razuma," *Poleznoe uveselenie*, April 1760, pp. 139–57.

73. S[emen] N[aryshkin], trans., "Iz mnenii Oksenshtirna o dvukh putiakh, kotorymi liudi v svoiu zhizn' idyt'," *Trudoliubivaia pchela*, September 1759, pp. 549–54.

74. Ibid., pp. 550–52.

75. Ibid., pp. 552–55.

76. "Pis'mo liubeznoi drug," *Nevinnoe uprazhnenie*, May 1763, pp. 195–203.

77. Ibid., pp. 195–96.

78. Ibid., p. 198.

79. Ibid., p. 201.

80. S[ergei] D[omashnev], "Iz sokratovykh razgovorov. Razgovor chetvertoi. O pritvorstve," *Poleznoe uveselenie*, February 1762, pp. 81–92.

81. I. Bogdanovich, "Pis'mo o bezsmertii dushi," *Poleznoe uveselenie*, October 1761, pp. 137–41.

82. For a good example of the opinion that reason was a gift from God, see "Pis'mo k A . . . N . . . ," *Poleznoe uveselenie*, August 1761, p. 51.

83. "O nespokoistvii," *Prazdnoe vremia v pol'zu upotreblennoi*, February 1760, pp. 95–107.

84. Ibid., p. 107.

85. "Eliseiskiia polia," *Nevinnoe uprazhnenie*, May 1763, pp. 215–26.

86. Ibid., p. 220.

87. Ibid., p. 221.

88. Ibid., p. 222.

89. "Zdravoe rassuzhdenie ukrashaet cheloveka," *Vsiakaia vsiachina*, March 1769, p. 113.

90. "Eliseiskiia polia," *Nevinnoe uprazhnenie*, May 1763, p. 225.

91. "O nespravedlivykh osnovaniiakh," *Trudoliubivaia pchela*, May 1759, p. 276. For similar opinions, see "Poslovitsa kakov v kolybelku, takov i v mogilku," *Prazdnoe vremia v pol'zu upotreblennoe*, February 1760, pp. 101–16, 117–32; March 1760, pp. 133–43, 149–60, 164–70, pagination corrected; Nikita Khrushchev, "Opyt o zhelaniiakh," *Poleznoe uveselenie*, January 1760, pp. 33–45.

92. "O nespavedlivykh osnovaniiakh," *Trudoliubivaia pchela*, May 1759, pp. 276–77.

93. Rzhevskii's sentiments, as well as those of Kheraskov, reflect an eighteenth-century tradition of idealizing the countryside in a pre-Romantic ruralism. See H. Rogger, *National Consciousness in Eighteenth-Century Russia*, p. 128.

94. A[leksei] R[zhevskii], "Stans sochinen 1761 goda iiulia 19. dnia po vyezde iz derevni G . . . Kh . . . ," *Poleznoe uveselenie*, August 1761, p. 54. See also idem, "Stansy," *Poleznoe uveselenie*, December 1761, pp. 189–91; P. Fon-Vizin, "Basn' pastukh i Sirena," *Dobroe namerenie*, August 1764, pp. 343–45.

95. P.Zh. [?], "O uedinenii," *Poleznoe uveselenie*, December 1761, p. 204.

96. P[aul] F[onvizin], "Prikliuchenie miridasa," *Dobroe namerenie*, August 1764, pp. 357–61.

97. "Fata viam invenient. Sud'ba naidet sebe put'. Persidskaia povest'," *Nevinnoe uprazhnenie*, June 1763, pp. 243–55.

98. "Pis'mo, v kotorom dokazyvaetsia chto neumerennoe uedinenie i neumerennoe soobshchestvo, ravno dlia cheloveka vredny," *Nevinnoe uprazhnenie*, pp. 286–97.

99. Ibid., pp. 286–87.

100. Ibid., p. 291.

101. Ibid., p. 288.

102. Ibid., p. 297.

103. "Society" is a translation of "*svet*." Occasionally the students used the word "*obshchestvo*," and, in those cases, the word will appear in transliteration. "*Svet*" was used casually in many instances. Apparently, it implied those educated elements in the capitals who shared the students' general values. The linguistic symbolism is quite limited because they used the word vaguely.

104. Ia. Bulgakov, trans., "O druzhestve," *Poleznoe uveselenie*, October 1760, p. 151.

105. Ibid., p. 153.

106. I. Bogdanovich, "Epigrammy," *Poleznoe uveselenie*, October 1761, p. 144. Bogdanovich's remark is similar to many assumed by Zapadov to be typical of the mood of all the *Kheraskovtsy* and characteristic of their sentimentalism. Their emphasis on the value of one's sensibilities was, according to Zapadov, proof that the students were Freemasons in

1760–1762. Zapadov's analysis would seem to obscure the difference between sentimentalism and moralism, and to assume the students were Masons in part because many of them later became Masons. See Kheraskov, *Izbrannye proizvedeniia*, pp. 15–16.

107. "O druzhbe," *Nevinnoe uprazhnenie*, June 1763, p. 279.

108. "Rech' o ravenstve sostoianii," *Nevinnoe uprazhnenie*, January 1763, p. 5.

109. Ibid., p. 10.

110. S. Domashnev, "Raznyia rassuzhdeniia," *Poleznoe uveselenie*, October 1761, p. 119.

111. "Rech' o ravenstve sostoianii," *Nevinnoe uprazhnenie*, January 1763, p. 7.

112. Dmitrei Anichkov, trans., "Rech' kotoruiu govoril odin razumnoi chelovek iz garamantov k Aleksandru velikomu," *Poleznoe uveselenie*, September 1761, p. 86. Pagination corrected. See also Khrushchev, "Opyt o zhelaniiakh," *Poleznoe uveselenie*, January 1760, pp. 43–44.

113. A. Rzhevskii, "Pis'mo k A . . . [leksei] N . . . [aryshkin]," *Poleznoe uveselenie*, January 1761, pp. 12–13.

114. Mikhailo Agentov, trans., "O upotreblenie vremeni," *Sobranie luchshikh sochinenii k rasprostraneniiu znaniia i k proizvedeniiu udovol'stviia*, January–March 1762, p. 124. Agentov used the word to single out those individuals who discarded the proper moral maxims and led dissolute, superficial lives.

115. A[leksei] R[zhevskii], "Stansy," *Poleznoe uveselenie*, December 1760, p. 236.

116. Ibid.

117. A[leksei] Naryshkin, "Pis'mo k . . . A . . . [leksei] R . . . [zhevskii]," *Poleznoe uveselenie*, January 1761, pp. 3–6.

118. Ibid., p. 3.

119. Ibid., p. 4. For other examples of this idea of divine investiture, see I. F. Bogdanovich, "Epistola," *Poleznoe uveselenie*, April 1761, pp. 126–28; and idem, "Pis'mo o bezsmertii dushi," *Poleznoe uveselenie*, October 1761, pp. 137–41.

120. Naryshkin, "Pis'mo k . . . A . . . [leksei] R . . . [zhevskii]," *Poleznoe uveselenie*, January 1761, p. 3.

121. Rzhevskii, "Pis'mo k A . . . [leksei] N . . . [aryshkin]," *Poleznoe uveselenie*, January 1761, p. 11.

122. Ibid., p. 12.

123. Aleksei Rzhevskii, "Sonet," *Poleznoe uveselenie*, March 1761, p. 96.

124. Demkov, *Istoriia*, p. 610. The influence of the Book of Psalms has been assessed in general terms. See "Upotreblenie knigi psaltyr v drevnem bytu russkogo naroda," *Pravoslavnyi sobesednik*, 1857, pp. 814–56.

125. The precise date is not known since the poem was not published until 1769. For the poem itself, see *F.S.S.*, I, 209–12.

126. Ibid., p. 209.

127. Ibid., pp. 210–11.

128. Ibid., pp. 211–12.

129. Ibid., p. 212.

130. Ibid.

131. Ibid., II, 95.

132. E. Simmons, *English Literature and Culture in Russia (1553–1840)*, p. 120.

133. Polovtsov, *Russkii biograficheskii slovar'*, XXI, 175; *F.S.S.*, II, 103–5; and Viazemskii, *Fon-Vizin*, p. 45. G. N. Teplov was a scholar who succeeded in state service because of his close ties with the Razumovskii family. He was a member of the Academy of Sciences and a senator. Most of his published works were moral tracts.

134. Paul Hazard, *The European Mind*, p. 262.

135. *F.S.S.*, II, 104–5. The summary has not been preserved. Its dating cannot be fixed any more precisely than the early 1760s.

136. Viazemskii, *Fon-Vizin*, p. 45.

137. Denis Fonvizin, "Pravosudnyi iupiter," *Poleznoe uveselenie*, November 1761, pp. 161–78. Pagination corrected. Fonvizin gave no indication of the original author of this article, signing only "Denis Fon-Vizin translated." See p. 178.

138. Ibid., p. 161.

139. Ibid., p. 162.

140. Ibid., p. 165.

141. Ibid., p. 178.

142. See C. leJeun, *Frantsuzskaia nyneshnego vremeni filosofiia*.

143. "Pis'ma k plemianniku," *Zhivopisets*, 1772, pp. 101–13.

144. Ibid., p. 107.

145. Ibid., p. 110.

146. *S.B.*, II, 325, 337. The utilitarian rationale for religion was more clearly argued in an unsigned article in *Idle Time Used for the Good*. See "Rassuzhdenie o dobrom upotreblenii strastei," *Prazdnoe vremia v pol'zu upotreblennoe*, October 1759, pp.241–50.

147. [Princess Catherine Dashkova?], "O istochnike strastei," *Nevinnoe uprazhnenie*, January 1763, pp. 28–32; February 1763, pp. 61–65; March 1763, pp. 136–44; April 1763, pp. 157–65; May 1763, pp. 232–40; June 1763, pp. 271–85.

148. *S.B.*, I, 243–51.

149. Bogdanovich, "Tablitsa dlia detei . . . ," *S.B.*, II, 338.

150. A. Sumarokov, "Epigramma," *Trudoliubivaia pchela*, July 1759, pp. 416–17.

Chapter III

1. Hajo Holborn, *History of Modern Germany 1648–1840* (New York: Knopf, 1964), p. 161.

2. Samuel Pufendorf, *Elementorum Jurisprudentiae Universalis*, II, 14.

3. Otto Gierke, *Natural Law and the Theory of Society 1500–1800*, p. 155.

4. Ibid., p. 143.

5. Christian Wolff, *Jus Gentium Methodo Scientifica Pertractatum*, II, 222.

6. Ibid., p. 313.

7. Christian Wolff, *Institutions du droit de la nature et des gens*, II, 179. For the original in Latin, see idem, *Institutiones Juris Naturae Et Gentium* in *Gesammelte Werke*, XXVI, 671–72.

8. Wolff, *Institutions*, II, 150–51; idem, *Gesammelte Werke*, XXVI, 613–18.

9. Wolff, *Institutions*, II, 148–49.

10. Ibid., pp. 150–51.

11. Gierke, *Natural Law and the Theory of Society*, pp. 118–19.
12. Wolff, *Institutions*, I, 21.
13. Ibid., II, 105.
14. Wolff, *Jus Gentium*, II, 334.
15. Wolff, *Institutions*, II, 138–40; idem, *Gesammelte Werke*, XXVI, 597–98. See also Samuel Pufendorf, *De Jure Naturae Et Gentium*, II, 959; idem, *Elementorum*, II, 286–87.
16. Samuel Pufendorf, *De Officio Hominis Et Civis Juxta Legem Naturalem*, II, 121. See also Wolff, *Institutions*, II, 152, 155, 179; idem, *Gesammelte Werke*, XXVI, 617–18, 624, 670.
17. Pufendorf, *De Officio Hominis*, p. 138. See also Wolff, *Jus Gentium*, II, 316.
18. Wolff, *Jus Gentium*, II, 402.
19. Ibid., p. 334.
20. Pufendorf, *De Officio Hominis*, II, 114.
21. Pufendorf, *Elementorum*, II, 76.
22. Ibid., pp. 287–88.
23. Wolff, *Institutions*, II, 180; idem, *Gesammelte Werke*, XXVI, 672–73.
24. Wolff, *Institutions*, II, 133; idem, *Gesammelte Werke*, XXVI, 589–90. The reference was to relations between masters and serfs on estates, but was used by Wolff inferentially as an example of the rights and duties of members of several types of associations such as the family, the estate, and the civil government.
25. Wolff, *Institutions*, II, 144–45; idem, *Gesammelte Werke*, XXVI, 605.
26. Wolff, *Jus Gentium*, II, 308.
27. James Billington, *The Icon and the Axe*, p. 236.
28. G. Makogonenko, *Denis Fonvizin*; K. V. Pigarev, *Tvorchestvo Fonvizina*; G. Gukovskii, *Ocherki po istorii russkoi literatury XVIII veka*.
29. Makogonenko, *Denis Fonvizin*, p. 4.
30. For a particularly engaging and persuasive argument about the nature of the influence of the German Enlightenment, see M. Raeff, "Les Slaves, les Allemands et les 'Lumières.' " Raeff's points were made with reference to late eighteenth-century Russia, not the 1760s (p. 544). For additional remarks, see idem, *Michael Speransky: Statesman of Imperial Russia 1772–1839*, 2d rev. ed. (The Hague: Nijhoff, 1969), pp. 41 ff., 214–27.
31. S. Domashnev, "Son," *Poleznoe uveselenie*, December 1761, pp. 209–20.
32. Ibid., p. 213.
33. Ibid.
34. Ibid., p. 209.
35. Ibid., pp. 215–18.
36. G[rigorii] K[ozitskii], trans., "Kratkoe izobrazhenie o estestve, pol'ze i neobkhodimoi potrebnosti voiny i ssor," *Trudoliubivaia pchela*, September 1759, pp. 571–74.
37. For example, see M. Permskoi, "Rech' nekotorogo krest'ianina . . . k rimskim senatoram," *Dobroe namerenie*, August 1764, pp. 372–83; September 1764, pp. 401–18. A later example of a distrust of rulers and the fear of wars is Bogdanovich's translation in 1771 of Rousseau's long commentary on the project for a "république européene" proposed by Charles Drénée Castel, Abbé de Saint Pierre (1658–1743). See J. J. Rousseau, *Extrait du Projet de Paix Perpétuelle de Monsieur l'Abbé de Saint-Pierre*. Only the original was available. For an excellent analysis of the origins and limitations of this plan, see Jean Goumy, *Etude sur la Vie et les Ecrits de l'Abbé de Saint Pierre*, pp. 72–93. See Chapter VI for details.

38. M. Permskoi, "Rech' nekotorogo krest'ianina . . . k rimskim senatoram," *Dobroe namerenie*, September 1764, p. 402.

39. Ibid., pp. 374–75.

40. Dmitrii Anichkov, trans., "Rech' kotoruiu odin razumnoi chelovek iz garamantov k Aleksandru velikomu," *Poleznoe uveselenie*, September 1761, pp. 81–91.

41. Ibid., p. 87.

42. Ibid., p. 88.

43. Ibid., p. 83.

44. Ibid., p. 90.

45. Ibid., p. 86.

46. Richard Wortman, *The Development of a Russian Legal Consciousness*, p. 97.

47. A. Vershnitskii, "Rech' Marka Avreliia imperatora rimskago, govorennaia im samim pri ego konchine, k synu svoemu i nasledniku prestola," *Dobroe namerenie*, September 1764, pp. 429–32; October 1764, pp. 449–75.

48. Vershnitskii, "Rech' Marka Avreliia imperatora rimskago," *Dobroe namerenie*, October 1764, p. 472.

49. Ibid., p. 455.

50. Ibid., pp. 461–62.

51. For other examples, see A. Karin, "Son: khram dobrodeteli," *Poleznoe uveselenie*, December 1761, pp. 249–59; Andrei Nartov, "Rech' skifskago posla k Aleksandru velikomu," *Poleznoe uveselenie*, January 1761, pp. 41–44.

52. Paul Jérémie Bitaubé, *Iosif*, translated with an introduction by D. Fonvizin, *F.S.S.*, I, 443. I am indebted to James Rice for his comments on the stylistic and political clues to the literary ancestry of Fonvizin's *Telemak*. Bitaubé (1732–1808) was a French enlightener who made his mark by his translations of the *Iliad* (1780) and the *Odyssey* (1785). His *Joseph* was first published in 1767 and was quite popular, going through several editions. Bitaubé was arrested during the Terror, but released during the Directory, and officially rehabilitated by Napoleon.

53. I. F. Bogdanovich, "Oda na den' vosshestviia na vserossiiskii prestol ego velichestva gosudaria imperatora PETRA FEODOROVICHA, samoderzhtsa vserossiiskogo," *Poleznoe uveselenie*, January 1762, p. 1.

54. Ibid., p. 4.

55. Ibid., p. 5.

56. A. Rzhevskii, "Oda vsepresvetleishemu derzhavneishemu velikomu i miloserdomu gosudariu, istinnomu ottsu poddannykh, imperatoru PETRU FEODOROVICHU, samoderzhtsu vserossiiskomu," *Poleznoe uveselenie*, March 1762, pp. 108–13.

57. Ibid., p. 109.

58. Ibid., p. 111.

59. Aleksei Naryshkin, "Na konchinu blazhennyia i vechnodostoinyia pamiati imperatritsy Elizavety Petrovny, i na vosshestvie na vserossiiskii naslednyi prestol gosudaria imperatora PETRA FEODOROVICHA," *Poleznoe uveselenie*, February 1762, pp. 49–57; idem, "Oda vsepresvetleishemu, derzhavneishemu, velikomu i miloserdomu gosudariu imperatoru PETRU FEODOROVICHU, samoderzhtsu vserossiiskomu," *Poleznoe uveselenie*, March 1762, pp. 129–35. See also A. Rzhevskii, "Oda ego velichestvu, vsepresvetleishemu, derzhavneishemu, velikomu i miloserdomu gosudariu, imperatoru PETRU FEODOROVICHU, samoderzhtsu vseros-

siiskomu na vseradostnoe vosshestvie na vserossiiskii prestol," *Poleznoe uveselenie*, March 1762, pp. 97–107.

60. For a famous statement on Peter written in obviously self-serving and invidious terms, see Catherine II, *Memoirs of Catherine the Great*. For the critical opinion of a well-known English historian, see R. Nisbet Bain, *Peter III Emperor of Russia*.

61. M. Raeff, *Imperial Russia 1682–1825*, p. 78. Raeff's point referred only to the sanction given by the tsar to conditions similar to those associated with *Bironovshchina*. For a recent reconsideration of Peter's reign, see idem, "The Domestic Policies of Peter III and His Overthrow."

62. I. F. Bogdanovich, "Oda eia imperatorskomu velichestvu, gosudaryne Ekaterine Alekseevne, samoderzhitse vserossiiskoi. Na novyi 1763 god," *S.B.*, I, 252–56. For the details on the dating of the ode, see idem, *Stikhotvoreniia*, note to pp. 150–53. See also A. Karin, "Oda na vosshestvie na prestol Ekateriny II," cited in Saitov, *Fedor Grigor'evich Karin*, p. 22, and S. Domashnev, "Oda na vosshestvie na prestol imperatritsy Ekateriny II," cited in M. N. Longinov, "Russkie pisateli XVIII veka," III, 206–7.

63. [Denis Fonvizin], "Rech' kotoruiu glavnoi zhrtes memfisa govoril pri pogrebenii egipetskoi tsaritsy, materi sifovoi," *Sobranie luchshikh sochinenii k rasprostraneniiu znaniia i k proizvedeniiu udovol'stviia*, July–September 1762, pp. 105–12. Jean Terrasson (1670–1750) was a French writer whose *Séthos* (1731) was an imitation of Fénelon's *Les Aventures de Télémaque, Fils d'Ulysse*. Fonvizin published his translation in four parts, between 1762 and 1768. See *F.S.S.*, I, xv.

64. [Fonvizin], "Rech' kotoruiu glavnoi zhrtes memfisa," *Sobranie luchshikh sochinenii k rasprostraneniiu znaniia i k proizvedeniiu udovol'stviia*, July–September 1762, p. 106.

65. Ibid., p. 108.

66. Ibid., p. 107.

67. M. N. Longinov, *Novikov i moskovskie martinisty*, pp. 11–12; G. Vernadskii, *Nikolai Ivanovich Novikov*, p. 4.

68. Longinov, *Novikov i moskovskie martinisty*, p. 13.

69. P. E. (?), "Predislovie," *Truten'*, pp. vii–xi. The editor, though not known, is probably Efremov.

70. M. D. Khmyrov, "Primechanie," in Longinov, "Russkie pisateli XVIII veka," III, 205, n. 3.

71. Longinov, "Russkie pisateli XVIII veka," II, 74.

72. For a recent interpretation of Catherine's intention of ruling by law, see D. Griffiths, "Catherine II: The Republican Empress."

73. *F.S.S.*, II, 94. See also Viazemskii, *Fon-Vizin*, p. 465.

74. I. F. Bogdanovich, "Avtobiografiia I. F. Bogdanovicha," p. 184.

75. Vernadskii, *Nikolai Ivanovich Novikov*, p. 4.

76. Longinov, "Russkie pisateli XVIII veka," II, 572.

77. Ibid., II, 74.

Chapter IV

1. David Ransel, *The Politics of Catherinian Russia*, p. 1. Aside from this study, the only attention to Panin is in a brief—and flawed—book by P. Lebedev, *Grafy Nikita i Petr Paniny*.

2. In a recent book, P. Dukes has claimed that the historiographical image of Panin as a contestant for power and a political adversary of Catherine originated with the historian S. M. Solov'ev and was continued by Korf and Shchlegov. However, the image of Panin-as-opponent originated with Denis Fonvizin's nephew, M. Fonvizin. Nonetheless, the assumption that an adversary relationship existed between the empress and her chief minister was also made by such scholarly writers as V. Iakushikin and D. Kobeko. See M. A. Fonvizin, "Zapiski Mikhaila Aleksandrovicha Fonvizina. Ocherki russkoi istorii. Primechaniia k 'Histoire philosophique et politique de Russie' par Enneaux et Chennechot." These articles were republications of the original edition printed in 1853. See also P. Dukes, *Catherine the Great and the Russian Nobility*, pp. 176–77.

3. Ransel, *Politics of Catherinian Russia*, p. 34.

4. The quote is from a memo dictated to the Danish diplomat Baron von Asseburg and entitled "Mémoire sur le détrônement de Pierre III," cited in Ransel, *Politics of Catherinian Russia*, pp. 62–63. The brackets are Ransel's.

5. Ibid., pp. 107–8.

6. V. A. Bil'basov, *Istoriia Ekateriny vtoroi*, II, 148.

7. David Ransel, "Nikita Panin's Role in Russian Court Politics of the Seventeen Sixties: A Critique of the Gentry Opposition Thesis," Ph.D. dissertation, Yale University, 1968, p. 120. Dispatch, dated October 9, 1762, of Breteuil to Choiseul.

8. Ransel, *Politics of Catherinian Russia*, pp. 79–80.

9. For the plan itself and associated documents, see "Bumagi, kasaiushchiiasia predpolozheniia ob uchrezhdenii imperatorskogo soveta i o razdelenii senata na departamenty v pervyi god tsarstvovaniia Ekateriny II," *Sbornik imperatorskogo russkogo istoricheskogo obshchestva* 7 (1871): 200–21. The council project itself is available in edited form in M. Raeff, ed., *Plans for Political Reform in Imperial Russia, 1730–1905*, pp. 63–68. See also Bil'basov, *Istoriia Ekateriny vtoroi*, II, 149–58; and N. Chechulin, "Proekt imperatorskogo soveta v pervyi god tsarstvovaniia Ekateriny II."

10. "Bumagi," *Sbornik imperatorskogo russkogo istoricheskogo obshchestva* 7 (1871): 212.

11. Ibid., pp. 210–11.

12. Ransel, *Politics of Catherinian Russia*, p. 136.

13. Ibid., p. 134.

14. For a complete list of the leading members of the Panin party, see Ransel, *Politics of Catherinian Russia*, pp. 107–13.

15. [Alexander Turgenev], *La Cour de la Russie Il y a Cent Ans 1725–1783. Extraits des Dépêches des Ambassadeurs Anglais et Français*, pp. 195–96; and E. R. Dashkova, *The Memoirs of Princess Dashkova*, pp. 10, 51.

16. [Turgenev], *La Cour de la Russie*, pp. 195–96.

17. D. Korsakov, "Stronniki votsareniia Ekateriny II (1757–1762 gg.)," p. 244.

18. Ibid., p. 232.

19. I. P. Elagin, "Zapiski I. P. Elagina," p. 588; for the important details of Elagin's relations

with Catherine, see the brief sketch by N. V. Drizen, "Ivan Perfil'evich Elagin (1725–1794)."

20. G. Makogonenko, *Denis Fonvizin*, p. 18.

21. K. V. Pigarev, *Tvorchestvo Fonvizina*, p. 57. For what little is known of Fonvizin's first trip abroad, see *F.S.S.*, II, 94, 317. The second reference is to two short letters, the first to M. Vorontsov and the other to A. M. Golitsyn, dated December 29, 1762, and January 14, 1763, respectively.

22. *F.S.S.*, II, 94. For the original play, see F. M. A. de Voltaire, *Oeuvres Complètes de Voltaire*, II, 385–436.

23. Pigarev, *Tvorchestvo Fonvizina*, p. 60.

24. *F.S.S.*, II, 343.

25. Ibid. Lukin probably gave Fonvizin reason to become agitated. When Lukin published his *Works* . . . in 1765, he dedicated the two-volume set to Elagin. Lukin even collaborated with Elagin on a translation of Prévost's *Mémoires et aventures d'un homme de qualité qui s'est retiré du monde*, published in Russian translation in six parts between 1756 and 1765. Fonvizin might very well have assumed he was not as successful as Lukin in winning Elagin's favor. See V. Lukin, *Sochineniia i perevody Vladimira Lukina*, I, 3–7; and Antoine-François, l'Abbé Prévost, *Mémoires et aventures d'un homme de qualité qui s'est retiré du monde*.

26. Ransel, *Politics of Catherinian Russia*, p. 1.

27. I. F. Bogdanovich, "Avtobiografiia I. F. Bogdanovicha," p. 184; idem, *Stikhotvoreniia*, p. 9.

28. Bogdanovich, "Avtobiografiia I. F. Bogdanovicha," p. 185.

29. Ibid.

30. S. M. Troitskii, *Russkii absoliutizm i dvorianstvo v XVIII v.*, p. 193.

31. Ibid., pp. 129–30.

32. Ibid., p. 254.

33. David Griffiths, "Russian Court Politics," pp. 20–21.

34. I. de Madariaga is cited in A. Weinbaum, "N. I. Novikov (1744–1818): An Interpretation of His Career and Ideas," p. 26, n. 26.

35. G. Vernadskii, *Nikolai Ivanovich Novikov*, pp. 6–7; and M. Makarov, "Bibliograficheskie redkosti: truten'," p. 27.

36. M. N. Longinov, "Russkie pisateli XVIII veka," III, 207. The information available on these minor writers is minimal. The best single source for all these men is Novikov, *Opyt istoricheskago slovaria*, in Efremov, *Materialy*, pp. 5–128.

37. Longinov, "Russkie pisateli XVIII veka," IV, 573–74.

38. Ibid., II, 77–78.

39. Ibid., pp. 78–80.

40. Fonvizin's earliest translations were Jean Terrasson's *Séthos* . . . (1762–1768), Ludvig Holberg's *Moral Fables* (1761), Cicero's *Pro Marcello* (1762), and several translations for *Useful Entertainment* and the *Collection of the Best Works for Spreading Knowledge and Bringing Pleasure*. In November 1761, Fonvizin's translation of an unidentified work appeared in *Useful Entertainment* as "The Just Jupiter." He also contributed four translations for the *Collection of the Best Works for Spreading Knowledge and Bringing Pleasure*. In the first number, January–March 1762, he had published "Mr. Menard's Search for Antique Mirrors" (pp. 1–8), an article that reveals Fonvizin's concerns about fops and their narcissism. The

article was taken from volume twenty-three of "Histoire des l'Academie des Inscriptions & Belles Lettres." In the same issue he published his translation of Johann Christian Kruger's moral tale, "The Seven Muses in the Marketplace" (pp. 74–83). In the second issue of the quarterly Fonvizin translated "The Discourse of Mr. Reitstein on the Rise of Drawing and Some Advice on Its Bases" (pp. 181–213), a short piece written in a question and answer format and concerned with the place of art in society. In the third issue, Fonvizin published the extract from Terrasson's *Séthos* . . . and an article on the didactic purpose of poetry, "The Discourse of Mr. Yart on the Purpose and Essence of Poetry" (pp. 120–43).

41. For Pososhkov's council, see the details and commentary in B. Kafenguaz, *I. T. Pososhkov. Zhizn' i deiatel'nost'*, pp. 106, 119, 124.

42. Christian Wolff, *Institutions du droit de la nature et des gens*, II, 179.

43. Ibid., p. 149.

44. Samuel Pufendorf, *De Officio Hominis Et Civis Juxta Legem Naturalem*, II, 144.

45. Ibid., p. 121.

46. I. F. Bogdanovich, *Istoricheskoe izobrazhenie rossii*, S.B., II, 145–231.

47. Ibid., p. 153.

48. Ibid., p. 203.

49. Ibid., p. 153.

50. D. Fonvizin, "M. Tulliia Tsitserona rech' za M. Martsella," *F.S.S.*, II, 618–21. This was a translation of *Pro Marcello*, delivered in 46 A.D. For the convenient Loeb edition of this speech, see Cicero, *The Speeches*, translated by N. H. Watts (London, 1931), pp. 422–51.

51. *F.S.S.*, I, x.

52. [N. I. Novikov], "Zaveshchanie Iundzhena kitaiskogo khana k ego synu," *Pustomelia*, July 1770, pp. 69–88; [idem], "Chenzyia kitaiskogo filosofa sovet, dannoi ego gosudariu," *Truten'*, February 1770, pp. 267–71.

53. For a splendid discussion of *chinoiserie* in eighteenth-century Russia, see Barbara Maggs, "China in the Literature of Eighteenth-Century Russia," pp. 215–62.

54. [N. I. Novikov], "Chenzyia kitaiskogo filosofa sovet, dannoi ego gosudariu," *Truten'*, February 1770, pp. 267–68, 270.

55. Ibid., p. 271.

56. Ibid., p. 269.

57. [Novikov], "Portrety," *Truten'*, January 1770, p. 241.

58. [Novikov], "Predislovie," *Truten'*, p. 8.

59. [Novikov], "Razgovor ia i truten'," *Truten'*, December 1769, pp. 194–95.

60. [Novikov], "V novoi god novoe shchastie," *Truten'*, January 1770, p. 230.

61. Novikov, ed., *Istoriia o nevinnom zatochenii blizhniago boiarina Artemona Sergeevicha Matveeva*, pp. vii–xiv.

62. Ibid., p. 337.

63. Ibid., pp. 355–56. For the same pairings in the works of Bogdanovich and Fonvizin, see *S.B.*, I, 390; II, 334–35; *F.S.S.*, I, 207–8, 331.

64. Denis Fonvizin, "Slovo na vyzdorovlenie ego imperatorskogo vysochestva gosudaria tsesarevicha i velikogo kniazia Pavla Petrovicha v 1771 gode," *F.S.S.*, II, 191.

65. For example, see ibid., p. 366. Letter to Peter Ivanovich Panin, dated January 4, 1772.

66. Fonvizin, "Zhizn' grafa Nikity Ivanovicha Panina," *F.S.S.*, II, 279–89. For a similar de-

scription of political personalities, see his short article, "Callisthenes." This work was probably not original. Fonvizin apparently learned of this topic through Elagin who in the 1750s had translated the "Ode à Priape," a famous poem by the French writer A. Piron (1689–1773). Coincidentally, Piron also wrote a five-act tragedy, *Callisthène*. The theme of the tragedy is close enough to that of Fonvizin's "Callisthenes" to suggest that Fonvizin simply paraphrased the original. See Longinov, "Russkie pisateli XVIII veka," II, 197–98; and A. Piron, *Oeuvres Complètes de Piron*, 7 vols. (Paris: M. Lambert, 1776), I, 163–290.

67. Fonvizin, "Zhizn' grafa Nikity Ivanovicha Panina," *F.S.S.*, II, 282.

68. Ibid., pp. 283–84.

69. Ibid., p. 284.

70. Ibid.

71. Ibid., p. 287.

72. [Turgenev], *La Cour de la Russie*, p. 242. See also Sabathier de Cabres, *Catherine II, Sa Cour et la Russie*, pp. 36, 50–51. For another example of the value of these descriptions, compare those of Elagin. To Fonvizin Elagin was one who "has reason enlightened by knowledge; he has a good heart by nature and follows strictly the rules of an honorable man. . . . The name of Elagin calls to mind the very epitome of an honorable man." Other observers, more impartial than Fonvizin, were quite direct in citing Elagin's faults. See *F.S.S.*, II, 343; M. N. Longinov, "Satiricheskii katalog pri dvore Ekateriny II-i," p. 2040; de Cabres, *Catherine II, Sa Cour et la Russie*, p. 41; and Catherine II, "Sobstvennoruchnaia zapiska Ekateriny II k Elaginu s vygovorom za lenost'," *Sbornik imperatorskogo russkogo istoricheskogo obshchestva* 7 (1871): 351.

73. N. Chechulin, *Vneshniaia politika rossii v nachale tsarstvovaniia Ekateriny II. 1762–1774*, p. 67, no. 2. Chechulin dated the dispatch "in February 1763."

74. [Turgenev], *La Cour de la Russie*, p. 241.

75. Of the Fonvizin group only Novikov dealt with Orlov with any degree of fairness. Even here, however, Pekarskii believed this impartiality was a trick and that Novikov coupled inflammatory articles with sops to Orlov to get both pieces by the censor. See [N. Novikov], "Razgovor ia i truten'," *Truten'*, December 1769, p. 196; "Pis'mo uezdnogo dvorianina k ego synu," *Zhivopisets*, 1772, p. 78; and P. Pekarskii, "Materialy dlia istorii zhurnal'noi literaturnoi deiatel'nosti Ekateriny II," app. 6, p. 9.

76. Ransel, *Politics of Catherinian Russia*, pp. 136–37.

Chapter V

1. *F.S.S.*, I, 263–411.

2. Ibid., p. 399.

3. Ibid., p. 304. See also pp. 283, 297–98.

4. Ibid., p. 274.

5. Ibid., pp. 376, 379, 380.

6. Ibid., pp. 387–89, 392–94, and for Makogonenko's comments, p. 623.

7. Ibid., p. 388.

8. Ibid., p. 389.

9. Since these satires on fops, provincial noblemen, and the like appeared in the journals with such repetitive vigor and exaggerated significance, there may have been an element of posturing involved. The students' would-be jaded observations ran counter to their age, experience, and knowledge.

10. This all but exclusively moral basis for social comment has been generally overlooked by scholars. Certain authors have asked how someone like Fonvizin could identify social ills without citing these abuses as flaws in imperial society. Others have not been bothered by this problem and have claimed that Fonvizin's criticisms were directed at the entire state and society. See E. Shumigorskii, "Gosudarynia-publitsist"; and N. Dobroliubov, "Russkaia satira v vek Ekateriny." For the second opinion, see G. Makogonenko, *Denis Fonvizin*; and K. V. Pigarev, *Tvorchestvo Fonvizina*.

11. *Polnoe sobranie zakonov rossiiskoi imperii*, XVI, 75–76, no. 11.578.

12. Ibid.

13. Ibid., p. 12, no. 11.597.

14. David Griffiths, "Catherine II: The Republican Empress," p. 331. See also Marc Raeff, "Random Notes on the Reign of Catherine II in the Light of Recent Literature."

15. Marc Raeff, "L'Etat, Le Gouvernement et la Tradition Politique en Russie Impériale Avant 1861," pp. 296–97.

16. Kerry Morrison, "Catherine II's Legislative Commission," p. 467.

17. Ibid., p. 468.

18. R. Jones, *The Emancipation of the Russian Nobility*, p. 92.

19. Ibid., pp. 92–93.

20. Ibid., pp. 107–16.

21. G. Gukovskii, *Ocherki po istorii russkoi literatury XVIII veka*, pp. 147, 150, 152, 161; G. Makogonenko, *Nikolai Novikov i russkoe prosveshchenie XVIII veka*, pp. 63–83, 100–101, 112; idem, *Denis Fonvizin*, pp. 91–104; Pigarev, *Tvorchestvo Fonvizina*, pp. 18–19.

22. For example, see Gukovskii, *Ocherki*, pp. 182 ff.

23. Jones, *Emancipation of the Russian Nobility*, pp. 110–11.

24. Gukovskii's use of the word *"frondeur"* conjures up images of the Panin party as representatives of a Russian *fronde*. According to Gukovskii, Panin was frightened both by the idea of a bureaucracy beyond the control of the upper echelons of the nobility and by the influence of courtiers (i.e., the Shuvalov brothers) whose interests were commercial and industrial rather than agrarian. Panin was a *frondeur* in planning for a government of laws that would reestablish an agrarian-oriented state. He was at once a "liberal" because of his political ideals and a "frondeur" because of the goals of these same ideals. For this strained exercise in linguistic artistry, see Gukovskii, *Ocherki*, p. 75.

25. David Ransel, "Catherine II's Instruction to the Commission on Laws: An Attack on Gentry Liberals?"

26. Ibid., p. 23.

27. For a review of the electoral procedures, see Paul Dukes, *Catherine the Great and the Russian Nobility*, pp. 56–57. The complete details are available in Florovskii's magisterial *Sostav zakonodatel'noi kommissii 1767–74 gg.*

28. A. Weinbaum, "N. I. Novikov (1744–1818): An Interpretation of His Career and Ideas," p. 23.

29. Ibid.

30. V. Bogoliubov, *N. I. Novikov i ego vremia*, p. 37.

31. Makogonenko, *Denis Fonvizin*, p. 94.

32. P. N. Berkov, *Vladimir Lukin, 1737–1794*, p. 15.

33. N. Karamzin, "O Bogdanoviche i ego sochineniiakh," pp. 13–14.

34. M. N. Longinov, "Russkie pisateli XVIII veka," II, 76–80; III, 205–7.

35. Novikov's journals are too well known to need review. For a summary of the contributors and topics, see P. Berkov, *Istoriia russkoi zhurnalistiki XVIII veka*, pp. 156–307.

36. The author of the letters to Falalei is not known. It is not possible to credit Novikov with these letters since the most reliable lists of his contributions to each of his journals, Vernadskii's compilation in *Nikolai Ivanovich Novikov*, Efremov's notes to the 1865 edition of the *Drone*, and, to a lesser degree, Makogonenko's comments in his monographs and edited works, yield no definite consensus.

37. "Pis'mo uezdnogo dvorianina k ego synu," *Zhivopisets*, 1772, p. 77.

38. Ibid.

39. Ibid., p. 76; and [Letter from Ermolai to the *Painter*], pp. 95–96.

40. "Synu moemu Falaleiu," *Zhivopisets*, 1772, pp. 82–83.

41. For an enlightening description and analysis of the customs and particular interests of the provincial nobility in 1767, see Wilson Augustine, "Notes toward a Portrait of the Eighteenth-Century Russian Nobility." For a short, first-rate survey, see the collection of articles republished as N. Chechulin, *Russkoe provintsial'noe obshchestvo vo vtoroi polovine XVIII veka*.

42. *F.S.S.*, I, 45–103.

43. Ibid., p. 51.

44. Ibid.

45. Ibid., p. 47.

46. Fonvizin originated neither the literary stereotype of the dandy nor the characteristics that identified him. The figure's earliest appearance was in Kantemir's first satire, written in late 1729, which criticized the fop Medor, who "would not trade a pound of good powder for Seneca; . . . nor his tailor for the praise of Cicero." Ivanushka's distinguishing features were borrowed from Elagin's play, a *French-Russian* (*Frantsuz-russkii*), which was first presented on October 17, 1765. This play was, in turn, a translation of Holberg's *Jean de France*. See Longinov, "Russkie pisateli XVIII veka," II, 199; and Antiokh Kantemir, *Sobranie stikhotvorenii*, pp. 59–60.

47. *F.S.S.*, I, 81.

48. Ibid., pp. 54–55.

49. Ibid., pp. 73–74, 84.

50. Louis Perlman, *Russian Literature and the Business Man*, p. vi.

51. Ibid., pp. 21–22.

52. Fonvizin was commissioned to translate Justi's *Grundsätze der Policey-wissenschaft* by the Academy of Sciences in 1765. However, the translation was never published, and the manuscript has not been found. See Makogonenko, *Denis Fonvizin*, p. 27; and Pigarev, *Tvorchestvo Fonvizina*, p. 65.

53. Armand-Leon de Madaillan de Lesparre, Marquis de Lassay (1652–1738), was known primarily for his marital and military affairs. Married and widowed three times, he was

more fortunate in his military duties with the duke of Condé. His conduct during Louis XIV's invasion of Franche-Condé in 1674 earned him considerable admiration from his contemporaries. He also enriched himself in the speculative affairs of John Law and eventually retired to his estate in Lassay in Normandy. It was here he established a press, which published his only other known work, *Recueil de différentes choses*, a book of reflections written at the time of the capture of Valenciennes by the French army.

54. Gabriel-François Coyer (1707–1782) was the author of several books that had a certain popularity in eighteenth-century France. A member of l'Académie de Nancy, the Accademia in Rome, and the London Academy, Coyer was known by many of the *philosophes*, particularly Voltaire. The work cited above was followed by supplemental arguments in 1757 entitled *Développement et défense du système de la noblesse commerçante*. His other books include a translation of Blackstone's *Commentaries on the Laws of England* and original pieces on a wide variety of topics, from his *Histoire de Jean Sobieski, roi de Pologne* (1761) to a *Dissertation sur la différence des religions grecque et romaine* (1755).

55. Denis Fonvizin, trans., *Torguiushchee dvorianstvo protivupolozhennoe dvorianstvu voennomu, ili dva rassuzhdeniia o tom, sluzhit li to k blagopoluchiiu gosudarstva, chtoby dvorianstvo vstupalo v kupechestvo? S pribavleniem osoblivogo o tom zhe rassuzhdeniia g. Iustiia*, F.S.S., II, 117–86. For an earlier example of a "trading nobility" advocated with the same rationale as that used by Fonvizin, see "O kommertsii," *Nevinnoe uprazhnenie*, February 1763, pp. 86–89.

56. Fonvizin, *Torguiushchee dvorianstvo*, F.S.S., II, 155.

57. Ibid., p. 131.

58. Ibid., pp. 129–30.

59. Ibid., pp. 156–57.

60. Ibid., p. 163.

61. Ibid., p. 122.

62. Ibid., p. 135.

63. Ibid. See also p. 146.

64. Ibid., p. 168.

65. Dukes, *Catherine the Great and the Russian Nobility*, p. 103.

66. Sebastien Le Prestre de Vauban (1633–1707) wrote many works on military science but also one, *Le Système de la Dîme Royale* (1707), that proposed an overhaul of the tax system in France. It was this work that prompted Coyer to write his essay on the trading nobility.

67. Quoted in W. F. Reddaway, ed., *Documents of Catherine the Great*, p. 267.

68. Catherine's wavering attitude toward a trading nobility has been documented in detail. See N. Lavrovskii, "K biografii Fon-Vizina."

69. Ibid., p. 210. See also Dukes, *Catherine the Great and the Russian Nobility*, p. 227.

70. Lavrovskii, "K biografii Fon-Vizina," p. 214.

71. *F.S.S.*, I, 90.

72. (Untitled), *Vsiakaia vsiachina*, no. 93, pp. 241–46.

73. "O nespravedlivykh osnovaniiakh," *Trudoliubivaia pchela*, May 1759, p. 278.

74. Quoted in N. Dubrovin, *Pugachev i ego soobshchniki*, I, 289.

75. For an example of this argument see "Istoricheskoe prikliuchenie," *Pustomelia*, June 1770, pp. 28–48.

76. For examples, see "Primechanie o vospitanii," *Poleznoe uveselenie*, November 1760, pp. 161–67; (untitled), *Vsiakaia vsiachina*, no. 122, pp. 324–27; and P.P. (?), trans., "Poslovitsa kakov v kolybelku, takov i v mogilku," *Prazdnoe vremia v pol'zu upotreblennoe*, March 1760, p. 170.

77. [N. I. Novikov], "Opyt modnago slovaria shchegol'skago narechiia," *Zhivopisets*, 1772, pp. 49–50.

78. (Untitled), *Vsiakaia vsiachina*, no. 93, pp. 241–46; and "Istoricheskoe prikliuchenie," *Pustomelia*, June 1770, pp.30–31.

79. La Messelière's remarks on his years in Russia are contained in his *Voyage à Sainte-Petersbourg ou sur nouveaux mémoires sur la Russie*, published in Paris in 1803.

80. Cited in Leonce Pingaud, *Les Français en Russie et les Russes en France*, p. 78.

81. E. Haumant, *La Culture Française en Russie (1700–1900)*, p. 46.

82. Ibid., p. 86.

83. L. N. Kirpichnikov, "Pedagogii proshlogo veka," p. 433; and A. Pypin, *Istoriia russkoi literatury*, III, 455.

84. For an excellent example, see Dubrovin, *Pugachev i ego soobshchniki*, I, 275.

85. (Untitled), *Zhivopisets*, 1773, pp. 102–3.

86. Ibid., p. 103.

87. *F.S.S.*, I, 329–30.

88. Haumant, *La Culture Française en Russie*, pp. 88–89; and A. Veidemeier, *Tsarstvovanie Elisavety Petrovny*, II, 119.

89. For example, see "Razmyshlenie zhenshchiny o vospitanii docherei," *Prazdnoe vremia v pol'zu upotreblennoe*, October 1759, pp. 233–38.

90. [N. I. Novikov], "Vedomosti iz tveri," *Truten'*, June 1769, pp. 56–57.

91. "Istoricheskoe prikliuchenie," *Pustomelia*, June 1770, p. 30. See also I. Bogdanovich, "Epistola," in *Stikhotvoreniia*, pp. 133–34; and "Pis'mo," *Truten'*, February 1770, p. 272.

92. "Istoricheskoe prikliuchenie," *Pustomelia*, June 1770, pp. 31–32.

93. [N. I. Novikov], "Opyt modnago slovaria shchegol'skago narechiia," *Zhivopisets*, 1772, p. 50.

94. [N. I. Novikov], (untitled), *Truten'*, June 1769, p. 38. Among numerous other satirical descriptions, see *F.S.S.*, I, 399; (untitled), *Vsiakaia vsiachina*, no. 13, pp. 38–40.

95. [N. I. Novikov], "Stat'i iz ruskago [sic] slovaria," *Truten'*, May 1769, pp. 32–33.

96. For examples see A. Naryshkin, "O mnogogovorlivom," *Trudoliubivaia pchela*, September 1759, pp. 560–61; Paul Fonvizin, "Razgovor mezhdu uchenym i shchegolem," *Dobroe namerenie*, September 1764, p. 400; and Vasilii Sankovskii, "Razgovor mezhdu uchenym i shchegolem," *Dobroe namerenie*, September 1764, p. 400.

97. For example, see "Vtoroe puteshestvie," *Nevinnoe uprazhnenie*, February 1763, pp. 66–76.

98. (Untitled), *Vsiakaia vsiachina*, no. 96, pp. 252–53. See also *Vsiakaia vsiachina*, no. 144, pp. 385–90; and P. P. (?), "O khudom vospitanii bol'shikh synovei dvorian zhivushchikh v derevne s primerom khoroshogo vospitaniia syna Evdoksa i docheri Leontina," *Prazdnoe vremia v pol'zu upotreblennoe* 2 (June 1760): 372.

99. *F.S.S.*, I, 73.

100. Ibid., p. 98.

101. Ibid., pp. 73, 76–77.

102. Ibid., pp. 72, 77–78.

103. Ibid., p. 72

104. [N. I. Novikov], "Pis'mo," *Truten'*, February 1770, p. 257.

105. Chechulin, *Russkoe provintsial'noe obshchestvo*, pp. 10–27.

106. H. Rogger, *National Consciousness in Eighteenth-Century Russia*, p. 60.

107. I. F. Bogdanovich, "Blazhenstvo narodov," in *Stikhotvoreniia*, p. 190.

108. Fonvizin also publicized the image of a virtuous serf in his translation of one of Holberg's fables. See *F.S.S.*, I, 387–89.

109. Ibid., p. 9.

110. Ibid., p. 18, see also pp. 42–43.

111. Ibid., p. 13.

112. V. I. Semevskii, *Krest'ianskii vopros v rossii v XVIII i pervoi polovine XIX veka*, I, 48.

113. Ibid., pp. 63–64.

114. I. F. Bogdanovich, "Perevod stikhov Marmontelia," *S.B.*, I, 273–74.

115. [N. I. Novikov], "Satiricheskiia vedomosti," *Zhivopisets*, 1773, pp. 78–80.

116. Ibid., p. 79.

117. Denis Fonvizin, *Sokrashchenie o vol'nosti frantsuzskogo dvorianstva i o pol'ze tret'ego china*, *F.S.S.*, II, 109–16.

118. The date of Fonvizin's translation has been a matter of dispute. The French original carried the date of February 12, 1763. Without specific knowledge of this date, Pigarev claimed that Fonvizin's signature on the manuscript copy "translated by D. I. Fonvizin, translator" was the telling point. Since Fonvizin was promoted to the rank of titular councilor under Elagin, this signature placed the document between October 1762 and October 1763 when Fonvizin was a translator in the College of Foreign Affairs. Makogonenko, however, found that Fonvizin continued to sign official papers this way after his appointment to work with Elagin. Moreover there is no convincing evidence that Fonvizin actually completed the translation in 1763, although he certainly had the linguistic ability in 1763 to translate from a French original, as his version of *Alzire* shows. Nonetheless, there is sufficient reason to date the translation in the period 1764–1766. Fonvizin's duties under Elagin (1763–1769) were so defined as to include the possibility of doing such a translation. Fonvizin endorsed by his translation arguments similar to those he made in the *Trading Nobility*. Given the possible interest of the *Précis* shortly before the Legislative Commission, it is reasonable to conclude that, though the evidence is circumstantial, the *Précis* was translated by 1766. It is definite that the work, whenever translated, was finished in 1767 and in circulation at the Legislative Commission. See Makogonenko, *Denis Fonvizin*, pp. 26–27; David Griffiths, "Eighteenth-Century Perceptions of Backwardness: Projects for the Creation of a Third Estate in Catherinean Russia," p. 458, n. 14.

119. *F.S.S.*, II, 116.

120. Ibid., p. 115.

121. For another example of the state's interest in stimulating trade, see Liubomudrov (pseud.), (untitled), *Zhivopisets*, 1773, pp. 48–52.

122. *F.S.S.*, II, 116.

123. I*** T*** [N. I. Novikov], "Otryvok puteshestviia v***," *Zhivopisets*, 1773, p. 168.

124. [N. I. Novikov], "Kakovy moi chitateli," *Truten'*, December 1769, pp. 218–19.

125. [N. I. Novikov], "V novyi god novoe shchastie," *Truten'*, January 1770, p. 230.

126. (Untitled), *Vsiakaia vsiachina*, no. 85, p. 221.

127. [N. I. Novikov], "V novyi god novoe shchastie," *Truten'*, January 1770, p. 232. See also (untitled), *Vsiakaia vsiachina*, no. 29, pp. 84–85.

128. "Otpiska gosudariu grigor'iu sidorovichu," *Truten'*, October 1769, pp. 158–62.

129. [N. I. Novikov], "Angliiskaia progulka," *Zhivopisets*, 1772, p. 64. Fonvizin also raised the specter of a peasant rebellion. See the relevant fable he translated from Holberg: *F.S.S.*, I, 275–78.

130. I*** T*** [N. I. Novikov], "Otryvok puteshestviia v***," *Zhivopisets*, 1773, pp. 161–62.

131. *F.S.S.*, I, 107–77.

132. Ibid., p. 124.

133. Ibid., p. 117.

134. Ibid., p. 172.

135. Ibid.

136. Ibid., p. 173.

137. Reddaway, *Documents of Catherine the Great*, p. 257.

138. Ibid., p. 256.

139. (Untitled note from the editor), *Vsiakaia vsiachina*, 1769, no. 149, p. 404.

140. Ibid., no. 53, pp. 140–43; no. 114, pp. 302–4.

141. Ibid., no. 94, p. 247.

Chapter VI

1. Had Catherine wished to intervene, she could have accepted Z. Chernyshev's proposal of October 17, 1763, to take advantage of the interregnum by redefining Russia's border with Poland and permanently annexing Polish Livonia and several adjacent provinces. Catherine rejected this recommendation but did so only on the grounds that it was impractical. See H. Kaplan, *The First Partition of Poland*, p. 28.

2. Quoted (with no date given) in David Griffiths, "Russian Court Politics," p. 35, n. 3.

3. Bil'basov, *Istoriia Ekateriny vtoroi*, II, 406.

4. In a letter Catherine wrote Panin shortly after the election of Poniatowski, she referred to the event in a vague and mischievous way: "I congratulate you on [the election of] a king whom we have made." Quoted in ibid., p. 447. The letter was undated. Bil'basov suggested it was written immediately after the election.

5. Kaplan, *Poland*, p. 134.

6. Ibid., pp. 137–38.

7. Note of Prince Henry to Frederick II, dated from St. Petersburg on January 11, 1771, *Politische Correspondenz Friedrichs des Grossen*, XXX, 417, as quoted in Griffiths, "Russian Court Politics," p. 45, n. 1.

8. Griffiths, "Russian Court Politics," p. 45.

9. Alan Fisher, *Russian Annexation of the Crimea 1772–1783*, pp. 29–32.

10. A. Barsukov, "Kniaz' Grigorii Grigor'evich Orlov (1734–1783)," pp. 59–67, 69.

11. The references to the treaty signed at Kuchuk Kainardji rely on the careful analysis of Roderic Davison; see " 'Russian Skill and Turkish Imbecility': The Treaty of Kuchuk Kainardji Reconsidered."

12. Ibid., p. 464.

13. G. F. Martens, ed., *Recueil de Traités . . . des Puissances et Etats de l'Europe*, II, 297, 301.

14. Davison, " 'Russian Skill and Turkish Imbecility,' " p. 475.

15. Griffiths, "Russian Court Politics," p. 95.

16. For a careful scrutiny of the plan for Armed Neutrality, see I. de Madariaga, *Britain, Russia and the Armed Neutrality of 1780* (New Haven: Yale University Press, 1962). For details of the empress's reshuffling of allies in the early 1780s, see David Ransel, *The Politics of Catherinian Russia*, pp. 251–54.

17. The statement was apparently made in the early 1780s. See Griffiths, "Russian Court Politics," pp. 169–70.

18. S. P. [N. I. Novikov], (untitled), *Pustomelia*, June 1770, p. 6. The signature "S. P." quite probably means "*Sochinitel' Pustomeli*" ("The Author of the Babbler"). The military figure, called "Nkl lksvch ldzhnskm," is not identifiable.

19. [N. I. Novikov], "Vedomosti iz konstantinopolia," *Pustomelia*, June 1770, p. 51.

20. G. V. [N. I. Novikov], "Poema o nyneshnykh delakh, ili uveshchanie o vospriiatii protiv turok [sic] oruzhiia," *Parnasskii shchepetil'nik*, 1771 (app. B), pp. 35–48. Vernadskii identified this piece as Voltaire's poem which Novikov did translate. See G. Vernadskii, *Nikolai Ivanovich Novikov*, p. 12; and F. M. A. de Voltaire, "Ode XVIII. Sur La Guerre Des Russes Contre Les Turcs en 1768," in Voltaire, *Oeuvres Complètes*, VIII, 489–90.

21. G. V. [N. I. Novikov], "Poema o nyneshnykh delakh, ili uveshchanie o vospriiatii protiv turok oruzhiia," *Parnasskii shchepetil'nik*, 1771, p. 47.

22. Ibid., p. 42.

23. I. F. Bogdanovich, "Perevod stikhov Vol'tera," in *S.B.*, I, 268–72. For the original, see Voltaire, *Oeuvres Complètes*, VIII, 533.

24. Bogdanovich, "Stansy," *S.B.*, I, 288; idem, "Oda sochinennaia ochakovskikh polei pastushkoiu na vziatie ochakova," *S.B.*, I, 274–76; and idem, "Pesn' na mir mezhdu rossieiu i ottomanskoiu portoiu 1792 goda," *S.B.*, I, 283–87.

25. Quoted in Jean Goumy, *l'Abbé de Saint-Pierre*, p. 83.

26. J. J. Rousseau, *Extrait Du Projet de Paix Perpétuelle de Monsieur l'Abbé de Saint-Pierre*, p. 69. Bogdanovich's translation was not available.

27. Ibid., p. 40.

28. Ibid., p. 75.

29. Ibid., pp. 98–99.

30. I. F. Bogdanovich, *Istoricheskoe izobrazhenie rossii*, *S.B.*, II, 178.

31. Ibid., p. 171.

32. I. F. Bogdanovich, *Slaviane*, *S.B.*, II, 6.

33. Ibid., p. 7.

34. Ibid. The same point was made in the *Historical Depiction of Russia*; see *S.B.*, II, 159.

35. This same comparison was also present in Bogdanovich's translation of Vertot's *Histoire des révolutions arrivées dans le gouvernement de la République Romaine*. The work was translated between 1771 and 1775.

36. *F.S.S.*, II, 381, Fonvizin's emphasis. The bracketed words were added by Makogonenko.

37. Ibid., p. 384.

38. Ibid. Letter to Peter Panin, dated May 2, 1772. This letter has been dated by Viazemskii and Vvedenskii as May 29, 1772. Since Makogonenko is a poor editor, a definite date cannot be established. See P. Viazemskii, *Fon-Vizin*, pp. 100–101; and Denis Fonvizin,

Sochineniia D. I. Fonvizina. Polnoe sobranie original'nykh proizvedenii, pp. 276–77.

39. For the clearest example of this interpretation, see G. Makogonenko, *Denis Fonvizin*, pp. 160 ff. It should be added that the "crisis" of 1772 was important as an example of the empress's *modus operandi*. Catherine confronted not one but three succession crises, that is, the abortive one of 1756–1758, the actual one of 1762–1764, and the mythical one of 1771–1773, and appears to have dealt with each in a similar manner. There is a pattern to her engagement of warring court parties, use of diplomatic issues to tip the balance in the rivalry of court factions, replacement (in 1762 and 1771) of both contending parties and reestablishment of the bases of her internal and foreign policies. Let the privacy of a footnote serve to invite the reader to test the number of particulars on all three occasions where Catherine acted in similar sequential fashion. For reviews of the facts of the cases, see Herbert Kaplan, *Russia and the Outbreak of the Seven Years' War*, pp. 103–11; Bil'basov, *Istoriia Ekateriny vtoroi*, I, 367–86; II, 6–94; and Makogonenko, *Denis Fonvizin*, pp. 152–63.

40. Novikov, *Opyt istoricheskago slovaria*, in Efremov, *Materialy*, p. 3.

41. Ibid., p. 5.

42. I. F. Bogdanovich, "Stikhi na sluchai brachnago torzhestva ikh imperatorskikh vysochestv, gosudaria tsesarevicha, velikago kniazia Pavla Petrovicha i gosudaryni velikoi kniagini Natalii Alekseevny v 1773 . . . ," *S.B.*, I, 294–95; and idem, (untitled), *S.B.*, I, 296–99.

43. Bogdanovich, "Primechaniia o germanskikh pravakh," *S.B.*, II, 243. There is no evidence as to when Bogdanovich wrote the work, but the choice of topic and the contents of the essay would suggest that he did not write it before the 1770s.

44. Ibid., pp. 247–48.

45. Ibid., p. 268. This reference to the people was vague and made only in passing.

46. Bogdanovich, "Blazhenstvo narodov," in *Stikhotvoreniia*, pp. 187–94.

47. Ibid., pp. 192–93.

48. *F.S.S.*, II, 98.

49. Ibid., p. 99.

50. Quoted in Makogonenko, *Denis Fonvizin*, p. 157.

51. *F.S.S.*, II, 364. Letter to P. Panin, dated November 21, 1771.

52. Fonvizin, "Slovo na vyzdorovlenie ego imperatorskogo vysochestva gosudaria tsesarevicha i velikogo kniazia Pavla Petrovicha v 1771 gode," *F.S.S.*, II, 187–93.

53. Ibid., p. 187.

54. Ibid., p. 193.

55. Ibid., p. 191.

56. Ibid., p. 188.

57. Ibid., p. 189.

58. Ibid., p. 193.

59. Leonard Krieger, *The Politics of Discretion*, p. 142.

60. [N. I. Novikov], "Avtor k samomu sebe," *Zhivopisets*, 1772, pp. 6–7.

61. Novikov, ed., *Drevniaia rossiiskaia vivliofika ili sobranie raznykh drevnikh sochinenii*.

62. [Novikov], "K chitateliu," *Drevniaia rossiiskaia vivliofika*, I, v–vi.

63. [Novikov], (untitled), *Koshelek*, 1774, pp. 28–29.

64. Ibid., pp. 29–30.

65. Ibid., pp. 28–29.

66. [Novikov], (untitled), *Zhivopisets*, 1773, pp. 35–36.

67. Ibid., p. 38.

68. [Novikov], "Razgovor II. Mezhdu nemtsom i frantsuzom," *Koshelek*, 1774, p. 25.

69. Ibid., p. 23.

70. Ibid., p. 24.

71. Novikov, *Matveev*, pp. vii–xiv.

72. Ibid., p. iv.

73. Vernadskii, *Nikolai Ivanovich Novikov*, pp. 26 ff.; M. N. Longinov, *Novikov i moskovskie martinisty*, p. 33; V. Bogoliubov, *N. I. Novikov i ego vremia*, pp. 8, 123.

74. [Novikov], "Razgovor II. Mezhdu nemtsom i frantsuzom," *Koshelek*, 1774, pp. 26–27.

75. Bogoliubov, *Novikov i ego vremia*, pp. 87–89.

76. I. F. Bogdanovich, "Blazhenstvo narodov," in *Stikhotvoreniia*, p. 188.

77. Ibid., p. 189.

78. Ibid., p. 191.

79. For example, see Bogdanovich, *Istoricheskoe izobrazhenie rossi*, S.B., II, 181.

80. Bogdanovich, "Blazhenstvo narodov," in *Stikhotvoreniia*, p. 192.

81. Ibid., pp. 192–93.

82. Fonvizin's anticipations are, in the most general of terms, similar to those expressed by another Russian traveler, Alexander Herzen, on his own journey to Paris in 1847–1850. See A. Herzen, *Pis'ma iz frantsii i italii*, in Herzen, *Sobranie sochinenii*, edited by V. P. Volgin et al., 30 vols. (Moscow: Izdatel'stvo akademii nauk, 1954–1966), V, 7–224.

83. *F.S.S.*, II, 493. Letter to Ia. I. Bulgakov, dated January 25, 1778. For another example, undated and vague in composition, see Fonvizin, "Politicheskoe rassuzhdenie o chisle zhitelei u nekotorykh drevnikh narodov," *F.S.S.*, II, 616–17.

84. S. L. Peshtich, *Russkaia istoriografiia XVIII veka*, II, 256–57.

85. Quoted in ibid., p. 259.

86. *F.S.S.*, II, 679; David Ransel, *The Politics of Catherinian Russia*, p. 272.

87. These documents were published by Shumigorskii. See E. S. Shumigorskii, *Imperator Pavel Pervyi. Zhizn' i tsarstvovanie*, app. 1, pp. 2–35.

88. Ransel, *Politics of Catherinian Russia*, p. 272.

89. D. Fonvizin, "Rassuzhdenie o nepremennykh gosudarstvennykh zakonov," *F.S.S.*, II, 254. This article is available in translation without Fonvizin's explanatory notes in Marc Raeff, ed., *Russian Intellectual History: An Anthology*, pp. 96–105.

90. *F.S.S.*, II, 254–55.

91. Ibid., p. 256, Fonvizin's emphasis.

92. Ibid., p. 257.

93. Ibid., p. 256.

94. Ibid.

95. Ibid., p. 258.

96. Fonvizin, "Ta Gio, ili velikaia nauka, zakliuchaiushchaia v sebe vysokuiu kitaiskuiu filosofiiu," *F.S.S.*, II, 231–53. This article is also available in translation without Fonvizin's notes in Raeff, *Russian Intellectual History*, pp. 88–95.

97. *F.S.S.*, II, 237.

98. Ibid., p. 239.

99. Ibid., p. 265.

100. Ibid., p. 259.

101. See for examples M. A. Fonvizin, "Zapiski Mikhaila Aleksandrovicha Fonvizina. Ocherki russkoi istorii. Primechaniia k 'Histoire philosophique et politique de Russie' par Enneaux et Chennechot," pp. 35–36, 60–63; Makogonenko, *Denis Fonvizin*, pp. 197–208. The historiographical image of Denis Fonvizin as an opponent of Catherine and a proponent of constitutionalism has even endured in the works of those who do not accept it. Pigarev explicitly branded the Fonvizin-as-constitutionalist interpretation as "apocryphal," yet he also suggested that it was "possible" that the "Discourse" included, if only implicitly, plans for the gradual elimination of serfdom and the steady restoration of the Senate's powers. See Pigarev, *Tvorchestvo Fonvizina*, pp. 135, 146.

102. D. Fonvizin, "Rassuzhdenie o nepremennykh gosudarstvennykh zakonov," *F.S.S.*, II, 259.

103. Ibid., p. 262.

104. Ibid., p. 263.

105. Ibid.

106. Ibid.

107. Ibid., p. 255.

108. Ibid., p. 266.

109. Ibid., pp. 266–67.

110. Ibid., p. 267.

111. Ibid.

Chapter VII

1. *F.S.S.*, II, 29. For an intriguing analysis of the legends surrounding Callisthenes and Alexander, see G. Cary, *The Medieval Alexander* (Cambridge: Cambridge University Press, 1967), pp. 112–16.

2. *F.S.S.*, II, 29.

3. Ibid., p. 31.

4. Ibid., p. 37.

5. Ibid., p. 39.

6. Ibid.

7. Compare the highest ranks of the Fonvizin group with those of their friends from Moscow University—most of whom became by 1772 clients of Panin's opponents at the court. Paul Fonvizin was awarded the rank of privy councilor, second class (d. 1803); Domashnev the rank of state councilor, fourth class (d. 1796); Karin the rank of cornet, twelfth class at the time of his death on the field of battle in 1769; Rzhevskii the second class (d. 1804); Aleksei Naryshkin the second class (d. 1800), and his brother Semen the fourth class (d. 1807).

8. V. O. Kliuchevskii, *Ocherki i rechi. Vtoroi sbornik statei*, pp. 269–70.

9. J. L. Black, *Nicholas Karamzin and Russian Society in the Nineteenth Century*, p. 105.

10. Ibid., pp. 187–88.

11. E. Thaden, *Conservative Nationalism in Nineteenth-Century Russia*, p. 17.

Bibliography

Journals

Dobroe namerenie (*Good Intention*), 1764

Koshelek (*Purse*), 1774

Nevinnoe uprazhnenie (*Innocent Exercise*), 1763

Parnasskii shchepetil'nik (*Scrupulous Parnassian*), 1770

Poleznoe uveselenie (*Useful Entertainment*), 1760–1762

Prazdnoe vremia v pol'zu upotreblennoe (*Idle Time Used for the Good*), 1759–1760

Pustomelia (*Babbler*), 1770

Sobranie luchshikh sochinenii k rasprostraneniiu znaniia i k proizvedeniiu udovol'stviia (*Collection of the Best Compositions for Spreading Knowledge and Bringing Pleasure*), 1762

Svobodnye chasy (*Free Hours*), 1763

Trudoliubivaia pchela (*Industrious Bee*), 1759

Truten' (*Drone*), 1769–1770

Vsiakaia vsiachina (*Anything and Everything*), 1769

Zhivopisets (*Painter*), 1772–1773

Books and Dissertations

Alexander, John T. *Autocratic Politics in a National Crisis: The Imperial Russian Government and Pugachev's Revolt 1773–1775*. Bloomington: Indiana University Press, 1969.

Bain, R. Nisbet. *Peter III Emperor of Russia*. Westminster: Archibald Constable, 1902.

Berkov, P. N. *Aleksandr Petrovich Sumarokov 1717–1777*. Moscow-Leningrad: Gosudarstvennoe izdatel'stvo "iskusstvo," 1949.

———. *Istoriia russkoi zhurnalistiki XVIII veka*. Moscow-Leningrad: Izdatel'stvo akademii nauk s.s.s.r., 1952.

———. *Lomonosov i literaturnaia polemiki ego vremeni 1750–1765*. Moscow-Leningrad: Izdatel'stvo akademii nauk s.s.s.r., 1936.

———. *Vladimir Lukin 1737–1794*. Moscow: Iskusstvo, 1950.

———. *Vydenie v izuchenie istorii russkoi literatury XVIII veka*. Leningrad: Leningradskii gosudarstvennyi universitet imeni A. A. Zhdanova, 1964.

Bil'basov, V. A. *Istoriia Ekateriny vtoroi.* Vols. 1, 2, and 12. Berlin: Izdatel'stvo F. Gottgeinera, 1900.

Biliarskii, P. *Materialy dlia biografii Lomonosova.* St. Petersburg: Tipografiia imperatorskoi akademii nauk, 1865.

Billington, James. *The Icon and the Axe.* New York: Knopf, 1966.

Biograficheskii slovar' professorov i prepodavatelei imperatorskogo moskovskogo universiteta. 2 vols. Moscow: Universitetskaia tipografiia, 1855.

Black, J. L. *Nicholas Karamzin and Russian Society in the Nineteenth Century: A Study in Russian Political and Historical Thought.* Toronto: University of Toronto Press, 1975.

Blagoi, D. *Istoriia russkoi literatury XVIII veka.* 2d ed. Moscow: Gosudarstvennoe uchebno-pedagogicheskoe izdatel'stvo, 1951.

Blamburg, Margaret. "The Publicists of Peter the Great." Ph.D. dissertation, Indiana University, 1974.

Blum, Jerome. *The End of the Old Order in Rural Europe.* Princeton, N.J.: Princeton University Press, 1978.

Bobrinskoi, A. *Dvorianskie rody vnesennye v obshchii gerbovnik vserossiiskoi imperii.* 2 pts. St. Petersburg: Tipografiia M. M. Stasiulevicha, 1890.

Bogdanovich, I. F. *Sochineniia Bogdanovicha.* 2 vols. St. Petersburg: Izdatel'stvo A Smirdina, 1848.

———. *Stikhotvoreniia i poemy.* Edited by I. Z. Serman. Leningrad: Izdatel'stvo "sovet pisatel'," 1957.

Bogoliubov, V. *N. I. Novikov i ego vremia.* Moscow: Izdatel'stvo M. and S. Sabashnikovykh, 1916.

Bulich, N. *Sumarokov i sovremennaia emu kritika.* St. Petersburg: Tipografiia Eduarda Pratsa, 1854.

Catherine II. *Memoirs of Catherine the Great.* Edited by D. Maroger. New York: Collier, 1961.

Chechulin, N. *Russkoe provintsial'noe obshchestvo vo vtoroi polovine XVIII veka.* St. Petersburg: Tipografiia V.A. Balasheva, 1889.

———. *Vneshniaia politika rossii v nachale tsarstvovaniia Ekateriny II. 1762–1774.* St. Petersburg: Tipografiia glavnogo upravleniia udelov, 1896.

Cherniavsky, M. *Tsar and People. Studies in Russian Myths.* New Haven: Yale University Press, 1961.

Cizevskii, D. *History of Russian Literature.* The Hague: Mouton, 1962.

Confino, Michael. *Systèmes agraires et progrès agricole. L'assolement triennal en Russie aux XVIIIe–XIXe siècles.* The Hague: Mouton, 1969.

Dashkova, E. R. *The Memoirs of Princess Dashkova.* Translated and edited by Kyril Fitzlyon. London: J. Calder, 1958.

De Cabres, Sabathier. *Catherine II, Sa Cour et la Russie en 1772.* Berlin: A. Asher, 1869.

Demkov, M. I. *Istoriia russkoi pedagogii.* 3 vols. 2d ed. Moscow: Tipografiia G. Lissnera i D. Sobko, 1899–1909.

Dubrovin, N. *Pugachev i ego soobshchniki.* 3 vols. St. Petersburg: Tipografiia I. N. Skorokhodova, 1884.

Dukes, Paul. *Catherine the Great and the Russian Nobility. A Study Based on the Materials of the Legislative Commission of 1767.* Cambridge: Cambridge University Press, 1967.

Efremov, P. A., ed. *Materialy dlia istorii russkoi literatury.* St. Petersburg: Tipografiia I. I. Glazunova, 1867.

Feinstein, Stephen. "V. N. Tatishchev and the Development of the Concept of State Service in Petrine and Post-Petrine Russia." Ph.D. dissertation, New York University, 1971.

Fisher, Alan. *Russian Annexation of the Crimea 1772–1783.* Cambridge: Cambridge University Press, 1970.

Florinsky, Michael T. *Russia: A History and an Interpretation.* 2 vols. New York: Macmillan, 1964.

Florovskii, A. *Sostav zakonodatel'noi kommissii 1767–74 gg.* 3 pts. in 1. Odessa: Tipografiia "Tekhnik" ekaterininskaia, 1915.

Fonvizin, D. I. *Izbrannye sochineniia i pis'ma.* Edited by L. B. Svetlov. Moscow: Gosudarstvennoe izdatel'stvo "iskusstvo," 1947.

————. *Sobranie sochinenii.* Edited by G. Makogonenko. 2 vols. Moscow-Leningrad: Gosudarstvennoe izdatel'stvo khudozhestvennoi literatury, 1959.

————. *Sochineniia D. I. Fonvizina. Polnoe sobranie original'nykh proizvedenii.* Edited by A. I. Vvedenskii. St. Petersburg: Izdatel'stvo A. F. Marksa, 1893.

Freeze, G. *The Russian Levites: Parish Clergy in the Eighteenth Century.* Cambridge, Mass.: Harvard University Press, 1977.

Garrard, J., ed. *The Eighteenth Century in Russia.* Oxford: Oxford University Press, 1973.

Gierke, O. *Natural Law and the Theory of Society 1500–1800.* Translated by E. Barker. Cambridge: Cambridge University Press, 1958.

Goumy, Jean. *Etude sur la Vie et les Ecrits de l'Abbé de Saint Pierre.* Paris: Bordier, 1859.

Green, Michael. "Mixail Xeraskov and His Contribution to the Eighteenth Century Russian Theater." Ph.D. dissertation, University of California at Los Angeles, 1973.

Grekov, B. *Izbrannye trudy.* 4 vols. Moscow: Izdatel'stvo akademii nauk s.s.s.r., 1957–1960.

Griffiths, David. "Russian Court Politics and the Question of an Expansionist Foreign Policy under Catherine II, 1762–1783." Ph.D. dissertation, Cornell University, 1967.

Gukovskii, G. *Ocherki po istorii russkoi literatury XVIII veka. Dvorianskaia fronda v literature 1750 -kh- 1760 -kh godov.* Moscow: Izdatel'stvo akademii nauk s.s.s.r., 1936.

————. *Russkaia literatura XVIII veka*. Moscow: Gosudarstvennoe uchebpedagogicheskoe izdatel'stvo, 1939.

Gurvich, G. *"Pravda voli monarshei" Feofana Prokopovicha i eia zapadnoevropeiskie istochniki*. Iur'ev: K. Mattisena, 1855.

Haumant, E. *La Culture Française en Russie (1700–1900)*. Paris: Librairie Hachette, 1910.

Hazard, Paul. *The European Mind, The Critical Years, 1680–1715*. Translated by J. Lewis May. New Haven: Yale University Press, 1953.

Jones, Robert. *The Emancipation of the Russian Nobility 1762–1785*. Princeton, N.J.: Princeton University Press, 1973.

Kafenguaz, B. *I. T. Pososhkov. Zhizn' i deiatel'nost'*. Moscow: Izdatel'stvo akademii nauk s.s.s.r., 1950.

Kamenskii, Z. A. *Filosofskie idei russkogo prosveshcheniia*. Moscow: Izdatel'stvo 'mysl'," 1971.

Kantemir, Antiokh. *Sobranie stikhotvorenii*. Edited by Z. I. Gershkovich. 2d ed. Leningrad: Sovetskii pisatel', 1956.

Kaplan, Herbert H. *The First Partition of Poland*. New York: Columbia University Press, 1962.

————. *Russia and the Outbreak of the Seven Years' War*. Berkeley: University of California Press, 1968.

Karnovich, E. P. *Zamechatel'nyia bogatstva chastnykh lits v rossii*. St. Petersburg: Tipografiia K. P. Plotnikova, 1885.

Kheraskov, M. M. *Bakhariiana ili neizvestnyi volshebnaia povest', pocherpnutaia iz russkikh skazok*. Moscow: Tipografiia P. Beketova, 1803.

————. *Drug neshchastnykh*. St. Petersburg: n.p., 1774.

————. *Izbrannye proizvedeniia*. Edited by A. V. Zapadov. Leningrad: Izdatel'stvo "sovetskii pisatel'," 1961.

Kizevetter, A. *Istoricheskie siluety liudi i sobytiia*. Berlin: "Parabola," 1931.

Kliuchevskii, V. O. *Ocherki i rechi. Vtoroi sbornik statei*. Petrograd: Literaturno-izdatel'skii otdel komissariata narodnogo prosveshcheniia, 1918.

Kobeko, D. *Tsarevich Pavel Petrovich (1754–1796)*. St. Petersburg: Tipografiia gratsianskogo, 1882.

Korovin, G. *Biblioteka Lomonosova*. Leningrad: Izdatel'stvo akademii nauk s.s.s.r., 1961.

Krieger, Leonard. *The Politics of Discretion. Pufendorf and the Acceptance of Natural Law*. Chicago: University of Chicago Press, 1965.

Lauber, Jack M. "Merchant-Gentry Conflict in Eighteenth-Century Russia." Ph.D. dissertation, University of Iowa, 1967.

Lebedev, P. *Grafy Nikita i Petr Paniny*. St. Petersburg: Izdatel' stvo D. E. Kozhanchikova, 1863.

leJeun, C. *Frantsuzskaia nyneshnego vremeni filosofiia, sakrashchena vypisana iz knigi Variétés d'un Philosophe Provincial* par M. Ch. leJeun. Translated by N. I. Novikov. St. Petersburg: n.p., 1772.

Lomonosov, M. V. *Polnoe sobranie sochinenii.* Edited by S. I. Vavilov et al. 10 vols. Moscow-Leningrad: Izdatel'stvo akademii nauk s.s.s.r., 1950–1959.

Longinov, M. N. *Novikov i moskovskie martinisty.* Moscow: Tipografiia Grachkva i comp, 1867.

Lukin, V. *Sochineniia i perevody Vladimira Lukina.* 2 pts. St. Petersburg: n.p., 1765.

Maggs, Barbara. "China in the Literature of Eighteenth-Century Russia." Ph.D. dissertation, University of Illinois, 1973.

Makogonenko, G. *Denis Fonvizin. Tvorcheskii put'.* Moscow-Leningrad: Leningradskoe gosudarstvennoe izdatel'stvo khudozhestvennoi literatury, 1961.

————. *Nikolai Novikov i russkoe prosveshchenie XVIII veka.* Moscow: Gosudarstvennoe izdatel'stvo khudozhestvennoi literatury, 1951.

————. *Ot Fonvizina do Pushkina.* Moscow: Khudozhestvennaia literatura, 1969.

————. *Radishchev i ego vremia.* Moscow: Gosudarstvennoe izdatel'stvo khudozhestvennoi literatury, 1956.

Marker, Gary. "Publishing and the Formation of a Reading Public in Eighteenth-Century Russia." Ph.D. dissertation, University of California, Berkeley, 1977.

Martens, G. F., ed. *Recueil de Traités . . . des Puissances et Etats de l'Europe.* 8 vols. Göttingen: Dieterich, 1817–1835.

Meinecke, Friedrich. *Cosmopolitanism and the Nation State.* Translated by B. Kimber. Princeton, N.J.: Princeton University Press, 1970.

Melnikov, N. N. *Izdaniia moskovskogo universiteta 1756–1799.* Moscow: Izdatel'stvo moskovskogo universiteta, 1955.

Menshutkin, B. M. *Russia's Lomonosov.* Translated by J. Thal and E. Webster. Princeton, N.J.: Princeton University Press, 1952.

Meynieux, A. *La Littérature et le Métier d'Ecrivain en Russie avant Pouchkine.* Paris: Librairie des Cinq Continents, 1966.

Miliukov, P. N. *Ocherki po istorii russkoi kul'tury.* 3 vols. Paris: Izdatel'stvo "sovremennyia zapiski," 1930.

Mirsky, D. S. *History of Russian Literature from Its Beginnings to 1900.* New York: Vintage, 1960.

Morane, Pierre. *Paul Ier de Russie Avant L'Avènement 1754–1796.* Paris: Librairie Plan, 1970.

Moser, Charles. *Denis Fonvizin.* Boston: Twayne Publishers, 1979.

Nezelenov, A. *Nikolai Ivanovich Novikov, izdatel' zhurnalov 1769–1785gg.* St. Petersburg: Tipografiia V. S. Balasheva, 1875.

Novikov, N. I. *Dramaticheskoi slovar'.* Moscow: U universitetskoi tipografii u N. Novikova, 1787.

————. *Drevniaia rossiiskaia vivliofika ili sobranie raznykh drevnikh sochinenii.* 11 vols. in 6. 2d ed. Moscow: Tipografiia kompanii tipograficheskoi, 1788–1791. Reprint ed. 20 vols. The Hague: Mouton, 1970.

————, ed. *Istoriia o nevinnom zatochenii blizhniago boiarina Artemona Sergeevicha Matveeva.* St. Petersburg: Izdannaia Nikolaem Novikovym, 1776.

————, comp. *Rodoslovnaia kniga kniazei i dvorian rossiiskikh i vyezzhikh.* 2 pts. Moscow: U universitetskoi tipografii u N. Novikova, 1787.

Pekarskii, P. *Istoriia imperatorskoi akademii nauk v peterburge.* 2 vols. St. Petersburg: Tipografiia imperatorskoi akademii nauk, 1870–1873.

Penchko, N. A. *Osnovanie moskovskogo universiteta.* Moscow: Izdatel'stvo moskovskogo universiteta, 1952.

Perlman, Louis. *Russian Literature and the Business Man.* New York: Columbia University Press, 1937.

Peshtich, S. L. *Russkaia istoriografiia XVIII veka.* 3 vols. Leningrad: Izdatel'stvo leningradskogo universiteta, 1961–1971.

Pigarev, K. V. *Tvorchestvo Fonvizina.* Moscow: Izdatel'stvo akademii nauk s.s.s.r., 1954.

Pingaud, Leonce. *Les Français en Russie et les Russes en France.* Paris: Perrin et Cie., 1886.

Pokrovskii, V., ed. *Aleksandr Petrovich Sumarokov. Ego zhizn' i sochineniia.* Moscow: G. Lissner i D. Sobko, 1905.

Prévost, Antoine-Francois. *Mémoires et aventures d'un homme de qualité qui s'est retiré du monde.* 2 vols. Amsterdam: Chez Arkstee, 1742.

Prokopovich, F. *Sochineniia.* Edited by I. Eremin. Moscow-Leningrad: Izdatel'stvo akademii nauk, s.s.s.r., 1961.

Pufendorf, Samuel. *De Jure Naturae Et Gentium.* Translated by C. J. and W. A. Oldfather. 2 vols. Oxford: Clarendon Press, 1934.

————. *De Officio Hominis Et Civis Juxta Legem Naturalem.* Translated by Frank Gardner Moore. 2 vols. Oxford: Oxford University Press, 1927.

————. *Elementorum Jurisprudentiae Universalis.* Translated by W. A. Oldfather. 2 vols. Oxford: Clarendon Press, 1931.

Pypin, A. *Istoriia russkoi literatury.* 4 vols. St. Petersburg: Tipografiia M. M. Stasiulevicha, 1907.

Radishchev, A. *A Journey from St. Petersburg to Moscow.* Translated by Leo Weiner. Edited by R. Thaler. Cambridge, Mass.: Harvard University Press, 1958.

Raeff, Marc. *Imperial Russia 1682–1825. The Coming of Age of Modern Russia.* New York: Knopf, 1971.

————. *Origins of the Russian Intelligentsia: The Eighteenth-Century Nobility.* New York: Harcourt, Brace & World, 1966.

————, ed. *Plans for Political Reform in Imperial Russia, 1730–1905.* Englewood Cliffs, N.J.: Prentice-Hall, 1966.

————, ed. *Russian Intellectual History: An Anthology*. New York: Harcourt, Brace & World, 1966.

Ransel, David. *The Politics of Catherinian Russia: The Panin Party*. New Haven: Yale University Press, 1975.

Ranum, Orest, ed. *National Consciousness, History, and Political Culture in Early Modern Europe*. Baltimore: Johns Hopkins Press, 1975.

Reddaway, W. F., ed. *Documents of Catherine the Great*. Cambridge: Cambridge University Press, 1931.

Rogger, H. *National Consciousness in Eighteenth-Century Russia*. Cambridge, Mass.: Harvard University Press, 1960.

Rousseau, J. J. *Extrait du Projet de Paix Perpétuelle de Monsieur Abbé de Saint Pierre*. N.p., 1761.

Ryu, In-Ho Lee. "Freemasonry under Catherine the Great: A Reinterpretation." Ph.D. dissertation, Harvard University, 1967.

Saitov, V. I. *Fedor Grigor'evich Karin*. St. Petersburg: Izdanie redaktsii zhurnala "bibliograf" (N. M. Lisovskago), 1893.

Semevskii, V. I. *Krest'iane v tsarstvovanie imperatritsy Ekateriny II*. 2 vols. St. Petersburg: Tipografiia M. M. Stasiulevicha, 1888.

————. *Krest'ianskii vopros v rossii v XVIII i pervoi polovine XIX veka*. 2 vols. St. Petersburg: Tipografiia "obshchestvennaia pol'za," 1888.

Shchipanov, I. Ia. *Filosofiia russkogo prosveshcheniia. Vtoraia polovina XVIII veka*. Moscow: Izdatel'stvo moskovskogo universiteta, 1971.

————, ed. *Moskovskii universitet i razvitie filosofskoi i obshchestvenno – politicheskoi mysli v rossii*. Moscow: Izdatel'stvo moskovskogo universiteta, 1957.

Shumigorskii, E. S. *Imperator Pavel Pervyi. Zhizn' i tsarstvovanie*. St. Petersburg: Tipografiia V. D. Smirnova, 1907.

Simmons, E. *English Literature and Culture in Russia (1553–1840)*. Cambridge, Mass.: Harvard University Press, 1935.

Slany, William. "Russian Central Governmental Institutions 1725–1741." Ph.D. dissertation, Cornell University, 1958.

Solov'ev, S. M. *Istoriia rossii s drevneishikh vremen*. 30 vols. in 15. Moscow: Izdatel'stvo sots-ekonomicheskoi literatury, 1959–1966.

Strycek, Alexis. *Denis Fonvizine*. Paris: Librairie des Cinq Continents, 1976.

Sumarokov, A. P. *Polnoe sobranie vsekh sochinenii v stikhakh i proze*. Edited by N. I. Novikov. 10 vols. Moscow: U universitetskoi tipografii u N. Novikova, 1781.

Sychev-Mikhailov, M. V. *Iz istorii russkoi shkoly i pedagogiki XVIII veka*. Edited by N. A. Konstantinov and M. F. Shabaev. Moscow: Izdatel'stvo akademii pedagogicheskikh nauk r.s.f.s.r., 1960.

Thaden, E. *Conservative Nationalism in Nineteenth-Century Russia*. Seattle: University of Washington Press, 1964.

Tikhomirov, M. N., ed. *Istoriia moskovskogo universiteta.* 2 vols. Moscow: Izdatel'stvo moskovskogo universiteta, 1955.

Troitskii, S. M. *Russkii absoliutizm i dvorianstvo v XVIII v.: formirovanie biurokratii.* Moscow: Izdatel'stvo "nauka," 1974.

[Turgenev, Alexander.] *La Cour de la Russie Il y a Cent Ans 1725–1783. Extraits des Dépêches des Ambassadeurs Anglais et Français.* Berlin: F. Schneider, 1858.

Veidemeier, A. *Tsarstvovanie Elisavety Petrovny.* 2 vols. St. Petersburg: n.p., 1834.

Vengerov, S. A., ed. *Russkaia poeziia.* St. Petersburg: A. E. Bineke, 1897.

Vernadskii, G. *Nikolai Ivanovich Novikov.* Petrograd: Izdatel'stvo "nauka i shkola," 1918.

Vertot, René Aubert de, Abbé. *A History of the Revolutions That Happened in the Government of the Roman Republic.* Translated by John Ozell. 2 vols. London: Printed for J. and J. Knapton, 1732.

Viazemskii, P. *Fon-Vizin.* St. Petersburg: V tipografii departamenta vneshnei torgovli, 1848.

Voltaire, F. M. A. de. *Oeuvres Complètes de Voltaire.* Edited by Louis Moland. 52 vols. Paris: Garnier Frères, 1877–1885.

Von Morenschildt, D. *Russia in the Intellectual Life of 18th-Century France.* New York: Columbia University Press, 1936.

Weinbaum, A. "N. I. Novikov (1744–1818): An Interpretation of His Career and Ideas." Ph.D. dissertation, Columbia University, 1975.

Welsh, D. J. *Russian Comedy 1765–1823.* The Hague: Mouton, 1966.

Wolff, Christian. *Gesammelte Werke.* Edited by M. Thomann. 36 vols. Hildesheim: Georg Olms, 1964–.

————. *Institutions du droit de la nature et des gens.* Translated by Mr. M***. Edited by Elie Luzac. 2 vols. Leiden: Chez E. Luzac, 1772.

————. *Jus Gentium Methodo Scientifica Pertractatum.* Translated by Joseph H. Drake. 2 vols. Oxford: Clarendon Press, 1934.

Wortman, Richard. *The Development of a Russian Legal Consciousness.* Chicago: University of Chicago Press, 1976.

Yaney, George. *The Systematization of Russian Government. Social Evolution in the Domestic Administration of Imperial Russia, 1711–1905.* Urbana: University of Illinois Press, 1973.

Articles

Alefirenko, P. K. "Obshchestvennoe dvizhenie v moskve vo vtoroi polovine XVIII stoletiia." *Izvestiia akademii nauk s.s.s.r. Seriia istorii i filosofii* 4 (1947): 521–35.

Augustine, Wilson. "Notes toward a Portrait of the Eighteenth-Century Russian Nobility." *Canadian Slavic Studies* 4 (1970): 373–425.

Barsukov, A. "Kniaz' Grigorii Grigor'evich Orlov (1734–1783)." *Russkii arkhiv,* 1873, pp. 1–146.

Batenkov, G. A. "Ivan Elagin." *Russkaia starina* 53 (1887): 319–21; 55 (1887): 202.

Berkov, P. N. "English Plays in St. Petersburg in the 1760's and 1770's." *Oxford Slavonic Papers* 8 (1958): 90–97.

———. "Neizdannoe ranee stikhotvorenie Kheraskova." *Russkaia literatura* 1960, pp. 194–95.

———. " 'Rassuzhdenie o rossiiskom stikhotvorstve' neizvestnaia stat'ia M. M. Kheraskova." *Literaturnoe nasledstvo* 9–10 (1933): 287–94.

Bogdanovich, I. F. "Avtobiografiia I. F. Bogdanovicha." *Otechestvennye zapiski* 87 (1853): 181–86.

———. "Liubopytnye dokumenty iz portfelei Millera." *Moskvitianin* 1 (1854): 8.

Brown, F. Andrew. "On Education: John Locke, Christian Wolff, and the 'Moral Weeklies.' " *University of California Publications in Modern Philology* 36 (1952): 149–72.

Burgess, M. "Russian Public Theater Audiences of the 18th and Early 19th Centuries." *Slavic and East European Review* 37 (December 1958): 160–83.

Chechulin, N. "Proekt imperatorskogo soveta v pervyi god tsarstvovaniia Ekateriny II." *Zhurnal ministerstva narodnogo prosveshcheniia* 292 (March 1894): 68–87.

Confino, Michael. "On Intellectuals and Intellectual Traditions in Eighteenth and Nineteenth-Century Russia." *Daedalus* 101 (Spring 1972): 117–49.

Davison, Roderic. " 'Russian Skill and Turkish Imbecility': The Treaty of Kuchuk Kainardji Reconsidered." *Slavic Review* 35 (September 1976); 463–83.

Diderot, D. "Sur la Princesse Dashkof." *Oeuvres Complètes de Diderot*. Edited by J. Assézat and M. Tourneux. 20 vols. Paris: Garnier Frères, 1875–1877, XVII, 487–94.

Dobroliubov, N. "Russkaia satira v vek Ekateriny." *Sovremennik* 77 (October 1859): 267–356.

Drizen, N. V. "Ivan Perfil'evich Elagin (1725–1794)." *Russkaia starina* 80 (1893): 117–143.

Elagin, I. P. "Zapiski I. P. Elagina." *Russkii arkhiv*, 1864, pp. 586–604.

Fonvizin, M. A. "Zapiski Mikhaila Aleksandrovicha Fonvizina. Ocherki russkoi istorii. Primechaniia k 'Histoire philosophique et politique de Russie' par Enneaux et Chennechot." *Russkaia starina* 42 (1884): 31–66, 281–302.

Griffiths, David. "Catherine II: The Republican Empress." *Jahrbücher für Geschichte Osteuropas* 21 (1973): 323–44.

———. "Eighteenth-Century Perceptions of Backwardness: Projects for the Creation of a Third Estate in Catherinean Russia." *Canadian-American Slavic Studies* 13 (1979): 452–72.

Ilovaiskii, D. I. "Ekaterina Romanovna Dashkova." *Otechestvennye zapiski* 126 (1859): 195–260.

Kallash, V. V. "Ocherki po istorii russkoi zhurnalistiki." *Russkaia mysl'*, (February 1903): 1–15.

Kaplan, Frederick. "Tatishchev and Kantemir, Two Eighteenth-Century Exponents of a Russian Bureaucratic Style of Thought." *Jahrbücher für Geschichte Osteuropas* 13 (1965): 497–510.

Karamzin, N. "O Bogdanoviche i ego sochineniiakh." *Vestnik evropy* 9 (May 1803): 3–18, 75–111.

Kirpichnikov, L. N. "Pedagogii proshlogo veka." *Istoricheskii vestnik* 21 (September 1885): 433–43.

Kizevetter, A. A. "Moskovskii universitet (istoricheskii ocherk)." In *Moskovskii universitet 1755–1930*, edited by V. B. Eliashevich, A. A. Kizevetter, and M. M. Novikov, pp. 1–140. Paris: Izdatel'stvo sovremennyia zapiski, 1930.

Korsakov, D. "Stronniki votsareniia Ekateriny II (1757–1762 gg)." *Istoricheskie zapiski* 15 (1884): 231–60.

Kruglyi, A. "I. P. Elagin (biograficheskii ocherk)." *Ezhegodnik imperatorskikh teatrov* 4 (1893–1894) app. 2: 96–118.

Lang, D. "Boileau and Sumarokov, the Manifesto of Russian Classicism." *Modern Language Review* 43 (1948): 500–506.

Lavrovskii, N. "K biografii Fon-Vizina." *Zhurnal ministerstva narodnogo prosveshcheniia* 160 (March 1872): 208–19.

Lenin, V. I. "Ot kakogo nasledstva my otkazyvaemsia?" in *Polnoe sobranie sochinenii*, II, 507–50. 55 vols. Moscow: Gosudarstvennoe izdatel'stvo politicheskoi literatury, 1958–1965.

Longinov, M. N. "Mikhail Matveevich Kheraskov." *Russkii arkhiv*, 1873, pp. 1453–79.

————. "Poslednie gody zhizni Aleksandra Petrovicha Sumarokova (1766–1777)." *Russkii arkhiv*, 1871, pp. 1637–1717.

————. "Russkie pisateli XVIII veka." *Russkaia starina* 1 (1870): 463–70; 2 (1870): 74–80, 194–200; 3 (1871): 205–7; 4 (1871): 571–77, 681–82.

————. "Satiricheskii katalog pri dvore Ekateriny II-i." *Russkii arkhiv*, 1871, pp. 2039–54.

McArthur, Gilbert. "Catherine II and the Masonic Circle of N. I. Novikov." *Canadian Slavic Studies* 4 (1970): 529–46.

Makarov, M. "Bibliograficheskii redkosti: truten'." *Otechestvennye zapiski* 5 (1839): 27.

[Miliutin, V. A.] "Ocherki russkoi zhurnalistiki, preimushchestvenno staroi." *Sovremennik* 25 (1851): 1–52, 151–82; 26 (1851): 1–48.

Mochul'skii, V. "K istorii zhurnalistiki XVIII v." *Russkii filologicheskii vestnik* 69 (1913): 114–29.

Morozov, A. A. "M. V. Lomonosov i teleologiia Kristiana Vol'fa." In *Literaturnoe tvorchestvo M. V. Lomonosova*, edited by P. Berkov and I. Serman, pp. 163–96. Moscow-Leningrad: Izdatel'stvo akademii nauk s.s.s.r., 1962.

Morrison, Kerry. "Catherine II's Legislative Commission: An Administrative Interpretation." *Canadian Slavic Studies* 4 (1970): 464–84.

"Otryvki iz perepiski A. P. Sumarokova." *Otechestvennye zapiski* 116 (1858): 579–98.

Pekarskii, P. "Materialy dlia istorii zhurnal'noi i literaturnoi deiatel'nosti Ekateriny II." *Zapiski imperatorskoi akademii nauk* 3 (1863): 1–87.

———. "Redactor, sotrudniki i tsenzura v russkom zhurnale 1755–1764 godov." *Zapiski imperatorskoi akademii nauk* 12 (1868): 1–56.

Petrovskii, N. "Bibliograficheskie zametki o russkikh zhurnalakh XVIII veka." *Zhurnal ministerstva narodnogo prosveshcheniia* 315 (January 1898): 85–107.

Pypin, A. N. "Do-petrovskoe predanie v XVIII-m veke." *Vestnik evropy* 3 (June 1886): 680–717; 4 (July 1886): 306–45.

Raeff, Marc. "The Domestic Policies of Peter III and His Overthrow." *American Historical Review* 75 (June 1970): 1289–1310.

———. "L'Etat, le Gouvernement et la Tradition Politique en Russie Impériale Avant 1861." *Revue d'Histoire Moderne et Contemporaine* 9 (1962): 295–307.

———. "Random Notes on the Reign of Catherine II in the Light of Recent Literature." *Jahrbücher für Geschichte Osteuropas* 19 (December 1971): 541–56.

———. "Les Slaves, les Allemands et les 'Lumières.'" *Canadian Slavic Studies* 1 (1967): 521–51.

———. "Staatsdienst, Aussenpolitik, Ideologien (Die Rolle der Institutionen in der geistigen Entwicklung des russischen Adels im 18. Jahrhundert." *Jahrbücher für Geschichte Osteuropas* 7 (1959): 147–81.

———. "The Well-Ordered Police State and the Development of Modernity in Seventeenth and Eighteenth-Century Europe: An Attempt at a Comparative Approach." *American Historical Review* 80 (1975): 1221–43.

Ransel, David. "Catherine II's Instruction to the Commission on Laws: An Attack on Gentry Liberals?" *Slavonic and East European Review* 50 (1972): 10–28.

———. "The 'Memoirs' of Count Münnich." *Slavic Review* 30 (December 1971): 843-52.

Serman, I. Z. "I. F. Bogdanovich-zhurnalist i kritik." *XVIII vek* 4 (1959): 85–103.

Ševčhenko, Ihor. "A Neglected Byzantine Source of Muscovite Political Ideology." *Harvard Slavic Studies* 2 (1954): 141–79.

Shaeffer, A. "Iz poslednikh dnei russkoi imperatritsy Elisavety." *Chteniia v moskovskom obshchestve istorii i drevnosti* 2 (1877): 1–16.

Shamrai, D. D. "Ob izdateliakh pervogo chastnogo russkogo zhurnala." *XVIII vek* 1 (1935): 377–85.

Shumigorskii, E. "Gosudarynia-publitsist." *Russkii arkhiv*, 1890, pp. 5–52.

———. "'Vsiakaia vsiachina' i 'spektator.'" *Zhurnal ministerstva narodnogo prosveshcheniia* 279 (January 1892): 125–56.

Solntsev, V. F. "Smes." *Bibliograf* 1 (1893): 21–42.

Solov'ev, S. M. "Imperatorskie sovety v rossii v XVIII veke." *Russkaia starina* 2 (1870): 463–68.

Stankevich, A. " 'Alzire' vol'tera v perevod Fon-Vizina." *Russkii arkhiv*, 1887, pp. 304–12.

"Upotreblenie knigi psaltyr v drevnem bytu russkogo naroda." *Pravoslavnyi sobesednik*, 1857, pp. 814–56.

Vasetskii, G. "Filosofskie vzgliady M. V. Lomonosova." In *Iz istorii russkoi filosofii. Sbornik statei.* Edited by I. Shchipanov, pp. 96–121. Moscow: Gosudarstvennoe izdatel'stvo politicheskoi literatury, 1951.

Veselovskii, A. N. "Zapadnoe vliianie v russkoi literature." *Vestnik evropy* 6 (November–December 1881): 25–58.

Wolff, Robert Lee. "The Three Romes: The Migration of an Ideology and the Making of an Autocrat." *Daedalus* 88 (Spring 1959): 291–311.

Zabelin, I., and Tikhonravov, N. "Biograficheskiia zametki o russkikh pisateliakh XVIII veka." In *Letopisi russkoi literatury i drevnosti*, edited by N. Tikhonravov. 4 vols. I, 198–202. Moscow: n.p., 1859.

Reference Works

Bantysh-Kamenskii, D. *Biografiia rossiiskikh generalissimusov i general-fel'dmarshalov.* 5 vols. St. Petersburg: Tipografiia tretiago departamenta ministerstva gosudarstvennykh imushchestv, 1840.

———. *Slovar' dostopamiatnykh liudei.* 5 vols. Moscow: Izdan A. Shiriaevym, 1836.

Brokgauz, F. A., and Efron, I. A. *Entsiklopedicheskii slovar'.* 43 vols. St. Petersburg: Semenovskaia tipo-litografiia (I. A. Efrona), 1890–1906.

Evgenii, Mitropolit. *Slovar' russkikh svetskikh pisatelei.* 2 vols. Moscow: V universitetskoi tipografii, 1845.

Gennadi, G. *Spravochnyi slovar' o russkikh pisateliakh i uchenykh.* 3 vols. Berlin and Moscow: Rosenthal & Co., 1876–1908.

Gerbel, N. B. *Russkie poety v biografiiakh obraztsakh.* Edited by P. Polevoi. St. Petersburg: Tipografiia M. Stasiulevicha, 1888.

Guberti, N. B. *Materialy dlia russkoi bibliografii.* Moscow: Universitetskaia tipografiia, 1878.

Polovtsov, A. A., ed. *Russkii biograficheskii slovar'.* 25 vols. St. Petersburg: Izdanie imperatorskogo russkogo istoricheskogo obshchestva, 1896–1913.

Vengerov, S. A. *Istochniki slovaria russkikh pisatelei.* 4 vols. St. Petersburg: Tipografiia akademii nauk, 1900–1917.

Index